PLOTS AND CHARACTERS
IN THE FICTION AND SKETCHES
OF NATHANIEL HAWTHORNE

PRESENTED TO
Cardinal Gibbons
Library
From:
Mr. & Mrs. Ray Daley

PLOTS AND CHARACTERS
IN THE FICTION AND SKETCHES
OF NATHANIEL HAWTHORNE

Robert L. Gale

with a Foreword by
Norman Holmes Pearson

14540

The MIT Press
Cambridge, Massachusetts, and London, England

First published 1968 as an Archon Book by The Shoe String
Press, Inc., Hamden Ct. This MIT Press edition published
by arrangement with The Shoe String Press, Inc.

First MIT Press paperback edition, October 1972

Printed and bound in The United States of America

Library of Congress Cataloging in Publication Data

Gale, Robert L.
    Plots and characters in the fiction and sketches of Nathaniel
Hawthorne.

    Bibliography: p.
    1. Hawthorne, Nathaniel, 1804–1864—Plots. 2. Hawthorne, Nathaniel,
1804–1864—Characters. I. Title.
[PS1891.G3   1972]   813′.3   72–6779
ISBN 0–262–57030–0 (pbk.)

To Gale, Miriam (nee Fisher) and Erie
Admirable parents

TABLE OF CONTENTS

Foreword   ix

Preface   xiii

Chronology   xvii

Chronological List of Hawthorne's
  Fiction and Sketches   xix

Plots   1

Characters   173

FOREWORD

Even to the man who has read all of Hawthorne, Professor Gale's book has its evident and welcome uses. *Plots and Characters in the Fiction and Sketches of Nathaniel Hawthorne* is not simply a reference book, although it is invaluably that. Indeed, only the luckiest memory can retain all of the data Professor Gale has so meticulously abstracted, arranged, and made available. They cover the span from Hawthorne's earliest literary efforts to the days of his greatest achievement and beyond that to the weaker but still interesting products of his failing power. To be able to turn to alphabetical indexes of them is to become abler. Half-memory is never enough for student, teacher, or scholar.

But the book, to repeat, is not simply a reference book. It is a volume which can profitably be read as a whole. The very convenience of alphabetized characters and plots serves an unexpected end. What we are also given is a stimulating scramble. The reader is not following Hawthorne's compositions in the sequence of their creation, although one can do that with the help of the chronological list which Professor Gale also includes. What we have instead is an inescapable emphasis on the scope and variety of Hawthorne's literary world, his landscape and the people in it. We jump without pattern from plot to plot and person to person. The juxtapositions are sometimes startling; they are, frequently, highly suggestive.

Normally, especially as teachers, we read the same few stories by Hawthorne again and again. They may well be the best, but they narrowly define and confine. Because the literary essay as a form is neither pedagogically nor critically popular, except when it is literary criticism by ourselves, Hawthorne's own essays are more and more ignored. Yet they were an essential factor in his literary development. I am delighted that Professor Gale included these sketches among his summaries. He reminds us both of the breadth and the variety of Hawthorne's writing, indeed of what it was necessarily like to be a professional writer in Hawthorne's time.

Perhaps it is to the summaries of the lesser known works of Hawthorne that the reader of this book will most frequently return. Nevertheless, even among the somewhat better known it is no mean accomplishment and convenience to have made a resumé of *Dr. Grimshawe's Secret* with all of the fumbling annotations and emendations by the aging Hawthorne taken into account. I am grateful too for being shown by the summary of "The Devil in Manuscript," where in Gale's words "Oberon has lost his peace of mind and has become lonely through surrounding himself only with the shadows of his imagination," how closely the theme of this work is related to that of "Young Goodman Brown." Both were published the same year. There are many benefits of this kind to be gained from *Plots and Characters in the Fiction and Sketches of Nathaniel Hawthorne.*

Not everything is to be found there, of course. One does not get at the deftness of Hawthorne's style which was so remarkable an achievement. Nor can a summary do more than hint at the sensitivity of Hawthorne's psychological understanding which converted natural facts into personal symbols and made for each character his myth. Nor is one given the gradual construction of Hawthorne's own ethic, his total myth. But the reader is at least always led toward Hawthorne's works, which is precisely Professor Gale's intention and his accomplishment.

Norman Holmes Pearson

Yale University
March, 1968

Life figures itself to me as a festal or funereal procession. All of us have our places, and are to move onward under the direction of the Chief Marshal. The grand difficulty results from the invariably mistaken principles on which the deputy marshals seek to arrange this immense concourse of people . . . Its members are classified by the merest external circumstances, and thus are more certain to be thrown out of their true positions than if no principle of arrangement were attempted.

— Nathaniel Hawthorne, "The Procession of Life"

PREFACE

This handbook, a companion to my *Plots and Characters in the Fiction of Henry James*, also available in paperback from The MIT Press, should prove useful in several ways. The reader may wish to have some understanding of the plot or contents of a certain Hawthornean novel, short story, or sketch before reading it, or he may wish to review the contents of a work after — perhaps long after — he has read it. If he is a specialist, he may wish to review the plots of several works to compare Nathaniel Hawthorne's treatment of certain subjects and themes early in his career and later, or perhaps to compare Hawthorne's treatment of some element with that of another writer, American, British, or Continental. It may be that the reader will wish to refresh his memory of a certain name or the function of a certain character in Hawthorne's pageant of persons. If he remembers the work in which the name figures, he can easily find the name in the alphabetized list of characters after the summary of the given work. If he remembers the character but not the work, he can find what he needs in the alphabetized list of all named or namable persons in Hawthorne's fiction and sketches; the entry there will also enable him to recollect where the character may be found in Hawthorne. If he wants to review Hawthorne's activity during a certain phase of his career, he may well begin by consulting the chronology of Hawthorne or the chronological list of his novels, short stories, and sketches.

The diligent reader of Hawthorne's plots summarized here will be struck by the truth of Randall Stewart's conclusion that Hawthorne was concerned during his entire professional life with the virtues and vices of Puritanism, the extreme difficulty of personal and social reform, the distinction between emotional and intellectual sins, the dangers of isolation and pride and scientism, the need in all persons for domestic love and confession and a connection with the outside world, and the enigma of evil.[1] These are serious, somber themes. As Mark Van Doren

[1] Randall Stewart, *Nathaniel Hawthorne: A Biography* (New Haven: Yale University Press, 1948), pp. 242-265.

reminds us, Hawthorne's "one deathless virtue is that rare thing in any literature, an utterly serious imagination. It was serious [he adds], and so it was loving; it was loving, and so it could laugh; it could laugh, and so it could endure the horror it saw in every human heart."[2]

Please note that I have summarized and identified all named or namable characters — well over nine hundred in all — only from the novels, short stories, and sketches of Hawthorne. Names in brackets are supplied from sources other than Hawthorne. I do not treat any of his non-fictional books or trivial informational essays. Thus, I omit consideration of items in the *American Magazine of Useful and Entertaining Knowledge*, 1836[3] (except for a few pieces reprinted from it in Hawthorne's Autograph Edition [Boston and New York: Houghton, Mifflin and Company, 1900]), and *Peter Parley's History*, 1837; all non-fictional parts of *The Whole History of Grandfather's Chair*, 1841 (although I summarize the fictional introduction and links, and identify the characters therein); non-fictional parts of the *Biographical Stories*, 1842; *True Stories from History and Biography*, 1851; the *Life of Franklin Pierce*, 1852; *Our Old Home*, 1863; and all of the *Notebooks*, prefaces, letters, and reviews. Any reader interested in locating material in most of the above books should consult Evangeline M. O'Connor's valuable index to Hawthorne.[4] I include all fiction and sketches

[2] Mark Van Doren, *Nathaniel Hawthorne* (New York: William Sloane Associates, 1949), p. 267.

[3] See Arlin Turner, *Hawthorne as Editor: Selections from His Writings in The American Magazine of Useful and Entertaining Knowledge* (University, Louisiana: Louisiana State University Press, 1941.)

[4] Evangeline M. O'Connor, *An Analytical Index to the Works of Nathaniel Hawthorne* (Boston: Houghton, Mifflin and Company, 1882; reprinted Detroit: Gale Research Company, 1967). It should be noted, however, that this book does not index all of the minor characters in Hawthorne's fiction and sketches, and further that it was first published before all of his minor fiction and sketches were identified. Finally, I have ignored Hawthorne's juvenile "Spectator" (see Elizabeth L. Chandler, "Hawthorne's 'Spectator,' " *New England Quarterly*, IV [April, 1931], 288-330) and his rather unimportant contributions to the Salem *Advertiser* (see Randall Stewart, "Hawthorne's Contributions to *The Salem Advertiser*," *American Literature*, V [January, 1934], 327-341).

appearing in Hawthorne's Riverside Edition (Boston and New York: Houghton, Mifflin and Company, 1883) and his Autograph Edition, even though a couple of slight pieces in the latter edition may not be by Hawthorne.

Also please note that dates in parentheses in the chronological list of Hawthorne's fiction and sketches are dates of first book publication of short stories and sketches. No such dates appear after the titles of short pieces which remain uncollected in book form. Titles in italics are of works more than about 50,000 words in length; titles in quotation marks are of works under about 50,000 words in length. Deceased characters in the fiction are named and identified if, in my opinion, they have a direct bearing on the plot.

It is a pleasure to acknowledge most gratefully the prompt and professional assistance given to me by librarians of the Library of the University of Pittsburgh, especially Miss Hazel Johnson. I am also indebted to the Harvard University Press and Edward H. Davidson, for permission to summarize their definitive edition of *Dr. Grimshawe's Secret* by Hawthorne,[5] which supersedes the inaccurate one prepared by Hawthorne's son Julian for publication in 1883.

Robert L. Gale

University of Pittsburgh
Pittsburgh, Pennsylvania

---

[5] Edward H. Davidson, editor, *Hawthorne's Dr. Grimshawe's Secret*, Cambridge, Mass.: Harvard University Press, Copyright, 1954, by the President and Fellows of Harvard College.

CHRONOLOGY

1804   Nathaniel Hawthorne (ne Hathorne) born July 4 in Salem, Massachusetts, son of Nathaniel Hathorne, sea captain, and Elizabeth Clarke Manning Hathorne.

1808   Father dies in Dutch Guiana.

1813   Hawthorne injures foot.

1818   Moves with mother and two sisters, Elizabeth Manning (born 1802) and Maria Louisa (born 1808), to Raymond, Maine.

1819   Returns to school in Salem.

1821-1825 Attends Bowdoin College, in Brunswick, Maine.

1828   Publishes *Fanshawe: A Tale.*

1836   Edits the *American Magazine of Useful and Entertaining Knowledge.*

1837   Publishes *Peter Parley's Universal History on the Basis of Geography,* in a children's series; publishes *Twice-Told Tales* (expanded edition, 1842).

1839-1840 Works as measurer of salt and coal in Boston Custom House.

1841   Publishes *The Whole History of Grandfather's Chair* (expanded editions, 1842, 1883) and lives at Brook Farm community, in West Roxbury, Massachusetts.

1842   Marries Sophia Peabody and lives (until 1845) at Old Manse, in Concord, Massachusetts (children: Una, born 1844; Julian, born 1846; and Rose, born 1851).

1845   Edits Horatio Bridge's *Journal of an African Cruiser.*

1846   Publishes *Mosses from an Old Manse.*

1846-1849 Works as surveyor in Salem Custom House.

1850   Publishes *The Scarlet Letter.*

1850-1851 Lives in Lenox, Massachusetts, near his friend Herman Melville.

1851   Publishes *The House of the Seven Gables, The Snow-Image and Other Twice-Told Tales,* and

	True Stories from History and Biography (incorporating *Grandfather's Chair*).
1851-1852	Lives at West Newton, Massachusetts.
1852	Publishes *The Blithedale Romance, A Wonder-Book for Girls and Boys,* and the *Life of Franklin Pierce.*
1852-1853	Lives at Wayside, in Concord, Massachusetts.
1853	Publishes *Tanglewood Tales, for Girls and Boys.*
1853-1857	Serves as U. S. Consul at Liverpool, England.
1857-1860	Travels and lives in England, France, and Italy.
1860	Publishes *The Marble Faun* (called *Transformation* in England) and returns to Wayside, in Concord, Massachusetts.
1863	Publishes *Our Old Home.*
1864	Dies May 19 at Plymouth, New Hampshire, and is buried in Concord, Massachusetts. His incomplete fragments include "The Dolliver Romance," 1864, 1876; *Septimius Felton: or, the Elixir of Life,* 1872; "The Ancestral Footstep," 1882-1883; and *Dr. Grimshawe's Secret,* 1883, 1954.

CHRONOLOGICAL LIST
OF HAWTHORNE'S FICTION
AND SKETCHES [1]

1828
Fanshawe: A Tale

1829
"The First and Last Dinner" (may not be by Hawthorne)

1830
"The Battle-Omen" (probably by Hawthorne)
"The Hollow of the Three Hills" (1837)
"An Old Woman's Tale" (1876)
"The Young Provincial" (1900) (may not be by Hawthorne)

1831
"Dr. Bullivant" (1876)
"The Haunted Quack: A Tale of a Canal Boat" (1900)
"The New England Village" (1900) (may not be by Hawthorne)
"Sights from a Steeple" (1837)

1832
"Hints to Young Ambition"

(1900) (may not be by Hawthorne)
'David Whicher: A North American Story" (may not be by Hawthorne)
"The Gentle Boy" (1837)
"My Kinsman, Major Molineux" (1851)
"Roger Malvin's Burial" (1846)
"The Wives of the Dead" (as "The Two Widows," 1843) (1851)

1833
"The Bald Eagle" (1900) (probably not by Hawthorne)
"The Canterbury Pilgrims" (1851)
"The Seven Vagabonds" (1842)
1834
"Passages from a Relinquished Work" (1854)
"Mr. Higginbotham's Catastrophe" (1837)

1835
"The Gray Champion" (1837)

[1] For details concerning most of the following items, consult Nina E. Browne, *A Bibliography of Nathaniel Hawthorne* (Boston and New York: Houghton, Mifflin and Company, 1905). For summaries of attributions to Hawthorne of several minor disputed pieces, see *Bibliography of American Literature,* compiled by Jacob Blanck (New Haven and London: Yale University Press, 1963), IV, 1-2.

"My Visit to Niagara" (1876)

"Old News" (1851)

"Young Goodman Brown" (1846)

"Wakefield" (1837)

"The Ambitious Guest" (1842)

"Graves and Goblins" (1876)

"A Rill from the Town Pump" (1837)

"The White Old Maid" (as "The Old Maid in the Winding Sheet") (1842)

"The Devil in Manuscript" (1851)

"Sketches from Memory" (1854, 1876)

"Alice Doane's Appeal" (1883)

"The Haunted Mind" (1842)

"Little Annie's Ramble" (1837)

"The Village Uncle" (as "The Mermaid") (1842)

1836

"Old Ticonderoga: A Picture of the Past" (1851)

"An Ontario Steamboat" (1900)

"Bells" (1900)

"The Duston Family" (1900)

"Nature of Sleep" (1900)

"A Visit to the Clerk of the Weather" (may not be by Hawthorne)

"The May-Pole of Merry Mount" (1837)

The Minister's Black Veil" (1837)

"The Wedding Knell" (1837)

1837

"Fancy's Show Box: A Morality" (1837)

"The Vision of the Fountain" (1837)

"A Bell's Biography" (1851)

"Dr. Heidegger's Experiment" (as "The Fountain of Youth") (1837)

"Fragments from the Journal of a Solitary Man" (1876)

"David Swan: A Fantasy" (1837)

"Edward Fane's Rosebud" (1842)

"The Toll-Gatherer's Day: A Sketch of Transitory Life" (1842)

"Endicott and the Red Cross" (1842)

"The Great Carbuncle: A Mystery of the White Mountains" (1837)

"The Man of Adamant: An Apologue" (1851)

"Monsieur du Miroir" (1846)

"Mrs. Bullfrog" (1846)

"The Prophetic Pictures" (1837)

"Sunday at Home" (1837)

1838

"Time's Portraiture . . . " (1876)

"Footprints on the Sea-Shore" (1842)

"Snowflakes" (1842)

"The Threefold Destiny: A Fairy Legend" (1842)

"Howe's Masquerade" (1842)

"Edward Randolph's Portrait" (as "Edward Randolph's Portrait: Province House") (1842)

"Chippings with a Chisel" (1842)

"Lady Eleanore's Mantle" (as "Lady Eleanore's Mantle: Province House") (1842)

"Night Sketches Beneath an Umbrella" (1842)

"Peter Goldthwaite's Treasure" (1842)

"The Shaker Bridal" (1842)

"Sylph Etherege" (1851)

1839

"The Sister Years . . . " (1842)

"The Lily's Quest: An Apologue" (1842)

"Old Esther Dudley" (as "Old Esther Dudley: Province House") (1842)

1840

"John Inglefield's Thanksgiving" (1851)

1841

The Whole History of Grandfather's Chair

1842

Biographical Stories

"A Virtuoso's Collection" (1846)

1843

"The Old Apple Dealer" (1846)

"The Antique Ring" (1876)

"The Hall of Fantasy" (1846)

"The New Adam and Eve" (1846)

"The Birthmark" (1846)

"Egotism: or, the Bosom Serpent" (as "Egotism: or, the Bosom Serpent: from the Unpublished Allegories of the Heart") (1846)

"The Procession of Life" (1846)

"The Celestial Railroad" (1846)

"Buds and Bird Voices" (1846)

"Little Daffydowndilly" (1851)

"Fire Worship" (1846)

1844

"The Christmas Banquet" (as "The Christmas Banquet: from the Unpublished Allegories of the Heart") (1846)

"A Good Man's Miracle"

"The Intelligence Office" (1846)

"Earth's Holocaust" (1846)

"The Artist of the Beautiful" (1846)

"Drowne's Wooden Image" (1846)

"A Select Party" (1846)

"A Book of Autographs" (1876)

"Rappaccini's Daughter" (1846)

1845

"P.'s Correspondence" (1846)

1846
"The Old Manse" (1846)

1849
"Main Street" (1851)

1850
"The Great Stone Face" (1851)
"The Custom House" (1850)
The Scarlet Letter
"The Snow-Image: A Childish Miracle" (1851)

1851
The House of the Seven Gables
"Ethan Brand: A Chapter from an Abortive Romance" (1851)
Biographical Stories

1852
"Feathertop: A Moralized Legend" (1854)
"*A Wonder-Book for Girls and Boys*
The Blithedale Romance

1853
Tanglewood Tales, for Girls and Boys: Being a Second Wonder-Book

1860
The Marble Faun: or, the Romance of Monte Beni (as *Transformation* in England)
" 'Browne's Folly' " (1876)

1862
"Chiefly about War Matters, by a Peaceable Man" (1883)

1864
"Pansie: A Fragment" (the first chapter of "The Dolliver Romance") (1864)
"The Dolliver Romance" (1864, 1876)

1872
Septimius Felton: or, the Elixir of Life

1882
"The Ancestral Footstep," 1882-1883 (1883)

1883
Dr. Grimshawe's Secret (1883, 1954)

1900
"The Ghost of Doctor Harris" (1900)

PLOTS

"Alice Doane's Appeal," 1835.

The author walks one pleasant June afternoon with two young ladies up Gallows Hill (outside Salem), which is covered with a noxious weed called wood-wax. Although guilt and frenzy once caused disgraceful deaths here, we are not a people of legend and therefore have not made the place a warning monument. The three try to imagine what the scene was like in 1692. The author seats the ladies on a rock near where the death tree stood and reads them his story, from the collection which he burned almost entirely.

Nearly a hundred and fifty years ago, the snow-covered body of a murdered man is discovered along a road three miles out of town. His face has a look of evil triumph. The author reads on. The victim is identified. The story concerns Leonard Doane, his affectionate sister Alice, and the jealous brother's comments to a certain wizard in his rock-sheltered hut concerning Walter Brome, who it seems resembles Doane in spite of superficial differences having to do with Brome's foreign education and the impurity of his passion for Alice. Doane and Brome meet on a lonely road. (The wizard listens, and his laugh sounds like the wind in his chimney.) Brome taunts Doane with proofs that his sister Alice has been shamed. Doane kills the mocker, feels his own spirit freed, but then grows torpid and curiously confuses his victim's face with that of his father, who was massacred on his hearth by night-striking Indians. Doane hears his sister's childish wail. The wind stirs not Brome's hair but that of Doane's father. Then Doane is on the icy road again, weeping on the face of his victim, whom he is frightened from burying under the frozen lake. Doane is confused: he thinks that Alice is guilty, then pure; he is sorry about Brome but shudders at the sense of deeper crime and also feels prompted by a fiend's whisper to kill Alice. So he visits the wizard, who must help under certain conditions. The author (with the bright eyes of his two auditors fixed upon him) evokes a ghostly atmosphere for his concluding action by describing the moonlit scene, with ice-sheathed trees and houses and streets, as Alice and her brother visit the village graveyard, all of whose tenants – all accursed – stream up above ground and stand in a pale group, wearing frightful expressions, like fiends pretending to be saints. The author gives the rest in summary. These devils and sinners are here to take delight in the discovery of a complex crime. It seems that all the incidents have been the results of a wizard, who saw to it that Brome should tempt Alice, his unknown sister, and then die by his twin-brother Doane's hand. The fiends are gleeful. At the end of the story, Alice appeals to the spectre of Brome, who absolves her from all stain; then the imps and shades flee from the presence of an angel.

The sun is down now. As the author reads about Alice and her brother, alone among the graves, his voice sighs with the sighing wind. He explains that the wood-wax here first grew from the wizard's nearby grave. The ladies start, then laugh, piquing the author, who decides to see whether truth is more powerful than fiction. While a twilight indistinctness envelopes buildings and tree-tops, he depicts a curious crowd from hoar antiquity following a group of condemned witches and wizards as they walk up Gallows Hill. Behind them come the triumphant avengers, led by diabolical Cotton Mather. The innocent will die; the guilty, grow old in remorse. And here the scaffold — but the author's pretty listeners are trembling and — sweet victory — crying at last. The past has now done all it can. As the three leave the hill, they see twinkling town lights and hear mirthful voices. But they regret the absence of any memorial on the hill, commemorating a grievous error and thus aiding the imagination in its appeal to the heart.

Walter Brome, Alice Doane, Leonard Doane, Cotton Mather.

"The Allegories of the Heart" — see "Egotism: or, the Bosom Serpent" and "The Christmas Banquet."

"The Ambitious Guest," 1835.

One night in September a family, including husband and wife, grandmother, and several children, gather about the hearth of their home in the Notch of the White Mountains. The place is a kind of tavern offering hospitality to travelers between Maine and the shore of the St. Lawrence. Suddenly a nameless young man enters, advances to the cheerful fire, and tells the family that he is on his way to Burlington, Vermont. When a rock falls from the cliff above the home, the father jokingly says that the mountain is nodding its head but adds that the family has a nearby refuge if any real slide should threaten. After supper the young man tells the group, especially the oldest daughter, that desire in him has become hope and now certainty, that though unknown now he will soon be gloriously well known. The father muses that if circumstances were different he might be a squire and a representative in the General Court. One of the smaller boys sings out that his ambition is to go out, late though it is, and have a drink at the Flume basin. A wagon comes by, and roughly singing men call out, uncertain whether to go on or put up at the tavern for the night. Since the landlord does not stir, they drive away. The daughter sighs, and the unknown youth hints that she might be in love. The wind wails, and they pile the fire higher. The grandmother says that her ambition is to have a mirror held before her when she is in her coffin, so that she may steal a glance at her funeral garb to make sure it is tidy. The young man wonders what drowning sailors think as they slide to watery graves. The roar outside increases. It is the Slide! They all rush out to their imagined sanctuary. The stream of roaring rocks divides and leaves the house untouched, as the people are swept to death, their bodies never found. In the morning, light smoke steals from the cottage chimney. Rumor has it that a stranger shared their catastrophe, but some deny it. His name remains unknown.

Esther.

"The Ancestral Footstep," 1882-1883.

I. Middleton, a young American, has been searching for some time through Eden-like England for the estate of his British forebears. For a while, he has been accompanied by an intelligent old man, whom he tells about his quest. Later he is entertained at the fine old estate of the Master, where he senses a mystery of hereditary sorrow or crime, and where he again sees the old man — now called Rothermel — and meets his daughter Alice. It seems that Middleton's first American ancestor, more than two hundred years ago, left a certain heirloom and a story about a criminally bloody footstep. At last a descendant has resolved to go to England to seek the truth; he learns that he is the rightful heir to a title and an estate, but decides to put faith in New World soil instead. Middleton and Alice talk. She feels that he holds the key to some blood-stained secret. He is ill at ease for challenging and upsetting these people. Next day he visits a hospital (later called Eldredge Hospital and also Pemberton's Hospital), where he sees the Master arguing with an angry gentleman, whom the Master soon describes to Middleton as the descendant of a sin-soaked family (which the Master has told Middleton about) and hence a claimant to the estate. Middleton sees that his own story and the Master's are probably linked. The Master explains that an ancient English family had three brothers. On the night of the wedding of the oldest, the second brother evidently spirited away the bride. She was never seen again, and the second brother — who also disappeared — was thought to have been murdered on the manor-house threshold. When the oldest brother died childless, the estate went to the third brother. Now an American, claiming to be a descendant of the second brother and the first brother's wife, appears and wants the estate. Middleton queries the Master briefly and then leaves, tempted to drop the entire matter. Instead, he walks through the woods near ---- Chace and is confronted by fierce Mr. Eldredge, who the Master has just explained lives in the contested manor-house and intends to claim the dormant title. Thinking Middleton is the annoying Yankee impostor, Eldredge tries to club him with his rifle butt but falls dead when the weapon accidentally discharges a bullet through his heart. (Later Hawthorne decides not to have Eldredge die.) Middleton apprehensively steps into the woods, as Roper passes by, checks the corpse, and then robs it. Then Alice happens by, and Middleton steps out, proclaims his innocence, and learns that this is the estate he seeks and deserves, further that the old man (already identified as Rothermel and Alice's father) was a swindler of many men (including Middleton's father) in America and has been more recently a canny but also slightly demented estate manager for Eldredge. Alice then takes Middleton into the old mansion, saying that it is his, and leads him to an ornate cabinet which looks like a miniature palace. He seems to recognize it from a dream, takes a key from his watch-chain, and opens a secret compartment containing – nothing but dust.

II. The family of the two feuding sons is shamed. The younger son wandered away. So the father founds the Eldredge Hospital for impoverished, educated wanderers. One old man there, named Hammond (Rothermel and Wentworth earlier) and apparently a student of American statesmanship, becomes Middleton's friend and one day offers to show him around the Eldredge manor-house. While the two men are talking, into Hammond's room comes a slight, healthy, free-stepping young lady (his daughter Alice) whom Middleton has already observed in the neighborhood, once in a barouche with another young lady (probably Eldredge's sister, judging from the family arms). Hammond speaks of the two quarrelsome brothers and the blood-stained threshold of their house; he adds that the title to the place is unsettled. Although Middleton is frequently tempted to get away from the whole affair, he goes — with a sort of shame — to Smithell's (here called Pemberton Manor) with the old hospitaler, is admitted, and is guided about by Squire Eldredge himself. Middleton takes no beer, feeling that he should not accept the hospitality of a place which he may try to claim, is told about the Ghost Chamber, and is there shown an elaborate cabinet of ebony and ivory carved to resemble a mansion. Eldredge explains that it is rumored to contain a family secret, which if shown would explain the fate of the estate. Middleton turns pale before it and soon leaves by another door with Hammond, who shows him the bloody footstep. Now Hawthorne summarizes his plot again. Middleton is the descendant of a man who stole his older brother's fiancee, married her (perhaps in Virginia), and changed his name in shame. His younger brother held the estate, and his heirs are claimants of the baronage. Middleton's ancestor left a document detailing the unsavory incidents and revealing his real name. The family may all be Catholic. Middleton, a rising Congressman, is alternately attracted and repulsed by the story but decides to visit the midland counties of England to seek his ancestral home. He meets old Hammond, a swindler who when in America knew Middleton's father. Eldredge is in possession of the estate, raves when he hears of pretenders coming over to investigate their rights, and even asks a lawyer's opinion on proceeding against Middleton illegally. Eldredge pursues lovely Alice, who warbles like a bird through the lovely English woods, as a possible instrument of nefarious aid for him. She tells perplexed Middleton that he should avoid tragedy and return to the New World. He should not open a pit of corruption which might infect all. Hawthorne now anticipates the conclusion by saying that enigmatic Alice proves an angel of light, the present possessor of the estate dies, and Middleton resigns his claims and, Adam-like, makes Alice his new-epoch Eve. Hawthorne plans to weave into his romance plot-strands dealing with various American expatriates whose woes he listened to at the [Liverpool] Consulate. His romance must have a grotesque, tragic, pathetic central scene; all else would then fall into place.

III. Middleton is happy in his present abode. He enjoys walking through the graveyards, the church, and especially the Eldredge grounds. He feels like the original emigrant of the ancestral family come home again. Eldredge, a lonely Catholic, is rumored to be strange, perhaps through looking for the track of the bloody footstep, as far away as Italy. One day while walking in the woods Middleton sees frail old Eldredge following his footsteps until the old man encounters him under an old oak tree. The two talk, and the American is able to convert the lonely old man's annoyance into curiosity by mentioning a New World family named Middleton with a secret two hundred years old. When Eldredge invites him to inspect his house, Middleton says that he is curious about the legend of its bloody footstep. Hawthorne again sketchily summarizes the story to this point: Middleton has met the hospitaler, visits the Eldredge mansion, sees the cabinet in the form of a small palace, and is later invited to dinner and to spend the night. One day while walking in the woods he encounters free, bright Alice, who asks him about American women, talks about women's rights, and urges him to value his part in the future of America above any social ambitions in England. Soon thereafter, Middleton goes to Smithell's to dine: present are his host's sister Miss Eldredge and a priest. Eldredge talks learnedly about paintings, serves a delicious Italian wine, and then reports the rumor that in America proof may exist to substantiate his claim to his estate. Middleton replies candidly that his father told him about the bloody footstep. That night he is assigned to a splendid old room, which contains the miniature palace. He muses in front of it until midnight, then retires to dream about it. In the morning he dreamily presses a square of the tiny palace floor, finds a recess beneath it, fits his key into it, and sees some sealed documents. But he does not examine them, feeling that he should not do so unless in his host's presence. Now Hawthorne summarizes the story again, this time stressing Eldredge's Italian and Catholic background. Middleton is appointed minister to a small Continental court. The neighborhood Mayor gives him a dinner, at which Eldredge sees the claimant and decides to plot murder. Hawthorne muses at length on Eldredge's subtle, anguished, half-insane nature. The murder attempt, perhaps by poison or by drowning in a moat, will fail and thus perhaps lead to Eldredge's suicide. The scene in which dreamy Middleton's suspicions will save him must be carefully wrought. Middleton, with Alice's encouragement, may resign the estate to Eldredge's very young, Italian-bred daughter. The old hospitaler is next resketched. After an active career as a swindler in America, he is now pathetically idle. Perhaps Alice should be his granddaughter, born in America but a sculptress in Rome for a few years. Hawthorne at the end wonders how to order the events: an introduction sketching consulate activities, an essay on various American expatriate claimants to English estates, then Middleton's arrival in the neighborhood of what he believes to be his ancestral home, the hospital, then the hospitaler taking him to the hall — the owner of which flits ahead of them like a ghost but is seen in mirrors — Middleton's appointment as ambassador, the Mayor's dinner at which Middleton meets Eldredge, that man's inviting the American to his hall, and finally events leading to the attempted murder.

Copley, Edward Eldredge, Squire Eldredge, Eldredge, Eldredge, Eldredge, Miss Eldredge, Alice Hammond, Hammond, Hopnort, the Master, the Mayor, Middleton, Middleton, Mrs. Middleton, Price.

"The Antique Ring," 1843.

Edward Caryl is a lawyer with few clients but some success already as a young American writer of poems, tales, and essays, some of which have been praised by Bryant, Griswold, Ticknor, and other authorities. When Caryl gives a star-bright diamond ring to his fiancee Clara Pemberton, she challenges him to compose a legend about it. A short while later, he reads her the following:

When the Earl of Essex is condemned to execution by Queen Elizabeth, he is visited by the deceitful Countess of Shrewsbury. He gives her a diamond ring and asks her to take it to the Queen and with it to beg her to forgive him and rescue him from disgrace. The Countess agrees. He tells her that the ring was once the property of Merlin and that his wizardry made it the home of a fiend which would do only good so long as the ring was a pledge of love and faith. But if either the giver or the receiver proved false, the evil spirit would flash red and work mischief until the ring was purified by being the medium of some holy act. The Countess takes the ring but fails to show it to the Queen, and Essex is beheaded. The ring burned the Countess's breast, went to her tomb with her, was stolen from the Shrewsbury burial vaults by Cromwell's desecrating soldiers, and was involved in evil during the reign of King Charles II and later in Sir Robert Walpole's times. The ring crossed the Atlantic Ocean and one night after an eloquent New England church service turned up, glowing white, among the copper coins in good Deacon Tilton's collection box. Offered thereafter for sale by a fashionable jeweler, it was purchased by the teller of this legend.

Clara Pemberton and her friends compliment Caryl on his charming tale. When the girl asks him the moral, he protests that he cannot separate idea from symbol but suggests that the gem may be likened to the human heart and the evil spirit to falsehood.

[William Cullen] Bryant, Edward Caryl, Queen Elizabeth, the Earl of Essex, [Rufus] Griswold, [Fletcher, James, John, and Joseph] Harper, [George Stillman] Hillard, Clara Pemberton, the Countess of Shrewsbury, [William Davis] Ticknor, Deacon Tilton, Deacon Trott, Sir Robert Walpole.

"The Artist of the Beautiful," 1844.

One day old Peter Hovenden, a retired watchmaker, walks with his pretty daughter Annie past the shop of his former apprentice and now his successor, Owen Warland. Peter jeers at the thin-fingered young man for having only ingenuity enough to make little Dutch toys and then walks on by the blacksmith's shop of brawny Robert Danforth, whose honest work he praises above that of any mere watchmaker, himself included. Owen made pretty things from his earliest butterfly-chasing days, loved to watch and imitate the beautiful movements of nature, and feared steam engines and other utilitarian monsters. He does not really like to mend timepieces, although he is adept at doing so, because he prefers the eternal to the temporal. He is now secretly occupied at fashioning a diminutive object of some mysterious sort. When Danforth the blacksmith delivers a tiny anvil to him, the deep-voiced fellow's presence so upsets delicate Owen that he spoils with a single movement of a steel instrument the work of months upon his secret creation. He turns sluggishly to his mundane work in the succeeding weeks, mends the clock in the church steeple so well that he is praised by the grateful townspeople and even by coldly sagacious old Hovenden. Soon thereafter, Owen goes wandering into the dark woods to pursue butterflies and watch water insects; he returns to his shop at night and begins working on his minutely beautiful conception. But one day Annie enters with a thimble needing repair, looks at his secret work without the loving sympathy which Owen craves and needs, and carelessly pushes with a needle point what she calls the whirligig which she sees — and thus ruins months of Owen's work. He spends the ensuing winter months riotously drinking, but then one warm spring day a butterfly flies through his open window and inspires him to return to his work again. The townspeople call him mad, and perhaps he is, to think that he can follow beauty along its airy track to heaven. One day Hovenden comes in to announce the engagement of his daughter Annie to Danforth. With one stroke of a small instrument, Owen shatters the delicate machinery of his tiny invention. He should not have forgotten Annie's lack of love for him. He grows sick, begins to gain weight, and starts to babble foolishly. Then one day, for what reason it is not recorded, he turns once more to the task of his life, certain that death will not overtake him before he has completed it. Much later, one winter night, Owen calls upon Danforth and his wife – who by now has given her brawny husband a stolid infant son – and crafty Hovenden. The artist of the beautiful presents Annie with a bridal gift. From within a cunningly carved box of ebony and pearl, which Danforth greatly admires, flies a mechanical butterfly with gorgeous purple wings and a halo of stardust. It flutters lifelike about the room but soon settles on the hand of the sly baby boy, who has a face sneeringly resembling his grandfather's. The child crushes the wondrous creation into glittering, useless fragments. Annie screams, while her father laughs scornfully. But Owen sits placidly by; since he has risen high enough to achieve the beautiful, its material symbol has little value for him now.

Mrs. Annie Hovenden Danforth, Robert Danforth, Danforth, Peter Hovenden, Owen Warland.

"The Bald Eagle," 1833 (probably not by Hawthorne).[1]

One summer day a coachman brings a report to the Bald Eagle, the tavern of a sleepy little Connecticut Valley village, that Marquis Lafayette is coming through on his way north. Immediately everyone prepares to welcome the hero. Jonathan Dewlap, the landlord of the Bald Eagle, and his wife bustle about, as do the town tailor, the oratorical lawyer, and the poetic schoolmaster. The local militia and a troop of horse wheel through various maneuvers. A Negro lookout is stationed on the highroad, falls asleep in the hot sun, and roused by a wagon rattling nearby fires his signal gun. But no Lafayette appears. Distant thunder is mistaken for a salute to the general, but it brings only rain and a dampening of spirits. At twilight the coachman returns with the report that Lafayette has gone north by another road.

Jonathan Babcock, Boaz, Caesar, Jonathan Dewlap, Mrs. Jonathan Dewlap, Marquis General Lafayette, Peleg Popgun, Tribulation Sheepshanks, Squire Wiggins.

[1] See Jacob Blanck, *Bibliography of American Literature,* IV, 2.

"The Battle-Omen," 1830 (probably by Hawthorne).[2]

One frosty winter evening, two young men are returning home after participating in a brief military encounter with some hostile Indians. As the wind wails over the frozen lake and enters the dark forest beyond, they begin to talk about omens in the sky believed by their New England forebears to presage battles and casualties. One of the men tells the other about a fisherman fifty years ago who once heard martial music in the air and the tread of soldiers yet to be killed in battle. While the two young men are talking, darkness falls and they suddenly hear ghostly music and drums pealing through the wilderness.

(No named characters.)

"A Bell's Biography," 1837.

One night the writer narrator decides to tell the life of the bell whose accents he hears. It is in an elevated position, makes a great noise in the world with its iron tongue, and hence deserves a biography. It was made by the French, partly of captured Spanish cannon, and was given to the Jesuits then converting the American Indians. It was in Our Lady's Chapel of the Forest, west of Lake Champlain, until the church was burned during the Old French War by some rangers, who wanted to take it home to their city but who were killed on the way back. The bell then lay concealed in the forest until found by some of Colonel Bradstreet's scouts on their way toward Lake Ontario toward the end of the War. They brought it to the narrator's town. Ever since, it has celebrated victories, tolled at funerals, and spoken at night to anxious men, workers, criminals, new mothers, lovers, and dying men.

Colonel [John] Bradstreet, [Marquis] Lafayette, Deacon Lawson, Rev. Mr. Rogers, [George] Washington.

"Bells," 1836.

Hawthorne discusses the loneliness of places without bells, the

[2]See Donald Clifford Gallup, "On Hawthorne's Authorship of 'The Battle-Omen,'" *New England Quarterly,* IX (December, 1936), 690-699.

influence of bells over various human feelings, the introduction of bells into Christian churches, the shape and size of bells, their tone, and the first bells in North America. He mentions having seen martyred Father Ralle's bell in the Bowdoin College Museum.

Father [Sebastien] Ralle [Rale].

Biographical Stories, 1842.

Edward Temple, aged about eight or nine years, is afflicted with a severe disorder of the eyes and must sit with bandaged eyes in a darkened room for several months. He is comforted by his kind mother, his brother George, who is three or four years older, and Emily Robinson, a seven-year-old orphan living with the Temples. Little Edward's father tells the boy many stories, based on fact but shaped into interesting narratives. First he tells the life of Benjamin West, which pleases Edward, who says that he can almost see the persons and events in the story. Next day Emily begins to teach him how to knit. In the evening, Mr. Temple tells the story of Sir Isaac Newton, which inspires George as well as Edward, who, however, wonders what star-gazing Newton would have done if he had been blind. Next day George refuses to sit with his eye-bandaged brother and instead plays all day. That night, Mr. Temple seems not to notice little expressions of hard feelings and instead tells the children about Samuel Johnson's penance for his not helping his father. The three children are moved; to Emily's delight, George and Edward make peace with one another. When Mr. Temple has to be away on a trip, Edward meditates, repeats poetry, solves arithmetical problems, learns to read with his fingers, and entreats his now kind brother to go out and play more often and spend less time amusing him with accounts of school events. Meanwhile, Emily tells him stories from a book about flowers which she has been reading. In due time Mr. Temple returns home and tells the children about Oliver Cromwell, who in his youth had a fist-fight with haughty Prince Charlie (later Charles I). Little Edward says that he would rather be blind than be a king. Gradually the boy learns to enjoy life without sight. One evening his father relates a story about Ben Franklin, who when ten years old stole some building stones to make a public wharf, was chastised by his rigidly moral father, a few years later contributed to his brother's newspaper, and much later became famous for his scientific experiments and his *Poor Richard's Almanac*. The following evening is devoted to an account of little Christina of Sweden, who became queen when her father was killed in victorious battle and who learned that power does not bring happiness. Emily is shocked at learning how mannish Queen Christina became. George shakes unseeing little Edward by the hand. Emily kisses him goodnight. Let us hope that he is happy when we meet him again.

  Emily Robinson, Edward "Ned" Temple, George Temple, Temple, Mrs. Temple.

"The Birthmark," 1843.

  Late in the last century a brilliant man of science named Aylmer leaves his beloved laboratory long enough to marry a beautiful young woman named Georgiana. Aylmer has devoted himself too unreservedly to science, and his love for his wife can become stronger only by intertwining itself with his professional devotion. One day shortly after their marriage, Aylmer tells her that her birthmark, a tiny hand on her left cheek, shocks him because it renders her imperfect. Georgiana is offended but gradually begins to hate the birthmark, which is really only a flaw of the sort by which Nature reminds everyone of his ineludible imperfection and mortality. After her husband talks in his sleep of operating on it with the aid of his laboratory assistant Aminadab, she agrees to let him try to remove it, even though she fears that the process may result in deformity or even death. Next day he secludes her in an underground boudoir near his laboratory, on the way to which they pass Aminadab. This shaggy, gross worker gazes on her beauty and says that if she were his wife he would never part with her birthmark. In the gorgeous boudoir, lit by perfumed lamps, Aylmer entertains his wife with magic shows and demonstrations, tries to take her portrait on a polished plate of metal, talks about alchemy and the elixir vitae, scatters pungent perfumes in the air, and tells her about a virulent poison he has developed and about a potent cosmetic. Her medicine must be even stronger. Georgiana feels that he is already treating her: her system seems stirred up. She reads in his library and in a large folio recording his own experiments, many of which, she notes, have ended in failure, since he ever aspires to the infinite. One day she visits him in his laboratory, against his wishes, and he is momentarily annoyed but praises her bravery and confesses that her birthmark has roots deeper in her being than he thought at first. He has a powerful if dangerous draught, which she eagerly volunteers to quaff, since she wants to satisfy, if only for a moment, his deepest conception. So she drinks it with a placid smile, speaks slowly for a moment, and falls asleep. Unaccountably, while watching her symptoms, Aylmer kisses her birthmark but then shudders. The mark is disappearing. He is ecstatic. Aminadab chuckles in the distance, and his master calls him a clod. Georgiana awakens, tells Aylmer that she is dying but that he must never repent for aiming loftily. The fatal hand has linked an angelic spirit with a mortal frame. Perfectly beautiful for a moment, she then dies. Gross Aminadab laughs again, thus exulting over earth's defeat of the immortal essence. If more profoundly wise, Aylmer would have woven his mortal life with the celestial, looked beyond time to eternity, and found the perfect future in the present.

Aminadab, Aylmer, Georgiana.

The Blithedale Romance, 1852.

Miles Coverdale, a poet in his late twenties, talks briefly to Old Moodie, who stands in the shade and mentions the Veiled Lady, a scientific mesmerist now in fashion, and then decides not to ask Coverdale a certain favor. So the young man goes home, has a cigar and a glass of sherry, and the next day, which is a snowy April one, goes out to rural Blithedale to start an experiment – without much hope of success but never repenting his idealism. Under the tutelage of lean, grim Silas Foster and his fat wife, a few city dwellers are establishing an agrarian commune. A statuesque, darkly beautiful writer who goes by the pen-name of Zenobia is there from town with a fresh flower in her hair. Soon Hollingsworth, a rugged, bearded young would-be reformer, stamps in through the wild snow, bringing a pallid, slender young woman named Priscilla with him. She was delivered to Hollingsworth by an old man who begged him to take her to Blithedale. She kneels weeping before Zenobia, who is rather imperious at first but then accepts her with a smile and a gesture. After supper, shared democratically by the city-folks and their countrified brethren – during which Coverdale feels slightly ashamed of his superciliousness – they all sit before the fire. Foster mends a shoe, his wife knits and naps, and the others talk while Priscilla gazes in rapture at Zenobia's majestic beauty. Finally they retire, Coverdale sleeping feverishly because he has caught a bad cold.

While Hollingsworth cares for him tenderly and Zenobia cooks him gruel – not very well, either – Coverdale slowly recovers; he overhears Hollingsworth's prayers and admires the man's apparent tenderness, although he deplores Hollingsworth's single-minded ambition to reform criminals and his inability to sympathize with Fourieristic reform theory. Coverdale certainly admires the mysteriously voluptuous Zenobia, whose fresh flower daily in her hair seems to symbolize her. He wonders if she has ever been married. By May-day, he is on his feet again and outside, where he notes an improvement in the appearance of Priscilla, who laughs gaily with Zenobia but seems sluggish in the presence of Hollingsworth. Coverdale, remaining outside the group, studies his three friends, although he knows that he should not. Hollingsworth seems inhuman through single-mindedness. Priscilla seems to be growing too happy too fast, and to be dangerously unaware that human relationships inevitably change. And enigmatic Zenobia seems jealous of the girl, although the gossips of the community, which is growing in numbers, link Hollingsworth and Zenobia as lovers. One day in July, Old Moodie mysteriously appears, asks whether Zenobia is acting friendly or imperious toward Priscilla, whom he calls his little girl, and then sees Priscilla drawing Zenobia along by the hands until the older woman looks haughtily down at her, on which Moodie shakes his head sadly and withdraws. A few days later, while rambling in the woods Coverdale is accosted by a devilishly handsome stranger, who asks pointed questions about the philanthropic blacksmith Hollingsworth, rich Zenobia, and nervous young Priscilla. Coverdale answers drily, and the stranger, who seems as false as his glittering false teeth and his metallic laugh, introduces himself as Professor Westervelt. Coverdale climbs a tree well known to him for its comfortable seclusion and chances to overhear Westervelt and Zenobia as they walk by beneath him. The professor seems to be urging her to abandon Priscilla, but Zenobia between sighs of anguish refuses.

The next evening Zenobia entertains her fellow transcendentalists with a story, "The Silvery Veil." One day Theodore wagered that he could learn the identity of the famous Veiled Lady. So he hid in her private room, and when she entered it after her demonstration, he seized her veil and got one glimpse of her beauty before she vanished. At the same instant, a pale maiden turned up amid some visionary people, who took her to their hearts and made her rosy. Among the group was a lady who was soon warned to cast a veil over the girl, since she was ordained by fate to be the lady's deadly enemy. When the lady did so, a bearded magician appeared and seized the girl, his slave forever. As Zenobia finishes the legend, she throws a fine gauze over Priscilla, who droops and seems on the point of fainting.

On Sundays, the Blithedale residents go various paths. One Sunday, Hollingsworth, Zenobia, Priscilla, and Coverdale go to the rock from which [John] Eliot is rumored to have preached to the Indians. There they harangue each other on the subject of women's rights. Zenobia vows to change the present set-up, at which point Coverdale unfortunately smiles but then adds that he feels women are better at religious sentiments then men are. When Hollingsworth says that women are really only men's helpers, Zenobia remains surprisingly mild, while Priscilla sits at

Hollingsworth's feet as though to prove his assertion. On the way back, Zenobia takes Hollingsworth's hand, and, although Priscilla could not have seen the movement, the girl begins to droop. Coverdale, who did see it, inquisitively and even maliciously asks Priscilla, to her annoyance, why she has a heavy heart.

Toward the end of the summer a crisis develops. While they are fence-mending, Hollingsworth with rough eloquence begs Coverdale to help him convert the whole farm area into a refuge for reclaimable criminals and hints that he has the money to do it. Suspecting that the single-minded reformer would use Zenobia's wealth and drop tender Priscilla, Coverdale accuses him of deviousness and moral obliquity, sees only loathsomeness in trying to reform vile sinners, and angrily refuses. Soon thereafter, in August, he leaves Blithedale, feeling unloved and wanting to get back to reality. He offers to be Zenobia's honest if unwise counselor but is haughtily refused. He cautions Priscilla to accept change. Walking past Hollingsworth without a word, he goes to town and takes up residence in the back room of a hotel, where he drearily muses through a rainy day until Blithedale seems unreal and the street noises are refreshing. He dreams that night of Hollingsworth and Zenobia passionately kissing over his bed. Next day he resumes a kind of Peeping-Tom observation of a fashionable boarding-house with its rear to his hotel. In its drawing-room he happens to see Zenobia, Priscilla, and Westervelt, the last of whom notices him at his window and points him out to regal Zenobia, who salutes and rebukes him at once by drawing the linen curtain as though ending an act at the theater. He spends some time in his hotel room nursing a sense of insult, until he decides to go call on Zenobia, which he does. In her drawing-room he is struck by her luxurious artificiality — indicated by a jeweler's flower in her hair now — and her shallow artiness. They talk about Blithedale, and in an attempt to shake her into sincerity he criticizes Hollingsworth for his impractical single-mindedness, which, however, Zenobia prefers to call greatness. So Coverdale changes the subject to Priscilla and suggests that she might impress Hollingsworth, whose powerful personality would fatally absorb the girl's. Zenobia now calls in

Priscilla, who passively takes Coverdale's hand and impresses him with her soft beauty, now seemingly finer than Zenobia's shinier splendors. When he brings up Hollingsworth's name again, Zenobia warns Coverdale to stop acting like a providential agent in the name of duty, welcomes oily Westervelt to her room (but with an averted face of hatred), and with passive, white-clad Priscilla leaves in that man's carriage. Instead of feeling unwanted and going to new scenes, Coverdale repairs to a colorful saloon frequented by Old Moodie, whom he spies behind a screen, then plies with claret and listens to. The sad old man confesses that twenty-five years ago he was a rich man in the Middle States, had a beautiful daughter, committed a crime to preserve the remnants of his squandered wealth and thus occasioned his wife's death, fled to Boston and let his family cover up for him, lived in a former gubernatorial mansion converted into an apartment house for innumerable poor Irish families, married a seamstress, had a pale daughter, lost his second wife to death, and told his daughter — Priscilla — about her beautiful half-sister, suffered when the younger daughter fell under the spell of a handsome wizard with false teeth and was taken away from him, and learned that his only brother — a bachelor — died leaving considerable wealth to his older daughter, Zenobia, rumored to have married and known to be financing the experiment at Blithedale out of hidden grief. Coverdale imagines the rest: Moodie sent for Zenobia and without telling her the truth warned her to be kind to Priscilla; he wants Zenobia's beauty to be set off by money but also wants security for Priscilla — now in danger again because of Westervelt.

Some weeks pass; then, one September day Coverdale witnesses a traveling show in a country-village hall, which advertises the Veiled Lady. Hollingsworth, who is also in the audience, tells Coverdale that Zenobia is back at Blithedale but then convulsively stares at the mention of Priscilla. When the bearded mesmerist, whose practice is loathsome to Coverdale, brings out his shrouded medium, the rugged blacksmith rises and breaks the spell by telling the girl that she is safe. A couple of days later Coverdale sets out to walk back to Blithedale and, though anticipating no warm welcome, soon feels exhilarated by autumnal nature all about him. When he draws near the farm where he toiled long and hard, it looks dead; but he sees a party of masqueraders. He laughs at their Arcadian garb and antics, runs off to Eliot's rock pulpit, and there encounters Hollingsworth, Priscilla, and Zenobia. They have been having a scene, which Coverdale interrupts. It evidently involved Hollingsworth's judgment and condemnation of Zenobia, who now in her turn voices some comments on Hollingsworth: he sought her for her money (which she now says is threatened), he tried to wreck the Blithedale venture in purer living, he dropped Coverdale as useless in his plan, he was ready to sacrifice even Priscilla (whom she forces him to admit he loves), and he is nothing but a cold and heartless egotist with a project. Priscilla kneels before Zenobia and says that they are sisters, which the older woman says that she has just learned. Then she tells Priscilla to leave with Hollingsworth. When the two have gone, Zenobia bursts into dry sobs. She recovers, suggests that Coverdale write up her story with the moral that a defenseless woman should neither fight nor stray from the beaten path, then criticizes Priscilla as pale and puny and hence not so good a woman for Hollingsworth as she, dishonored though she was earlier by a handsome villain. She looks gorgeous in her anguish as she gives Coverdale a cold hand in farewell. He lies listlessly beneath the pulpit rock, has a tragic dream, and starts up as the late moon is rising. Finding Zenobia's handkerchief by the river and fearing that she has drowned herself, he rushes to the farm and rouses Hollingsworth and garrulous old Foster, and the three take a boat to grapple at midnight for her body, find it, and carry it back to the farm. (For twelve years now Coverdale has remembered her grotesquely stiffened form.) To her burial Priscilla walks with muffled Moodie, and Coverdale with Hollingsworth. Westervelt is there too. He tells Coverdale that Zenobia was foolish to throw away her life, which might have included twenty more years of beauty and influence, just for a dreamy philanthropist. Coverdale quietly curses the mesmerist but recognizes a degree of truth in his words. Priscilla grieves but survives, since she is mainly devoted to Hollingsworth, whom, some years ago, Coverdale sought out in his cottage with Priscilla. The depressed man confesses in tears that he has not reformed a single criminal, not even his own murderous self. Coverdale moralizes that no one should be a single-minded reformer at the expense of his heart and the hearts of others near him. Coverdale has not returned to Blithedale, although when he feels world-weary he is sometimes tempted to do so. He is now a middle-aged bachelor, has traveled to Europe twice, has published a book of poems, disbelieves now in progress and lacks purpose, and has an explanatory secret — he is in love with Priscilla.

Miles Coverdale, Fauntleroy, Mrs. Fauntleroy, Mrs. Fauntleroy, Silas Foster, Mrs. Silas Foster, Dr. [Rufus] Griswold, Hollingsworth, Old Moodie, Priscilla, Theodore, Professor Westervelt, Zenobia.

"A Book of Autographs," 1844.

The author is studying a volume of autograph letters, mostly of Revolutionary War soldiers and statesmen and addressed to General Palmer. It is pleasant to think back three quarters of a century and imagine the circumstances surrounding the letters. There are several from earnest John Adams expressing uncertainty and awe, and later determination. One is from Washington, clear, calm, unvaryingly cool-headed. Two are from Franklin, one a homely one to his wife. Samuel Adams's fragmentary letter is utterly plain. Hancock's letter reveals a majestic but hardly real person. Patriotic General Warren's hand is ungraceful but courteous and efficient. Other letters are from Henry Laurens, Jefferson (very brief), Robert Morris, Judge Jay, General Lincoln, sturdy Baron Steuben, Lafayette, General Schuyler (about some Indians at the Salt Springs of Onondaga), the traitor Arnold, courteous and vigorous Hamilton, sternly simple Tim Pickering, mysterious old Aaron Burr, and soldier Henry Knox. Other letters are of later date and include samples from neat Henry Clay, Calhoun, and Andrew Jackson. Literary persons whose letters are included are Timothy Dwight, Colonel Trumbull, charming Washington Irving, Margaret Davidson, delicate Washington Allston, and Noah Webster (with an anecdote about General Washington). God has taught the human soul how to guard its secrets, or else it would be possible to read more deeply than we now have done into the characters of those whose autograph letters are in this volume.

> John Adams, Samuel Adams, Washington Allston, [Benedict] Arnold, [James] Bayard, [General John] Burgoyne, Aaron Burr, [John] Calhoun, Josias Carvill, Henry Clay, [George] Clinton, Margaret Davidson, Davies, Timothy Dwight, [Benjamin] Franklin, Madam [Benjamin] Franklin, [General Thomas] Gage, Colonel Gridley, Haldiman, Acquilla Hall, [Alexander] Hamilton, [John] Hancock, [Sir William] Howe, Washington Irving, Andrew Jackson, Judge [John] Jay, [Thomas] Jefferson, Henry Knox, [Marquis] Lafayette, Henry Laurens, General [Henry] Lee, Leroy, General [Benjamin] Lincoln, Robert Morris, General Palmer, Timothy "Old Tim" Pickering, Polly, Sally, General [Philip] Schuyler, J. T. Smith, Baron [von] Steuben, Mrs. Stevenson, Colonel [John] Trumbull, General [Joseph] Warren, General [George] Washington, Noah Webster.

" 'Browne's Folly,' " 1860.

Nathaniel Hawthorne writes a letter from the Wayside, August 28, 1860, to his cousin [Richard Manning of Salem], telling of a hill near Salem on which a royalist named Browne once built a foolishly magnificent pleasure-house which was shaken by an earthquake in 1755 and which was thereafter moved down the hill. Browne fled to England during the Revolution, and the mansion was cared for by Richard Derby, an in-law of Browne. In time the house fell into ruins. Once, some schoolboys explored it and opened a supposedly haunted closet, in which they found some old family portraits. Hawthorne closes by saying that he has forgotten what story he once planned to write about "Browne's Folly."

Browne, Richard Derby.

"Buds and Bird Voices," 1843.

When balmy spring comes at last to the narrator and peeps into his study, his thoughts take wing and he determines to be nothing but happy. The snow leaves the corpse-like earth like a white napkin taken from its face. Bits of green appear. The trees are still naked but give promise of foliage. The narrator delights in his willow, lilac shrubs, and apple trees. He notices the disarray of nature when the snow retreats. Cluttering the brown ground are last year's leaves, dead branches, a ruined bird's nest, and dead vegetation from the garden. In the soil of the mind and the garden of the heart are withered things too, but no wind is strong enough to sweep them away. The birds are now a delight, even the crow (a thief and probably an infidel), certainly gulls, ducks, and the many smaller songsters, and wasps, bees, and butterflies. It is pleasant to climb a nearby hill and view the region, which is partly flooded by the river. Thank God for spring, which renews our greenness.

(No named characters.)

"The Canterbury Pilgrims," 1833.

One moonlit summer evening, Miriam and Josiah stop at a beautiful fountain which fills from the hillside but never overflows. They love one another and are therefore leaving their nearby Shaker community to marry and live in the outside world. They are soon joined at the cistern by a group of six disillusioned people, who decide to pause on their way up to the Shaker village, tell their worldly stories, and thus perhaps persuade the lovers to return home. First a disappointed poet explains his pangs and how unappreciated he is. Then a ruined merchant speaks of his failure, adding, however, that he hopes to organize the finances of the Shakers on a profitable basis and could help Josiah if he turns back. Next a yeoman bitterly tells the couple how hard he worked but how much smaller his earnings grew year by year. Finally the yeoman's wife warns Miriam and Josiah that if they marry they will gradually become gloomy and peevish. She points to her two fretful children and adds that two more were blessedly taken by God. At this point, the exchange of a few kind words, or even a mutually confidential glance, might have renewed the love between the yeoman and his wife. But no, the moment passes. Josiah and Miriam are moved by the parable-like accounts of the strangers. But they embrace one another and announce that the world will never be dark for them, because they are in love.

Father Job, Josiah, Miriam.

"The Celestial Railroad," 1843.

The narrator recently dreamed of visiting the City of Destruction, between which and the Celestial City the Celestial Railroad has been built. The narrator goes by coach with one of its directors, Mr. Smooth-it-away, over a bridge across the old Slough of Despond to the station-house, where John Bunyan's old friend Evangelist is the ticket agent. The passengers are ready, since their burdens have all been deposited in the baggage car. Apollyon, the engineer, seems to breathe fire and smoke as they start. Soon they pass two old-fashioned pilgrims with cockle shells, staffs, rolls of parchment, and packs. Apollyon flirts scalding steam over them. Smooth-it-away explains that Bunyan's old Interpreter's House has been sidetracked. A tunnel passes through the Hill of Difficulty. The narrator is sorry not to be able to see beautiful Miss Prudence, Miss Piety, and Miss Charity, until he learns that they are now dry old maids. Next the train speeds through the Valley of the Shadow of Death, radiantly lit by gas collected from the hellish soil. The passengers are assured that the mouth of Hell is only a half-extinct old volcano. They drop some people off without taking on any newcomers, then speed on. Sinful faces thrust themselves at the seated passengers — mere freaks of the imagination, no doubt. Going past the cavern where Bunyan's Pope and Pagan dwelt, they see a misty giant, called Transcendentalism, fed on moonshine and shapeless. Then they arrive at Vanity Fair, where the narrator spends many days happily wandering, since there is no longer any animosity between residents there and pilgrims to the Celestial City. Many are the items purchased there by giving bits of conscience, and sermons of the various ministers there are so easy that no one needs to read anything to become wise. Some sell their places in the Celestial City for tracts of land in the city of Vanity. But one day when the narrator sees the two old-fashioned pilgrims, Stick-to-the-right and Foot-it-to-heaven, they impress him and he decides to travel farther. So he and Smooth-it-away take the train again, soon going past the reputed door to Hell. The narrator later drowses, passes the lovely land of Beulah, then surmises from a shriek of steam that the train is approaching the final station-house. He hears celestial music coming from the other side of the river bordering the Celestial City. The music greets the two old-fashioned foot pilgrims. The narrator hopes for the same reception, and Smooth-it-away smoothly reassures him and tells him to take the ferry-boat. The narrator hurries on board, is laughed at smokily by Smooth-it-away from the far shore, and is dumped into the cold water. He awakens from his dream with a shudder of relief.

Apollyon, Prince Beelzebub, Rev. Mr. Bewilderment, Miss Charity, Rev. Mr. Clog-the-spirit, Evangelist, Flimsy-faith, Foot-it-to-heaven, Greatheart, Hide-sin-in-the-heart, Live-for-the-world, Lord of the Celestial City, Lord of Vanity Fair, Miss Piety, Miss Prudence, Scaly-conscience, Rev. Mr. Shallow-deep, Smooth-it-away, Stick-to-the-right, Rev. Mr. Stumble-at-the-truth, Take-it-easy, Rev. Mr. That-tomorrow, Rev. Mr. This-to-day, Giant Transcendentalist, Rev. Mr. Wind-of-doctrine.

"Chiefly about War Matters, By a Peaceable Man," 1862.

Feeling it to be a kind of treason to go on writing at a time of national conflict, the author with a friend [William Davis Ticknor] leaves snowy New England in March [1862] and meets the spring half-way. As it advances north, they go south through Connecticut, New York, New Jersey, and Philadelphia, which is balmy. On they go, to Washington, which they just miss seeing as a camp, since the day before sixty thousand men crossed the

Potomac. They visit the Capitol, see Leutze – at work on a vast painting of the Rocky Mountains – Secretary Seward, and then President Lincoln at the White House. Uncle Abe is sallow, queer, sagacious, and utterly trustworthy. The travelers go on to Alexandria, see where Jackson shot Ellsworth, inspect an old slave-pen, and visit Fort Ellsworth – which in a century will be a historical monument and will contribute to our richer past – and the denuded woods around it. They see some Negro refugees from the South, and the author expresses his fear for their future. Next he sees a vigorous young officer on horseback, and the sight makes him conclude that war morally invigorates youth. He visits McClellan's headquarters, observes the general as he reviews his troops, and pronounces the dark, neat, strong commander courageous and honest in appearance. The next morning the author and his friend leave Washington over a newly laid railroad track for shabby, forlorn Harper's Ferry, where the author ruminates on the justice of the hanging of John Brown, visits a prison containing an assortment of captured rebel soldiers, and concludes that the South should hope for Northern victories to make it moral. Next he inspects obsolete Fortress Monroe, concludes that old ideas and old men are unfit for war, and suggests that if in the future wars were fought only by soldiers fifty years of age and older there would be fewer old maids. In the waters around the fortress is the outmoded flagship the *Minnesota,* which the author boards, only to lament the advent of the ironclad, one of which, the *Monitor,* he also boards. At Newport News he sees the remnants of the sunken *Congress* and *Cumberland,* more cause for the author to lament scientific improvements in warfare. Back to rainy Washington, and Willard's Hotel, a busy meeting-place of many types. How many of the drinking, smoking, office-seeking soldiers seen here are true in their hearts to the Union? If one looks at the whole subject generously he will forgive many pro-Southerners in the Federal city who would wish to see the Yankees driven north again and everything re-established on its old basis – or worse. Once, Washington was warm, gracious, and southern in character, they say, and the Union wrongly pushed the Southerners out and forced them to fight reluctantly against the Constitution. So they whisper tearfully, and the author is sorry for them. And now the North must woo the South as the lion does its bride, roughly but in the hope of a quiet household again at last.

[Emanuel] Leutze, President Abraham "Uncle Abe" Lincoln, General [George B.] McClellan, Major Ben Perley Poore, Secretary [William Henry] Seward.

"The Chimaera" (VI. in *A Wonder-Book for Girls and Boys*), 1852.

Handsome and brave young Bellerophon promises King Iobates of Lycia that he will rid his land of the destructive Chimaera, a goat-headed, lion-headed, snake-headed, fire-breathing monster with a wriggling tail. The young man comes to the Fountain of Pirene in Greece, to bridle and ride the winged horse Pegasus in his battle with the Chimaera. After waiting and waiting, he sees the spirited steed descend from the skies, drink at his favorite fountain, munch a little clover, and then caper about. Bellerophon waits for the right moment and then leaps astride the marvelous horse, which instantly bounds miles into the air in an effort to shake off his weighty rider. But the man bridles Pegasus, tames him, and the two become fast friends. Soon armed for the attack, Bellerophon tracks the Chimaera to its lair by following the trail of ruin which it has left in Lycia. In the fearful aerial battle which ensues, the hero chops off the goat head, then the roaring lion head, and finally, enveloped in flames from the third head, mortally wounds the monster, which uncoils its tail from Pegasus and drops from the sky like a meteor.

Bellerophon, King Iobates.

"Chippings with a Chisel," 1838.

Years ago, the narrator spent a summer at Edgartown, on the island of Martha's Vineyard. He becomes acquainted with a carver of tombstones named Wigglesworth, from central Massachusetts. The narrator studies the various styles of tombstones on the Vineyard: Gothic, plain, and rugged. Old Wigglesworth combines simplicity amounting almost to childishness with an almost unearthly wisdom. The two discuss many of his different tombstone customers: an old widow, who orders a stone for her first love, killed by a whale forty years before; an old man who, accompanied by his fourth wife, buys slabs for his first three wives; a rough old whaling captain whose wife has died; a woman who wanted a stone for her missing sailor husband who then turned up; and a mother, one of whose daughters died while the other came along to talk with Wigglesworth. He and the narrator discuss epitaphs, then other customers: a tavern woman who offers to pay Wigglesworth by boarding him for a while; a man who wants a marker for an enemy; an antiquarian who wants to honor an Indian; an old woman Bible-reader; an infidel; a rich man named Norton; a sick young maiden. The narrator voices the opinion that one should remember the dead, yes, but never by elaborate tombstones. Wigglesworth is aghast. Still, the narrator concludes, he has learned much from talking with the stone-cutter, among other things, that life's sorrows can comfort as much as its joys can.

Norton, Wigglesworth.

"The Christmas Banquet" ([II.] from "The Allegories of the Heart"), 1844.

Roderick [Elliston] is reading this story to his wife Rosina and their friend the sculptor [George Herkimer], as they sit in their summer-house.

A rich old man dies and leaves money for an annual Christmas banquet for the ten most miserable persons available — not to make them merry but to prove that their human discontent is real. Two trustees prepare the invitation lists. The banquet is presided over by a skeleton, reputedly that of the benefactor, with a wreath of cypress in its bony fingers. The first year the guests include a despondent man, one with an ulcerated heart, a hypochondriac, one whose trust in man turned sour, one whose earnest message none would listen to, an aged gallant, a distressed poet, a melancholy idiot, an almost perfectly beautiful lady with a cast in one eye, and finally Gervayse Hastings. This handsome though cold young man seems out of place, and he puzzles the talkative guests by saying that they seem only shadows to him. The next year a murderer, sick and quaking persons, frustrated couples, a miser, and the like are invited, and also Hastings again. Once more the guests object, but the trustees assure them that this cold guest deserves a place at the Christmas banquet, even that none of the others would exchange places with him. The talk around the macabre table indicates that sorrow has admitted them all to spiritual depths — all but Hastings. Many years pass. Hastings grows old and bald. Finally he attends the banquet at the age of eighty. His life has seemed illustrious but terribly cold and has never involved any warmth of intimacy, not even with his wife and children. He tells the other guests — who now include a straying clergyman, a disappointed theorist, a ruined millionaire, confused philanthropists and politicians, unproductive women, and a voiceless orator — that his misfortune is the worst. He feels chilly always, his heart is a mere vapor, and no one and nothing about him is more than a shadow. The presiding skeleton with its cypress falls in a dusty heap. When the guests look back at Hastings, his shadow has ceased to flicker on the wall.

When Rosina frankly criticizes her husband's story for not sufficiently describing the central character, Roderick admits as much but says that it is hard to dramatize a person who never partakes of a single human grief but remains instead outside everything.

Aaron Burr, Stephen Girard, Gervayse Hastings, [George Herkimer], Father [William] Miller, Roderick [Elliston], Rosina [Elliston], Smith.

Circe's Palace" (IV. in *Tanglewood Tales, for Girls and Boys*), 1853.

After the fall of Troy, Ulysses and his men have their troubles with Aeolus, the ruler of the winds, with Polyphemus the one-eyed Cyclops, and with the Laestrygons, and then arrive at a mysterious island. When his hungry men become impatient, Ulysses bravely explores the center of the island, finding a palace of white marble, which he is so suspicious of that he returns, killing a fat stag with his spear on the way back. The stag is soon devoured, and the men then divide into two groups, and half — under the leadership of Eurylochus — go to the palace in search of more food. Eurylochus hangs back while his hungry men enter and are royally entertained by smiling Circe the enchantress, four lovely maidens, and many servants. But at the touch of her wand, the twenty-two gluttons are turned into swine and go grunting and squealing off to their sty. Meanwhile Eurylochus, dismayed by the noise, has returned to report to his wily leader, who vows to rescue his men. On his way to do so, Ulysses encounters his friend Quicksilver, who plucks and gives him a unique flower, the fragrance of which will ward off Circe's most virulent poison. The enchantress and her crew welcome Ulysses, ply him with delicious but deadly wine — which, however, has no effect on him, since he is protected by Quicksilver's flower — and are dismayed when he retains his regal human shape. Seizing Circe by the hair and drawing his keen sword, Ulysses demands that she restore his men to human shape, which she does, although ever after that their voices seem grunty and squealy.

King Aeetes, Aeolus, Circe, Eurylochus, Medea, King Picus, Polyphemus, Quicksilver, Ulysses.

"The Custom House" (the prefatory essay to *The Scarlet Letter*), 1850.

Deciding to wax autobiographical, the author describes the custom house of his native Salem, with its flag and eagle over the entrance, and its square, lofty office where he is surveyor. Business is decaying, but there is still some bustle. He recalls his grim ancestors and then describes some of the customs officers under him: a collector, several tired old workers, a few others who are youthful and strong, an old inspector, one utterly honest fellow completely suited to his position, and others. While the author has this job, he finds himself unable to have anything to do with literature, which to the practical eye seems devoid of significance. He thinks ineffectually of the past. Then one day in a cluttered second-story room he finds a small package in which there is a piece of tattered scarlet cloth with a letter A embroidered in gold. When he puts it on his chest, it seems to burn him. With it is a roll of paper, on which a former surveyor, Jonathan Pue by name, dead these eighty years, recorded the story of Hester Prynne. Pue's shade gives the author a kind of ghostly permission to prepare Hester's story for publication, but he cannot seem to manage it while at the custom house. Not even moonlight and a coal-fire inspire his romantic imagination. He is turning witless because he is dependent upon Uncle Sam rather than upon himself. Then General Taylor is elected President, and the author is swept out of office in his third year at the custom house. Rusty though he has grown, he now turns to Pue's manuscript. Salem fades, and he becomes a citizen of somewhere else.

[Bronson] Alcott, Bertram, [Dr. William] Ellery Channing, Deputy Collector, King Derby, [Ralph Waldo] Emerson, Simon Forrester, Billy Gray, [George Stillman] Hillard, Hunt, Inspector, Inspector, Kimball, [Henry Wadsworth] Longfellow, General [James] Miller, the Naval Officer, P. P., Phillips, Pingree, Hester Prynne, Surveyor Jonathan Pue, Shepard, Governor [William] Shirley, President [Zachary] Taylor, [Henry David] Thoreau, Upton.

"David Swan: A Fantasy," 1837.
Young David Swan, aged twenty years, leaves his home in New Hampshire to go to work for his uncle, who is a grocer in Boston. David walks part way. Then, lying down at noon to wait for the stagecoach, he falls into a deep sleep. People pass him and comment in different ways about him. A merchant and his wife are so intrigued by his honest appearance that they are about to adopt him and shower him with gold, but their

coachman calls them away. Next a pretty girl comes by, blushing at his good looks and flicking a bee away from his eyelid. Then two would-be thieves and murderers approach and are about to rob him, prepared to kill him if he stirs; but a dog happens by and frightens them off from their purpose. David finally rouses and catches his stagecoach, little realizing that money, love, and death brushed close by him.

Henry, David Swan.

"David Whicher: A North American Story," 1832.[3]

Before a fire one July day, a group of auditors listen spellbound as a bespectacled little man, who praises the Indians at the expense of interloping white people and their false accounts, tells many vivid Indian stories, including one about David Whicher. About two centuries ago at Merry-Meeting Bay, Maine, where the Kenebeck and Androscoggin rivers meet, Whicher, a widowered basket-weaver, confidently leaves his daughter Judith and his infant son Joshua one summer afternoon to go to the woods to chop ash trees and split the wood with wedges and a hammer. Suddenly he is surrounded by four Indians, reeking with bloody scalps along with other trophies from their white victims. Whicher has always been peaceful, trustful of Jehovah and the golden rule, and unafraid. So he puts on a cheerful face, boldly asks for some beech-nuts from the youngest Indian, shows the group how to weave green withes into hand-cuffs, and almost manages to escape by playfully binding the wrists of two of his captors. But when one with a ready gun grows suspicious, Whicher diverts the attention of all by showing them how he weaves baskets. Suddenly he sees his daughter's chestnut hair tied across one tawny chest, together with the blue beads of his baby son. His faith in the goodness of all men is shaken. Shall he lie down and perish without fighting back? He contrives a plan. Showing the four savages how to split

[3] For details, see Nelson F. Adkins, "Notes on the Hawthorne Canon," *Proceedings of the Bibliographical Society of America,* LX (July-September, 1966), 367.

branches from a fallen sycamore with wedges and then beginning to split its tough trunk, he invites them to insert their hands in the split and try – two on each side – to pull the trunk apart. When they do so, Whicher hammers the wedge out, and the trunk springs shut, crushing and holding the Indians' hands. Whicher then wonders whether he has not been a born killer all along, merely awaiting sufficient opportunity. He inspects the booty of the four helpless redskins and finds his little son's locks on the youngest. He lifts his axe to brain them all, but stops, tells them that if they are innocent God will keep them from harm – even from the wolves now howling in the lengthening shadows nearby – and then leaves. He returns to the spot exactly one year later to weep on the anniversary of his terrible loss. He finds four skeletons pinned to the fallen log and still trying to pull it apart. The auditors of the story are amazed. One agrees that Indians take a great deal of killing.

David Whicher, Joshua Whicher, Judith Whicher.

"The Devil in Manuscript," 1835.

One bitterly cold December evening, the narrator goes to visit his friend Oberon, a disappointed author. In a typical lawyer's office the two sit before a raging fire. In getting there the narrator became so chilled by the freezing wind that he is momentarily tempted to roll among the blazing coals. Oberon suddenly tells him that he fancies that the devil is in his pile of manuscripts – tales in which he tried to embody his conception of the fiend represented in tradition and written accounts of witchcraft. Oberon has lost his peace of mind and has become lonely through surrounding himself only with the shadows of his imagination. All publishers have rejected his work. He is tempted to consign his whole sheaf of writings to the flames. When the narrator remonstrates, Oberon insists that there is a demon in his work, gets out a bottle of champagne and drinks liberally from it, recalls his various times of literary inspiration and their accompanying moods, and then flings the manuscript into the hottest part of the fire. The sheets shrink momentarily and then burn fervently. Oberon sees his glowing lovers, his hellish fiends, his martyred holy men, and even a city on fire. He imagines that a fiend glared at him from the fire and then rushed up the chimney. The frustrated author begins to repent and to anticipate only an obscure grave, when suddenly there is a cry of "Fire!" from outside. On such a wintry night the pumps will be frozen and the wooden town will become one great bonfire. Engines rattle. Church bells ring out the warning. The narrator suspects the cause of the fire. Oberon guesses the truth and leaps in frenzied joy. From his writings the fiend has gone forth to startle the whole region. Oberon is triumphant at last. His brain has set the town on fire!

Oberon.

"The Dolliver Romance," 1846, 1876.

One June morning, Dr. Dolliver, a gentle old man, rises to the happy shouts of his great-granddaughter Pansie, for whom he is responsible. His wife Bessie has been dead half a century, and all of his grandchildren are also dead. The venerable old fellow is rheumatic and infirm; but he puts on his many-colored, patched old morning-gown and hastens downstairs to share breakfast with his beloved Pansie and their kitten. He sometimes confuses the charming little three-year-old with his buried grandchildren. He is not a real doctor but rather an apothecary, apprenticed ages ago to Dr. John Swinnerton, who bequeathed him a brazen serpent for a sign. Business declined, but after Pansie became his charge the old man dutifully and bravely stirred himself and has lately been earning a little money along with much respect. Some townspeople are pleased to recall that patriarchal Governor Bradstreet once blessed him. They call the old man Grandsir Dolliver now, greet him loudly, and gladly shake his hand; but the greetings are faint and the handshake seems muffled. Sometimes the estranged old man fancies that he is young again, until he gazes at himself in the mirror. But Pansie's firm little hand warms him, and when he has put the child to bed at night and sits gazing into his cavernous fire, he looks reposeful, trusting, and even beautiful.

Grandsir Dolliver has now finished breakfast. He goes into his herb garden, inherited from learned old Dr. Swinnerton along with his dwelling and some abstruse old manuscripts, illegible and in Latin. Dr. Dolliver's brilliant grandson Edward — Pansie's father — made the garden produce repulsively luxurious blooms, deciphered a certain knotty manuscript, produced seemingly miraculous drugs as a result, and gained more money and fame than his grandfather. That is, until one dawn his young wife found Edward dead in his laboratory. Perhaps he sampled one of his curious drugs. He evidently burned all the old manuscripts before he died. His wife died soon thereafter and left Dr. Dolliver to care for her little daughter Pansie. The old man shouldered his burden bravely. This morning, while in the garden, he sees Pansie uproot a tropical plant and urges her to desist. She runs into the graveyard adjacent to their home. He follows, falls, frightens her, and leads her home again, on the way to which he pauses at a stone marked "Dr. John Swinnerton, Physician." Swinnerton was rumored to have had the power to avoid death. Having no grandchild to tease him, he chose death. Pansie drops the tropical flower into an open grave; once covered, the flower blooms no more.

The dose of the cordial which Dr. Dolliver took the night before makes him frolicsome, and he plays joyfully with Pansie. He recalls that he knows all of the ingredients of the cordial except one, which a strange-acting madman added to the bottle once, in the form of a powder. Now, Dr. Dolliver regularly, almost nightly, takes a single flashing drop of the ruby-colored liquid. When he does, he feels better; and when he does not, he sleeps badly and has many aches. He does it all for Pansie, so that he can work and provide for her. His eyes grow brighter, until they gleam and even frighten Pansie at times. He wishes that he had manufactured the cordial commercially; he might have made a fortune. One day wrathful Colonel Dabney enters the apothecary's shop, criticizes Dr. Dolliver for looking devil-ishly young and bright-eyed, speaks of a bloody footstep bearing its track through the Dabney family, and tells Dr. Dolliver that he knows about the mysterious stranger and the efficacious powder which he shook into the cordial some years ago. Suddenly the colonel argues that the cordial is his by the right of three hundred years, produces some gold and then a pistol, and demands the bottle. The terrified apothecary produces it, whereupon Colonel Dabney takes a huge drink from it, jumps high into the air vigorously, laughs rapturously, but then falls dead with a thump. Dr. Dolliver calls in the authorities, who believe his account and pronounce the much-disliked colonel's death due to a visitation of God. Dr. Dolliver is now outwardly quiet but is inwardly disturbed. Will he venture to sample the silver-cased bottle again?

The Black Man, Governor [Simon] Bradstreet, Colonel Dabney, Mrs. Bessie Dolliver, Edward Dolliver, Mr. Edward Dolliver, Pansie Dolliver, Dr. "Grandsir" Dolliver, Martha, Dr. Professor John Swinnerton.

"Dr. Bullivant," 1831.

A century and a half ago there flourished in Boston a fellow with abundant animal spirits — quite a contrast to our prejudiced notion of the Puritans, who in our pictures of them seem somber and gloomy. Imagine Cornhill in 1670. Most of the buildings are wooden, and the street signs are all strange. On one white post is the gilded bust of Aesculapius. Inside the apothecary's shop is a slender, tall, white-haired old man, the "Doctor" (Bullivant), who dispenses drugs and with them dry, salty, and racy quips. He also mimics departing customers. This generation of Puritans is more materialistic, international-minded, and independent. It includes freebooters and criminals, whom the licentious reign of Charles II does little to discourage. In 1679 a Synod convenes to try to renew the former sanctity. The result is a division of the people into two classes: the remnants of first settlers and others of gloomy temperament; and the new, thoughtless, evil, and unprincipled adventurers. During the despotic four-year rule of James II, acts of royal usurpation occur, and among the foremost people favoring them is Dr. Bullivant, who is influential in the detested government of Sir Edmund Andros and his cohorts. But with the first rumors of the attempt of the Prince of Orange to take the throne of England, Andros and many others of the court party find themselves in prison. One of their number is Bullivant, who for a time paces the floor of his ten-foot-square cell, looking very dingy and sheepish, and devoid of his usual stock of quips. Once the authority of William and Mary is quietly established, however, Dr. Bullivant is released and is tolerantly allowed to return to his shop, where until his death he again delights in making people laugh and then sneering at them up his sleeve.

Sir Edmund Andros, Dr. "'Pothecary" Bullivant, Increase Mather, Edward Randolph.

Dr. Grimshaw's Secret, 1883, 1954.[4]

[Preliminary Studies] Hawthorne sketches out his intention to show an American, perhaps a politician, returning to England two hundred years after his forebears have left England for America, and with a vague sense of wrong seeking his reputedly legitimate British title and lands, now in the hands of a sinful, perhaps slightly insane British nobleman, who is dramatically different from the American in character. The democratic American and the partly admirable British aristocrat should be contrasted; but the American must expose and ruin the Britisher and then perhaps make partial amends by marrying his daughter. The American, the rightful heir, should have a family resemblance but show the changes which American life and perhaps family misfortunes might produce. The American, Chatsworth by name, descends from some runaway outlaw of the family, comes to England expecting little but finds reality matching his dreams; he visits his ancestral home and also a hospital endowed by the Chatsworth family for poor travelers. The story will open at Salem in the home of an old antiquarian, who traces genealogies

[4]Summarized by permission of the publishers from Edward H. Davidson, editor, *Hawthorne's Dr. Grimshawe's Secret,* Cambridge, Mass.: Harvard University Press, Copyright, 1954, by the President and Fellows of Harvard College.

and has some medical knowledge and provides for a sprite-like girl and an incipiently noble young boy of obscure background and with a desire to go to England to seek the answer to some mystery. Time passes, and the boy, now grown, is in England dreamily following up the many hints and suggestions of his old guardian, now dead, but soon runs into trouble and lands in a hospital with pensioners and a kind warden. At the hospital, which he has memories of, the hero, Ethridge, may first meet the heroine; while there, he visits his ancestral lands, meets persons of the family, and while entertained by the incumbant nobleman may surprise some of the family by his knowledge of their history. Though the rightful heir, he generously refuses to claim the title and lands. He could meet the nobleman at a public dinner, where he might speak, since he is a distinguished politician. Hawthorne adds more jottings, about hair growing in a grave, churches, castles, a bloody footstep, hospitals, and English matters.

[First Draft] In a house near a graveyard, kind old Dr. Etherege lives with a pale, large-eyed little girl named Elsie and a proud, intelligent little boy named Ned. Etherege has many old books and cobwebs. One day Mountford, an English lawyer, visits the old man and asks his advice on tracing a man named Colcord, who was a seventeenth-century bondservant from England. They examine a certain grave to the location of which Mountford has directions but find only a rusty old sixteenth-century key, which he pays the sexton for and takes. Ned suddenly asks the Englishman if he knows about the bloody footstep, an ever-fresh print at an old British house, about which the strange boy has repeatedly dreamed.

Dr. Etherege continues to study his spiders. Also, he is rumored to keep a room in readiness for a mysterious guest. Will it be his absent brother, or a long-separated fiancee? Hawthorne tells himself that he must develop the shadowy, almshouse background of Ned. One night Dr. Etherege asks his two charges if they have been happy. When they say yes, he bids them goodnight, sits up with his manuscript and his huge African spider, and is found dead in the morning by the maid, who, after his funeral, sweeps out the cobwebs but finds that his great, intimate African spider is only an empty skin. Dr. Etherege by his will makes provision for Ned's education and leaves the small remainder to Elsie, with directions that she go to the doctor's brother James abroad. Now Hawthorne writes himself a long note telling how to start the novel, sketch the scene, play up Ned, and suggest the background of the brother in England – a speculator involved with an estate having a bloody footstep and now reduced to the status of a hospital pensioner. Hawthorne goes on to hint at the family sin, a maiden's corpse whose hair continues to grow, a silver key for her coffin, and the regenerative effects of spider webs.

One lovely summer day a plainly dressed but authoritative young man is traveling along delightful hedges and then an unfrequented path when he is set upon by rough strangers and knocked unconscious. When he awakens, he is in the plain room of a thoughtful-looking palmer who feeds him medicine with a spoon marked, as are many things about the place, with a leopard's head (later a wolf's head). The wounded invalid cannot seem to collect his wits, and everything seems like a half-recollected dream to him. Soon Dr. Blathwaite, the bachelor antiquarian warden of the place – which is a hospital for indigent gentlemen – visits the patient, whom the palmer, Pearson, identifies as Edward Etherege from his papers. Edward explains that he was on a walking tour and was exploring an old British estate which he had heard of when he was shot or struck by an unseen assailant. Later Dr. Brathwaite [sic], offers his guest Edward a big British lunch, and the two talk about aristocratic blood and antiquarianism, and then Edward reads in one of the books lining his host's study an account of the bloody footstep of the Grantly family, which intermittently claims a barony. When the warden takes him through the hospital, Edward is reminded of his past by a Saxon object held in the hand of a statue of the founder of the hospital, and then by cobwebs all over a venerable hall. Next they visit Pearson, the palmer who rescued the American; the secretive old fellow's schoolteacher daughter is just leaving his room, which is cluttered with ancient parchments.

The three men discuss American republicanism, British class distinctions, and reverence for the past. Edward senses that old Pearson, who admits that he lived in America long ago, knows something about him and is keeping it back.

One day, when Edward is feeling better, Warden Brathwaite takes him to the village of Brathwaite and shows him some thatched houses, gardens, and old families. They observe a dark, Italianate man on horseback whom the warden identifies as the present Brathwaite of Brathwaite Hall and as a villainous claimant to the title of Lord Hinchbrooke. He is Catholic and has sent a son and a daughter to school in America. Edward and the warden go on to a charming Norman church with a tower, half-obliterated graves, and a huge yew-tree. Then they talk with a pretty girl, named Miss Cheltenham, who is sketching the church. She looks like the person whom Edward saw in the room of the canny old palmer. When they look at a grave marked "Richard Oglethorpe 1613," Edward feels memories stirring, as he often does here. He thinks again of the bloody footstep and then wonders whether the pretty girl is Elsie somehow. The two men proceed to the lovely deer park near Brathwaite Hall. A little later, Edward receives a letter from the State Department asking him to become an ambassador (to the court of Hohen Linden, as is later revealed). He accepts, but with certain political misgivings, which Warden Brathwaite cannot understand. Much impressed and now less supercilious, the warden plans a dinner for his illustrious American guest, who spends some of his time while still recuperating in talking with the palmer about such antiquarian topics as ocean-separated families.

Now Hawthorne writes a long note to himself about how he must develop the story. Two hundred years ago three British brothers quarrel over a young lady and thus split the family and stain it with sin. Or two of the three sons may be in love with the lady, who dies faithful to the exiled brother and has buried with her some token useful as evidence. Catholicism will be involved. What about the warden and the old palmer? The latter might be the true heir. He should have some trait — perhaps a bloody foot — which causes him to be much observed and often jeopardized. He might descend from the masked Protestant beheader of Charles I or from a Quaker friend of George Fox. Next Hawthorne tells himself how to begin the story: with the cobwebby doctor and his wards, the little boy and girl ... Edward Etherege should then appear in England and be in danger of being poisoned by the Italian incumbant at Brathwaite Hall, who may be represented as having a nun-like daughter. The old pensioner should be cleverly portrayed as an indecisive victim of too much conscience, but the true heir of the Brathwaite title.

Now we see Edward interrupting the slightly repellent old palmer as he conscientiously tends his garden; the two debate the function of conscience and whether ends justify means. One day, while the hall is being tidied up for the banquet, Hammond calls upon Edward, reminding him that he (as Mountford) saw Edward in America when he was a boy. When the two see Pearson and his daughter, Hammond talks to the old pensioner rather unpleasantly, at which his daughter asks Edward to put a stop to it. Now Hawthorne advises himself to treat Pearson the palmer carefully — perhaps introducing him at the hour of his death — and then launches into another long note to himself on plot developments: the pensioner poisoned because he is the true heir, a silver key to be found in the growing hair of the coffined corpse, the pensioner partly crazy and working mischief through excessive would-be benevolence, the girl perhaps his grand-daughter, the pensioner perhaps a regicide — thus the bloody footstep — or a Quaker, the New England doctor the possessor of inheritances and secrets concerning the central family and in the habit of keeping a place in his home for an ever-absent relative, the doctor perhaps the former lover of the lady with the peculiar golden hair, the doctor's diabolical spider, the coffined lady perhaps the victim of murder, the British agent and his suspicions and machinations, the attempted assassination of Edward Ether-ege, the warden's grand dinner for Ambassador Etherege and the Italian's plot to poison him, and the benevolent interference by the feminine relative of the pensioner.

Now comes the great day of the warden's dinner in Etherege's honor. A tremendous variety of food and drink is offered to

many distinguished and very British guests, most of whom are
rather cold toward the American, especially at first. Brathwaite,
the Italian pretender to the title, is also there. After dinner there
is music, and a loving cup is passed. Then come many speeches;
Etherege speaks eloquently and successfully on relations between
England and America. Late in the evening, ominously dark
Brathwaite invites Etherege to spend a week at his remote estate.
The American reluctantly accepts. After the banquet, Etherege
has a midnight snack with his host and tells him about his
upbringing and his belief that he is entitled to the Brathwaite
title and lands. The warden believes that he knew Etherege's
foster-father, the learned doctor, a man named Archdale, who
left England after unsuccessfully courting a Brathwaite lady and
later through revenge wanted Etherege to take the title.

Though reluctant to accept Brathwaite's hospitality — if unafraid of it — Etherege decides to do so. A little later, in spite of a
severe warning from Pearson [who now seems to have merged
with the British agent who interviewed Etherege's foster-father,
the doctor in New England], Etherege finds himself in front of
the Brathwaite mansion. He calls it his home in a voice so loud
that Elsie (formerly Pearson's daughter), out sketching, hears and
warns him away yet again. He offers to return to New England,
where they used to be together. She says that it cannot be. Then
sarcastic-looking Brathwaite comes up. Next Hawthorne addresses
himself another note on ideas and difficulties. Elsie must know
that Etherege's claim is baseless. The founder of the American
line might be a wife-killer who takes his boy across the ocean.
The pensioner will be a saint with a legitimate claim. The Italian
might love Elsie and be unspeakably wicked in some terribly
depraved manner. And so one September day Etherege as a guest
goes to the manor-house of Lord Brathwaite, who is absent but
whose servant shows him to a large room — perhaps a room in
which his ancestors stayed before leaving forever. Etherege feels
no sense of homecoming. He wanders out, gets dreamily lost in
the house, and meets Father Angelo, the personal priest of the
place. He shows the American a musty library, in which an
enormous spider spins webs among the books. Is this spider

related to the one which Etherege's foster-father tolerated? Lord Brathwaite enters, gives his guest his left hand to shake, entertains him with a sociable luncheon, then lets him wander through the grounds. Torn between wanting to go back to America, a land of the future, and to remain in England, secure and peaceful, Etherege returns to the house by another path and finds the bloody-looking footstep on a threshold, glistening in the recent rain. Lord Brathwaite tells him that perhaps it was made by an agonized man leaving the place and destined to return later. Etherege ventures to doubt it.

Hawthorne now writes another long note to himself. The pensioner might be brought to the house or be shown as a kind of hired inmate there. The New England doctor should have been wronged thirty years ago in England; Hammond may now be the dead doctor's agent in this country. Perhaps the true heir seduced the wife of the doctor. She committed suicide and was buried in a curious coffer, and her body has turned to golden hair. The doctor might have paralyzed with spider venom his enemy, who is now confined in the mansion. The present Italianate resident hears of Etherege and plans to poison him or confine him with the other inmate. The horror of the story must be mitigated by surface bacchanals.

So Etherege is at the mansion, where he is interested in Hammond the steward, who acknowledges loyalty not to Lord Brathwaite but to the doctor of New England, gone now these twenty-nine years. The house seems to exert a baleful influence over all. Etherege feels that the house has captured him and that Lord Brathwaite is obligated to make him his victim. One evening when the two are having dinner, Etherege explains that he has come over to England as a possible aspirant to his host's title, at which Lord Brathwaite — first saying that he would demand firm proof before he would give up the estate — calls for a special bottle of wine, invites his guest to sit in the long-empty chair reserved for the wandering heir, and fills their glasses. As soon as Etherege drinks, his head swims. Later he awakens from what seems like a century-long sleep and finds himself in a dim old chamber with a terribly old man. Recalling the old family legend of an undying ancestor, he mentions the name of Sir Edward Brathwaite and speaks of Norman Hanscough (a variant name of the New England doctor), at which the old creature falls in a rattling heap.

Meanwhile the warden rides over to the mansion with a letter for Etherege from the President of the United States. On the way there, he encounters the pensioner and then Elsie, both of whom warn him of Etherege's danger. Once there, the warden is told that Etherege left that morning for London. He goes out, sees the pensioner again, and the two confront Brathwaite, who with Hammond beside him opens the house to them to search and seems confident until the pensioner goes straight to a secret stairway and soon finds Etherege, beside whom is the dead old man and an aged coffer. Etherege produces the silver key, and the chest reveals masses of golden hair. The pensioner, producing a matching lock of hair from his pocket, is proclaimed the true heir. Brathwaite is ashamed, and Hammond seems relieved.

Hawthorne now writes another long note to himself. He considers the opening of the novel at the Charter-Street burial ground where the doctor lives with the two children and the spider. He saved a partially hanged man (Hammond), who thereafter became his moral slave. A Brathwaite perhaps seduced the doctor's sister and thus started that man on his path of revenge. The seducer is now aged and imprisoned in a secret chamber of the English mansion. Etherege may see the senile creature. What about the girl? Should Etherege wish to marry her? As for the old pensioner — his ancestor might have beheaded his king and tracked blood everywhere. The girl may be committed to the pensioner's care. The man is impractical but occasionally forceful. And now back to the secret chamber (before Etherege's rescue). Within its webby confines sits a young man. A servant enters. Years later the man is still there, in a dressing gown and with a long beard. A servant enters with a package of poison. Near the coffer are pistols, a noose, and a grooved dagger. The servant leaves. The sullen man begins to scream, then stops.

[Second Draft] Early in the present century, grim, shaggy old

Dr. Ormskirk (soon called Grimshawe) lives by the cemetery in a comfortable house. With him are a beautiful and dreamy six-year-old boy named Ned (not his son), a merry little girl named Elsie (painfully related to the doctor) — two or three years younger than Ned — and their maid Crusty Hannah. The doctor is uncouth, ugly, non-religious, and addicted to brandy, pipe tobacco, and spiders. He especially loves in his cluttered study a gigantic spider, thought by some to be the devil. One day, when Ned asks where he came from, Dr. Grimshawe says from an almshouse but adds to the crying boy that he should dream that he has the same noble blood in his veins as has the original of a certain sad portrait on their wall. The doctor speaks of an English town, a hospital for old men, and an old ancestral house. The old Catholic family had a renegade Puritan son — said to have beheaded the king and walked in his blood — who was imprisoned in a secret room in the house, escaped, and was sold as a bond-slave to Virginia but went to New England and left children, including the true heir to the English estate. The doctor venomously hates all manor-house aristocrats and hopes that the hypocritical incumbant will have to welcome the heir to a chamber said to be ready for him. The doctor neglects Elsie's education but teaches Ned the classics, mathematics, and manners, enrolls him under M. le Grand to study dancing, fencing, the cudgels, and boxing, and once lectures him — and Elsie too — on Christian morality with memorably passionate eloquence. The children forever regard him as a saint.

There is talk of placing Ned and Elsie under a more suitable guardian, but the fierce doctor rebuffs all suggestions. When the three walk into town, vicious children yell at the red-nosed doctor and pelt him with mud. A riot starts, which a mild-mannered school teacher named Seymour tries to break up, only to be knocked senseless. The doctor takes Seymour to his cobwebby home, where the man recovers and begins to teach Ned and Elsie. The two totally different men talk of England, and Seymour reveals that he is the descendant of a gentle Quaker whose Catholic brothers cruelly imprisoned him in a forgotten chamber of their house. He escaped being murdered, left bloody footsteps from an incurably tortured foot, then married and fled alone to America. His wife sent him their son from England and then died. When the doctor shows Seymour the portrait on the wall, the schoolmaster weeps strangely and later indifferently shows his host some confusing family papers perhaps having to do with a claim on the ancestral estate. The doctor writhes in anguish over some sinful purpose in his life and one night emits curses which blast a fine old elm tree outside his window. Next is announced Seymour's disappearance, which saddens the children but pleases Crusty Hannah.

Time passes, and the doctor is more grim and reclusive, Ned stately and somber, and Elsie gentle but now showing a wild artistry in embroidery. One winter day a stranger named Mountford presents himself. He is a neat, sensitive British lawyer whose mission is to find a tombstone in this town marked with a foot. Ned and Elsie lead him to it and find the grave dug into for another tomb by the gravedigger, Ebenezer Hewen, who shows Mountford the original stone, with the name Thomas Colcord and the death date of 1687 on it. Mountford has dinner and conversation that evening with the doctor, and then, much smitten by the gentle children, leaves. In the spring Ned finds an old silver key near Colcord's ruined grave, suggests sending it to Mountford, but gives it instead to gruff Dr. Grimshawe, who hangs it around Ned's neck saying that the boy can be heir of whatever treasure it unlocks. Ned matures and becomes poetic. The gruff doctor argues with him for being dreamy, then apologizes, and tells him that he is meant to accomplish a long-cherished mission. The doctor sends Ned to a fine school, is lonely at home with only Elsie and Crusty Hannah, mumbles about Seymour and England, and keeps on drinking and smoking and communing with his huge spider. One day he tells Elsie that he will now die, confers with his lawyer Mr. Pickering, props himself up in his study chair with his brandy, and then dies. The doctor's will provides for Elsie and Hannah, but especially for the education of Ned, who is sent for, feels his old life totally broken off, and takes some family papers from the old study. Now much time passes, and Hawthorne writes himself a note telling how to touch up the first part of the story.

When the novel resumes, we find a traveler happily walking along an old path amid flowers and trees through the morning sunshine of late spring. The songs of birds delight him, and he thinks that he must have been born in this area. The path becomes tangled. A shot rings out. Later the traveler awakens in a strange room with furniture marked by heads of leopards (later identified as tigers) and tended by a gentle old palmer whose voice seems familiar. A surgeon named Portingale cares for the stranger's shoulder wound. The palmer reads beside the patient, and later the two talk. The place is a hospital refuge for unfortunates, but not, says the younger man – now named Edward Redclyffe – like the almshouse where he was born. The palmer turns out to be (Seymour) Colcord, who once tutored old Grimshawe's young charge and who was not done away with. Edward says that he has lived among hard men, has fought and been wounded, and now has achieved a position which would not disgrace his ancestry – if he could establish it. The warden of the hospital enters, inquires a little brusquely about Redclyffe, and tells him that the Redclyffe family owns Oakland Hall nearby. The American says that he intends to advance no claims to kinship. The warden transfers him to an apartment in his own house. Redclyffe strolls through the hospital library, a restful, musty old place smelling like Dr. Grimshaw's unforgotten study. The warden enters and greets his American guest most hospitably . . .

[Preliminary Studies] Mrs. Ainsworth, [Aaron] Burr, Chatsworth, William [Dawson], Earl, Etheridge, Captain Gibson, the Mayor, Judge Platt, Scarisbrooke.

[First Draft] Miss Alicampion, Father Angelo, Father Antonio, the Beauty of the Golden Locks, Miss [Ida] Blagden, Dr. Blathwaite, Sir Edward Brathwaite, Sir Humphrey Brathwaite, Lord Brathwaite, Brathwaite, Brathwaite, Miss Brathwaite, Miss Brathwaite, Warden Brathwaite, Sir Humphrey Brathwayte, President [James] Buchanan, [William] Calcraft, King Charles I, Miss Cheltenham, Colcord, Cram-

bo, Cunkey, Dobbin, Elsie, Edward Etherege, Edward
Etherege, James Etherege, Dr. Etherege, Mrs. Etherege,
Evelyn, George Fox, Dr. Gibber, Dr. Gibbins, Dr. Gibb[le]-
ler, Dr. Gibbliter, Grantly, Dr. Griffin, Hammond, Hannah,
Norman Hanscough, Lord Hinchbrooke, Mother Hubbard,
Miss [Susan?] Ingersoll, Dr. Inglefield, James, King James
I, King James II, Hannah Lord, Elsie Lyndhurst, James
Lyndhurst, James Mackintosh, Miss Mackintosh, The Mas-
ter, the Mayor, Moseby, Mountford, Mary Mumpson, Ned,
Richard Oglethorpe, Dr. Oglethorpe, the Palmer, Pearson,
Miss Pearson, the President of the United States, [David?]
Roberts, Rollins, Rollins, Marshall [Captain Isaiah] Rynders,
Stuart, Sukey, Uncle, the Warden.

[Second Draft] King Charles I, Seymour Colcord, Thomas
Colcord, Crusty Hannah, Elsie, Etherege, George Fox, M.
"Count" le Grand, Dr. Grim, Dr. Grimshawe, Dr. Grim-
south, Warden Hammond, Crusty Hannah, Ebenezer
Hewen, Mountford, Ned, Old Spiderbinder, Dr. Ormskirk,
Pickering, Dr. Portingale, Sir Edward Redclyffe, Edward
Redclyffe, Seymour, Dr. [John] Swinnerton.

"Dr. Heidegger's Experiment," 1837.
Dr. Heidegger invites four aged friends to his cobwebby old
study for an experiment. They are Mr. Medbourne, a formerly
prosperous merchant now ruined by speculation; Colonel Killigrew, a gouty old sinner; Mr. Gascoigne, a ruined politician with
an evil but fading reputation; and Clara Wycherly, a wrinkled
widow. The guests enter and look at Dr. Heidegger's rows of
books, his bust of Hippocrates, the skeleton in his closet, his
tarnished mirror, and the old portrait of a young lady on the
wall. The picture is of Sylvia Ward, whom the doctor would have
married fifty-five years ago but for her accidental death. Dr.
Heidegger tosses a faded rose, once held by Miss Ward, into a
vase of sparkling water, and it grows crimson and dewy. Then he
offers his four guests glasses of the fluid, telling them that it is
from the Fountain of Youth which Ponce de Leon vainly looked

for in Florida. They drink eagerly and begin to grow youthful. Although the doctor has just warned them to avoid the perils of youth, they soon begin to flirt and talk of political patriotism and get-rich-quick schemes. They mock old age, start to dance, begin to threaten one another, and soon upset the precious vase and spill the water of youth. Dr Heidegger, who has remained old and has observed his guests' antics, rescues his rose from the fragments of his vase. Twilight falls. He remarks that the rose is fading. His guests shiver. They have grown old again. The rejuvenating waters possessed a transient virtue after all. The doctor tells his friends not to bemoan the fact; he would not stoop to wet his lips if the Fountain of Youth gushed at his doorstep. He has learned a lesson from watching his guests. But they resolve to set out for Florida forthwith.

Gascoigne, Dr. Heidegger, Colonel Killigrew, Medbourne, Sylvia Ward, Mrs. Clara Wycherly.

"The Dragon's Teeth" (III. in *Tanglewood Tales, for Girls and Boys*), 1853.

Cadmus, Phoenix, and Cilix are the sons of King Agenor and Queen Telephassa of Phoenicia, who also have a daughter named Europa. One day while playing in the meadow, Europa encounters a beautiful white bull, becomes friendly with it, and rides off on its back into the foaming sea, to the consternation of her three brothers, who are chasing a butterfly not far away. When they report the girl's disappearance, King Agenor is so furious that he orders his sons to pursue Europa and never return until they find her. Their mother Queen Telephassa accompanies them, as does Thasus, a noble young friend of the children. The five become a kind of gypsy band, wandering unsuccessfully on and on, always asking the same question — has anyone seen a girl riding on a white bull? Finally Phoenix tires, builds a hut of branches in a solitary tract of country, and stays, eventually becoming the king of his neighbors. Next Cilix tires and does the same thing in another area. Then Thasus sprains his ankle, stops, and follows the example of Phoenix and Cilix. But Queen

Telephassa and her most loyal son, Cadmus, continue their search, until one day the old mother can go no farther, tells Cadmus to consult the Oracle at Delphi, and dies. Cadmus buries her reverently, goes to Mount Parnassus, and learns from the windy-voiced Oracle that he should seek his lost sister no more but should instead follow the straying cow and make his new home where she lies down. Seeing a brindle cow, he follows her mile after mile, gathering a horde of followers behind him, and plans a kingdom in the fertile valley where she stops. His cohorts are eaten by a wide-jawed dragon with vast rows of teeth. When Cadmus kills the creature in a rage, a mysterious voice tells him to plant its teeth. When he does so, armed soldiers push their grimy faces up from the earth and start killing each other, until only five remain. These Cadmus orders to desist, and they become the sturdy builders of his entire city — except for his palace, which miraculously one morning is there in shimmering marble, complete with dome, portico, and pillars. Inside is lovely Harmonia, who becomes his queen and the mother of his rosy little children. Later, Cadmus invents the alphabet.

King Agenor, King Cadmus, Cilix, the Oracle of Delphi, Queen Harmonia, Phoenix, Queen Telephassa, Thasus.

"Drowne's Wooden Image," 1844.

A long time ago in Boston one sunny day Captain Hunnewell, just returned from Fayal [in the Azores], goes to the shop of the wood carver Drowne to commission a fine figurehead for his beautiful new ship. Drowne agrees to stop working on his other statues, all competent but cold, and to proceed at once with the new figure, details of which the captain whispers in his ear. A little later the celebrated Boston painter Copley visits the fellow artist and observes that all of his works are dead looking. Drowne calls them all abortions, lacking as they do the touch which would make them lifelike. Surprised at Drowne's deepened intellect, Copley chances to see a half-developed figure surrounded by chips of fine oak. Questioned, Drowne says that he is freeing a creature which lives within the oaken block. As the painter leaves, Drowne almost embraces the half-created shape, which in due time assumes the form and colorful dress of a foreign lady with a flower-laden hat, a fan of pearl and ebony, and a haughty piquancy of expression. Although Copley urges him not to paint the wooden statue, Captain Hunnewell wants it painted. Drowne, who admits to being inspired by a gush of wisdom when he carved it, says that he also wants it painted. Copley feels abashed at Drowne's aesthetic independence and thinks that the sculptor must be inspired by love. Drowne paints his work in a very lifelike manner and then refuses to consider Copley's suggestion that he sell the breathing vision in England. His fame spreads around Boston and beyond. People file by the image with reverence and also something like fear. One morning Captain Hunnewell walks from his home to the ship, accompanied by a companion who makes the people rub their eyes. The companion is Drowne's wooden statue down to the last detail of dress and expression. The crowd follows, which vexes the haughty beauty, who flutters her fan and breaks it. The two enter the sculptor's shop by the water, leaving the crowd outside in awe. Copley enters, finds only Drowne – repairing the fan of his statue, which is broken, and looking rather stolid – and then hears the voice of Hunnewell beyond the shop ordering oarsmen to row him and his lady to the ship. Drowne expresses suspicion that he carved the image of the lady in a dream. Years pass, and he never does another piece of carving so magnificent. But is not the highest state which a human spirit attains its truest state? At about this time rumor has it that Hunnewell brought home an aristocratic young Portuguese lady as his ward, letting her stay at his home and aboard his ship.

[John Singleton] Copley, Deacon Drowne, Peggy Hobart, Captain Hunnewell.

"The Duston Family," 1836.

One day in March, 1698, Goodman Duston is returning to his home at Haverhill, in the Massachusetts Bay Colony, when he hears the war whoop of attacking Indians. He sees his seven children rushing out of their home, tells them to run to the garrison, and bursts into his wife's bedroom. Hannah Duston has just given birth to their eighth child. Confused by the approach of the bloodthirsty foe, Duston abandons his wife and her nurse, the widow Mary Neff, and saves his children by shooting at their pursuers and accompanying them to the garrison. Meanwhile, the Indians seize the two women, brain the baby, and take their captives a hundred miles northeast to an island (now called Hannah Duston Island) in the Contocook [Contoocook] River. There, while left unguarded one night, Hannah, Mrs. Neff, and an English lad also being held for ransom grab tomahawks and kill and scalp their captors. Accursed Hannah makes her way back home and receives bounties for the Indians she murdered.

Mrs. Hannah Duston, Goodman Duston, Duston, Duston, Duston, Duston, Duston, Duston, Duston, Duston, Mrs. Mary Neff, Cotton Mather.

"Earth's Holocaust," 1844.

The people of the earth decide to build a gigantic bonfire on the western prairie and in it destroy all the worn-out trumpery imaginable. The narrator, hopeful of being illuminated as to some moral truth, attends the festivities. First the crowd hurls all heraldic signs of aristocratic background into the blaze, in spite of a stately old man's objections. Then come robes of royalty and crown jewels, then barrels of liquor. One old toper sneaks a bottle of brandy from the flames just in time, and his red-nosed, gouty friends look morose. Minor items are tossed in next: an empty purse, counterfeit money, aged love letters, and the like. Some ladies even throw in their feminine attire and determine hereafter to wear only manly garb. All implements of war are wheeled up and hurled into the consuming flames, even though one lame old general soberly says that doing so only makes more work for the world's armorers. Now various instruments of capital punishment are burned: axes, guillotines, and the gallows. Excited now, the people toss in marriage certificates, ledgers, titles to property, and even gold coins. At this a pickpocket faints in the crowd. Now come books and pamphlets. Why should the weight of dead men's thoughts oppress the living? The works of Voltaire scatter brilliant sparks, German tales smell of brimstone, Milton glows powerfully, Shakespeare gushes marvelous flames, Mother Goose and pages of ballads burn longer than any popular works of the last century, longer even than epics. The narrator's own modest works contribute a glimmering spark or two. Fresh fuel next comes in the form of surplices, church crosses, and even humble New England communion-tables and pulpits. When the Bible is added to the fire, certain marginal notes are consumed in a twinkling but not a line of text is blackened. While the last hangman, thief, murderer, and drunkard mutter gloomily to each other, a red-eyed stranger begins to talk, saying that the world will be the old world yet, so long as no one hits upon a way of reforming that foul cavern, the human heart. The narrator, who has become increasingly worried, concludes that the evil principle may well mock at this bonfire, which has destroyed only outward examples of a deep-rooted, original wrong. The feeble intellect alone can effect no permanent reforms.

Father [Theobald] Matthew, Rev. Mr. Sydney Smith.

"Edward Fane's Rosebud," 1837.

It is hard to look at an old person and recreate his youth in one's fancy. Some old women look so old that they seem never to have been young and gay. Consider Widow Toothaker, for example. One chilly November day, she sits at her lonesome hearth, drinking Geneva and hot water. She has attended sick-chambers as a nurse for forty years. Yet once she was the blooming fiancee of Edward Fane, was in fact Rose Grafton, nicknamed his Rosebud. She was beside his three-year-old sister Mary when she died. Edward's rich and proud mother scorned the young nurse, however, and the two lovers parted, seldom seeing one another again. Rose married Mr. Toothaker, who soon grew infirm, halt, and palsied in mind and body. She nursed him unfailingly until his death. She might then have married again, but she grew to like frequenting sick rooms, where smallpox, typhus fever, and other maladies raged. Wherever she walks, coffin makers follow. Now here sits old Nurse Toothaker by her fire. Can any germ of bliss survive in her? A knock on her door. General Fane is dying and has summoned his Rosebud. She goes to him, happily.

General Edward Fane, Mary Fane, Mrs. Fane, Rose "Rosebud" Grafton Toothaker, Toothaker.

"Edward Randolph's Portrait" (II. in "Legends of the Province House"), 1838.

The narrator returns one January night to the Province House, has a glass of whiskey punch with Bela Tiffany, a talkative old man there, and hears the story of the mysterious black portrait which once hung in a room above the bar-room.

A picture, which time has rendered black as ebony, is hanging in the chamber of Lieutenant-Governor Thomas Hutchinson at the moment news is brought to him that three regiments of British troops are in Boston harbor to overawe the increasingly insubordinate people. With him are his charming young niece Alice Vane and his kinsman Francis Lincoln, the provincial captain of Castle William. They discuss the gloomy old picture, about which fables have grown. Lincoln says that it is rumored to be a portrait of the Devil, taken at a Salem witch meeting. It shows its face at times of public calamity. At the top of its frame are bits of black silk, as though it was once veiled. Alice says that in Italy, where she formerly lived, experts know how to restore time-blackened paintings. Hutchinson explains that the picture is of Edward Randolph, founder of the Province House. Lincoln reviles Randolph's memory, since the man obtained the repeal of the first provincial charter and hence earned the hatred of freedom-loving people. If his picture reflects his anguish at being cursed by those people, Lincoln adds, then it is well that time has eclipsed his features. Although he is uneasy, Hutchinson decides to sign the order bringing the British troops ashore. He is about to do so that evening, in spite of a plea and an eloquent protest from several selectmen of Boston, when Lincoln points up at the portrait. It is covered with black silk, which Alice removes: Randolph's face and upper figure seem to be pressing toward Hutchinson and writhing in anguished guilt. All the same, Hutchinson seizes his pen and signs the order. In the morning, rumors start about the picture, which is clouded again. Perhaps Alice renovated it only temporarily. Much later, when Hutchinson's dying hour is near, his features — at least according to Lincoln, who stands by — resemble Randolph's. The blood of the Boston Massacre chokes the guilty man.

A storm breaks over the Province House and makes its upper rooms rattle as though a political argument were going on upstairs. The narrator takes his leave and fights his way home through a snow storm.

Howorth, Lieutenant-Governor Thomas Hutchinson, Captain Francis Lincoln, the Selectman, Bela Tiffany, Alice Vane.

"Egotism: or, the Bosom Serpent" ([I.] from "The Allegories of the Heart"), 1843.

After five years the sculptor George Herkimer returns from Florence to try to help an acquaintance of his youth named Roderick Elliston, who for four years now has been separated because of jealousy from his lovely wife Rosina (and Herkimer's cousin). Elliston is now in dire straits, having — or imagining that he has — a serpent in his stomach. Like most chronically diseased persons, Elliston egotistically forces himself on strangers, then exhibits signs of insanity, and next begins to fancy that others also nourish snakes in their bosoms. He perceptively queries a brother-hater, an ambitious politician, a miser, a drunkard, a wrathful clergyman, a sullen recluse, a bickering husband and wife, an envious author, an impure man, an abandoned girl, a pair of spiteful women, and a jealous man. With a hiss — sometimes answered — he accuses each of harboring a serpent or a nest of snakes in his chest. Finally he is put into an asylum, grows black and sullen, then tries by starvation and poison and tobacco smoke and alcohol to kill his serpent. Released as not properly confinabie, he goes home to his family mansion, attended by his sympathetic Negro servant Scipio. When Herkimer approaches and tells him that he has a message from Rosina, Elliston contorts in pain, saying, "It gnaws me! It gnaws me!", and takes refuge near a beautiful fountain in a charming garden adjoining the house. Herkimer asks Rosina to wait, goes to his sick friend, and learns from him that Scipio thinks that a snake residing in the fountain afflicts members of the Elliston family and will do so until the possessed one forgets himself for one moment. At this instant Rosina's gentle voice urges her husband to forget himself and think of another. Touched, Elliston sits up, restored, and begs for her forgiveness. Did Herkimer see a waving motion through the grass and hear something plunge into the fountain? Rosina urges Elliston to be certain that he is purified of fiendish jealousy and that their past will not darken their future.

Roderick Elliston, Mrs. Rosina Elliston, George Herkimer, Scipio.

"Endicott and the Red Cross," 1837.

One autumn noon more than two centuries ago, John Endicott calls his soldiers into the main square of Salem. Times are uneasy, since Charles I and Archbishop Laud of Canterbury have begun to seem determined to rule Plymouth and Massachusetts tyrannically. Beneath Endicott's grizzled beard his polished breastplate reflects the scene: the rude church, a bleeding wolf's head nailed to the meetinghouse door, the whipping post, a suspected Catholic at the pillory, a rude royalist in the stocks, and on the meetinghouse steps a gossiping woman with a cleft stick on her tongue and a man labeled Wanton Gospeller. Other sinners are in the crowd, some with cropped ears, slit nostrils, and the like. A beautiful young woman wears the letter A fantastically embroidered in scarlet and gold on her dress, in token of her adultery. A few Indians are standing nearby. As the troops begin to drill, old Roger Williams walks into town in ministerial black and hands Endicott a sealed letter from Governor Winthrop of Boston. Reading it, Endicott grows furiously wrathful, then calls the soldiers and townspeople before him, and harangues them. He says that in spite of their having made this howling wilderness their home, in the name of civil and religious liberty (at this point the Gospeller boldly objects, causing old Williams to smile), "Papistical" Charles I and "idolatrous" Laud intend to send over a governor-general to deliver New England to the Pope. Then Endicott cuts the Red Cross from his standard-bearer's flag of England. The result becomes the ensign of New England, in which neither Pope nor Tyrant has a part. Thus begins the deliverance of New England.

John Endicott, Wanton Gospeller, Roger Williams, Governor [John] Winthrop.

"Ethan Brand: A Chapter from an Abortive Romance," 1851.

One cool August evening while Bartram, the rough and sluggish lime-burner, is watching his kiln near Graylock mountain, with his sensitive little boy Joe at his side, a former lime-burner Ethan Brand approaches the infernal-looking fire with a chilling laugh. Many years ago he went away in search of the unpardonable sin. Now he has returned. The furnace fire lights his thin, thoughtful face and grizzled hair. When asked, he tells Bartram that he found the unpardonable sin in his own heart and laughs again, mirthlessly. Bartram sends Joe down to the village to bring back some people. Brand tells Bartram that the unpardonable sin is the sin of an intellect which triumphs over the sense of brotherhood with man and reverence for God. He is proud of his discovery. The curious villagers swarm up the mountain side. Among them are the stage-agent, a wilted little cigar-smoking drunkard; Lawyer Giles, now a crippled soap-boiler but a courageous fellow; the village doctor, brandy-mad and unprofessional; and Old Humphrey, a white-haired relic demented because of his lost daughter Esther, whom Brand ruined in a psychological experiment and who is now a traveling circus performer. A German Jewish diorama showman entertains Joe with pictures of faraway cities and castles and famous battles on land and sea, until the little boy sees Brand's enormous eye looking through the glass. Then the man shows Brand something mysterious in his box and hints that the heavy unpardonable sin is in it. An old dog suddenly begins to chase its tail, faster and faster, only to stop as suddenly as it started. Brand sees an analogy to his own search and laughs so terribly that the people all leave. Telling the lime-burner that he will watch the fire, Brand soon stands alone at the top of the wildly dancing kiln flames. He was once a simple, loving man, but through intellectual curiosity and success he desecrated the divine heart of mankind, upset the balance of head and heart, and thus became a fiend. He is proud of it but knows now that Mother Earth has scorned him and fire is his only friend. In the morning, the lovely sun gilds all heights, and the stagecoach horn rings through the hills. Bartram goes to his fire, calls Joe, and lets his pole fall on a human skeleton lying on the snow-white lime. Within the skeleton is Brand's stony heart.

Bartram, Ethan Brand, Esther, Giles, Humphrey, the Jew of Nuremberg, Joe.

"Fancy's Show Box: A Morality," 1837.

Does the mere thought of committing a sin stain one's soul? Let us imagine old Mr. Smith, silver-haired and with a glass of Madeira, visited by Fancy, Memory, and Conscience. Fancy opens her picture box to the old man, showing him a girl prostrate at a proud young man's feet. Smith is the arrogantly smiling man. Recognizing the girl as Martha Burroughs, he denies having ruined her until Memory whispers something in his ear. Then Conscience stabs him. Fancy now shows him a vision of his lifelong friend Edward Spencer, dead at his feet with a wound in his head. Again Smith denies the charge until Memory reminds him that he once threw a bottle at his friend but missed. Conscience again smites him. Next he sees himself stripping the clothes from three starving children. Memory reminds the incredulous man that he once briefly tried to sue three orphans but failed, and Conscience tortures him once more. Let us hope that would-be sinners who have not committed their imagined deeds have incurred no guilt. All the same, unperpetrated sins need penitential tears.

Martha Burroughs, Conscience, Fancy, Memory, Smith, Edward Spencer, David Tomkins.

Fanshawe: A Tale, 1828.

Secluded in New England is Harley College, located in a narrow valley near a village of rough and hardy people, and presided over (some eighty years ago) by Dr. Melmoth, a learned divine of almost sixty years of age. He has a shrewish wife named Sarah, a study to which he can retreat, and no children. One day he receives a letter from an old friend named John Langton, a businessman abroad and now in trouble, asking him to become the guardian of his eighteen-year-old daughter Ellen. His wife agrees; so Dr. Melmoth journeys to the seaport where Miss Langton is living and brings her home. She is a pretty ray of sunshine in the house. One student quickly begins to like her. He is Edward Walcott, tall and handsome, of a well-to-do family, but a little wild. One day late in spring he goes riding with Ellen up the valley, beside a stream and near a lonely forest. They overtake a proud, pale, self-possessed scholar named Fanshawe, who has absently ridden farther than he intended. Then the couple stop at a neglected little cottage, inside which is a sick woman named Butler and her older, tough-looking sister. The demented invalid asks Walcott if he brings news of an absent person. Ellen and her escort soon leave, drink at a pure fountain nearby, and then return to Harley College. That night Fanshawe feels little like reading; instead, he reviews his solitary years of study and thinks of a certain gentle eye. Falling passively in love with Ellen, Fanshawe occasionally walks with her. One day in late summer, while he is out with her and with Walcott, they see a dark, coarse stranger, who boldly invites Ellen to try fishing with him alone. He whispers something to her which she resents, and she asks her escorts to take her back to Dr. Melmoth's house, where in the evening she grows restless. Suddenly she sees the stranger in the gloomy garden. He tells her that her father's safety depends on her. Fanshawe walks by, sees the man giving Ellen a letter from her father, hypnotically orders him to leave, and takes the girl back to the house.

Near Harley College is an inn called the Hand and Bottle, run by Hugh Crombie, about forty years of age, and his wife Sarah, the former Widow Hutchins, about fifty. Hugh grew up in taverns, was once a talented musician and poet, drank a good deal, but cared devotedly for his father. When the old man died, Hugh left for a wild life at sea, but two years ago he returned — seemingly reformed and religious — and soon married Sarah, who originally owned the tavern. On the afternoon of the day the stranger accosted Ellen, Hugh is sitting in the tavern yard drinking when a darkly tanned stranger, whom Hugh recognizes, rides up. The two exchange some grim banter, and then over a quart of local wine the stranger tells Hugh that he intends to marry Ellen Langton for her fortune, left her by her father, who, the stranger rejoices to add, is now in his watery grave. Having his former life of crime recalled to him, Hugh can do little but fearfully promise his passive cooperation in this deplorable scheme. When he asks the stranger whether he intends to visit the cottage where he used to live and where his mother — evidently crazed Mrs. Butler — still is, the dark man says no. The next night, Walcott, distressed by Ellen's sudden coolness, goes drinking with another student, named Glover, at Hugh's tavern. Glover drunkenly mentions the presence of a girl in a chamber of the inn. Then Fanshaws enters, apparently in search of the mysterious angler. While they are all singing, in comes Dr. Melmoth, on his way back from visiting a sick person (Mrs. Butler) and now driven to the tavern by a violent rainstorm. Hugh pacifies him when he notes the presence of wine-bibbing students by saying that they were out looking for Dr. Melmoth, who then opens the wrong door and finds Ellen. Fanshawe steps forward and eloquently defends her reputation. Melmoth then takes her home. Alone now, Walcott becomes violently drunk, hurls bottles and furniture about, and challenges to a duel the following morning the mysterious stranger, who suddenly appears in a hallway once Ellen is gone. Melmoth lets Ellen into his house without revealing what transpired to his wife, who sleepily says that the girl was sick and went to bed early. The following morning the fortnightly newspaper announces that the ship bringing Ellen's father John Langton home to New England has sunk. While Mrs. Melmoth goes to inform the girl, Melmoth opens a letter from Langton reporting that a delay prevented his taking the ship. Mrs. Melmoth rushes downstairs to announce that Ellen has disappeared and to send her impractical husband to the village to alert all and seek the missing girl.

The same morning, Walcott awakens with a raging thirst and a whirling head, learns from Dolly, one of the two college maids, that Ellen has disappeared, and rushes at once to see Hugh, who advises the young man to forget Ellen and then in a moment of conscience loans him a horse to pursue her. Walcott soon overtakes high-spirited Fanshawe, who is also seeking Ellen. Having a better mount, Walcott passes him and soon encounters Dr. Melmoth, who is worried but treats the mission as an aspect of knight-errantry. Next they encounter Ellen's father John Langton, who, with two servants, has just happened to come from the thriving little village which commands the only outlet from the valley. He is stunned by news of Ellen's disappearance but quickly recovers, returns with Melmoth and Walcott to the village, and begins an inquiry. Meanwhile Walcott, who has been rather ignored by Langton, decides to investigate alone. He learns from the reluctant answers of a suspicious-looking sailor that Ellen has not yet passed through the village.

And now back to the night before. Ellen is troubled, having no one to turn to: Mrs. Melmoth is stern, Dr. Melmoth is unworldly, Walcott is wild, and Fanshawe is absent. She feels that she is already dishonored through being found at Hugh's inn. So when she sees the stranger near Melmoth's front door, she joins him. They walk to the inn, where Hugh reluctantly gives them horses, and then ride beside the cottage where Mrs. Butler lies sick. Her sister urges the two to watch at the woman's deathbed. Raving about her dead husband and absent son, Mrs.

Butler has one moment of joy — when the gloomy angler steps forward and identifies himself as her son — and then she dies. He rushes Ellen out of the house, only to find that their horses are gone. The two take a hidden path parallel to the river until they are under a lofty precipice, beneath which the villain places poor Ellen in a rocky recess near a lovely spring while he looks about. She grows indifferent, even torpid, then begins to seek a means of escape. When he reappears, grinning viciously and threatening now, she kneels before him and asks him to think of his dead mother, which comment he says only turns his heart to stone. Suddenly a rock falls near them from the precipice.

Now back to Fanshawe. He has been riding on his sorry nag. He comes to the Butler cottage, now a scene of death. Hoping for news, he enters and soon learns from the dead woman's sister that he should follow the path toward the river. She hopes that Butler will be killed, so that she can inherit the cottage. Fanshawe soon becomes lost but goes on to the precipice, hears voices, sees Ellen and Butler, and drops a stone to attract their attention. Butler climbs toward the fearless student, determined to fling him from the cliff, but slips and falls to his death. Fanshawe cautiously descends, kisses Ellen, who has fainted, then revives her with water from the spring. They return to the cottage and send word to Dr. Melmoth. It seems that Butler ran away from his harsh father, was befriended by the merchant John Langton, but became indiscreet, and was abandoned. He grew utterly wicked, got wind of the false report of Langton's death, and plotted Ellen's ruin, as we know. The girl remains sick for some time. Her father offers to reward Fanshawe, who haughtily refuses. Walcott is anxious about her until she begins to recover; then he relinquishes the field to Fanshawe. One warm evening at sunset, Ellen steals upon Fanshawe at the oak tree where Butler first accosted her. She offers to marry the scholar and lead him into the world, but he says that the only way he can prove he deserves her generosity is by refusing. She kisses his hand and soon thereafter goes with her father to his seaport home. Fanshawe becomes a dedicated scholar and dies at the age of twenty. Hugh Crombie becomes honest. Dr. Melmoth's last years may be read in his biography, published by his successor about 1768. Four years after Fanshawe's death, Ellen marries Walcott, and they have a long life of unexceptional bliss.

Butler, Mrs. Butler, Butler, Hugh Crombie, Mrs. Sarah Crombie, Crombie, Dolly, Esther, Fanshawe, Mrs. Fowler, Miss Fowler, Glover, Hutchins, Ellen Langton, John Langton, Mrs. John Langton, Nathanael Mather, Mrs. Sarah Melmoth, Dr. Melmoth, Edward Walcott.

"Feathertop: A Moralized Legend," 1852.

The witch Mother Rigby calls her invisible helper Dickon for another coal to light her pipe with and then decides to make a scarecrow, to keep her corn from being nibbled further. She gets a broomstick and other bits of wood, a meal bag full of straw, a pumpkin, assorted old aristocratic clothes, and a three-colored hat with a rooster's tail feather. When she puts her pipe into the slit of a mouth cut into the pumpkin head, the scarecrow seems to come alive. Since Feathertop, as she christens him, is capable of better things than scaring blackbirds, she orders him to puff for his life on the pipe, which seems actually to give him life, then urges him to speak — which he does in simple set phrases — and finally tells him to go woo Polly Gookin, the rich merchant's pretty daughter. Feathertop loses his vitality until Mother Rigby fills another aromatic pipe for him. She gives him her staff, which immediately begins to look like a gold-headed cane; and he is off, walking rather stiffly to town. Soon the villagers are gazing in awe at the distinguished stranger, with a glittering star on his coat, his splendidly embroidered waistcoat, his snowy-plumed hat, and an exquisite pipe with a painted bowl. They try to guess what faraway country he is from. Only a cur, which snuffs at Feathertop's heels, and a child, who babbles about pumpkins, seem unimpressed. When the glittering figure stops to refill his pipe, he seems to grow hazy and then more refulgent than ever. He calls on the Gookins. The merchant is fearful, as though obliged to redeem an evil pledge by sacrificing his daughter. He spies on the couple after presenting Polly and supposedly leaving them alone. Polly is entranced. Everything her companion says and does seems wonderful to her. But suddenly they see themselves in a full-length mirror. Polly faints. Feathertop is in utter despair, rushes home to his mother, says that he has seen himself for the ragged and empty thing he is, and dashes his life-giving pipe to bits against the chimney. Mother Rigby calmly assigns the heap of rags and sticks to the field as a scarecrow, and calls her impish Dickon for another coal.

Dickon, Feathertop, Justice Gookin, Polly Gookin, Goodman Rigby, Mother Rigby.

"Fire Worship," 1843.

The narrator deplores the replacement of open fireplaces by cheerless stoves. It was better to turn from a cloudy sky to a brilliant fire, which we have now imprisoned in iron. Inventions are blotting out the picturesque and the poetic. Fire is a power, a god, a destroyer, and a worker. One who is true to fire is true to everything sacred. The old clerical predecessor in the narrator's mansion lit his morning fire, read and wrote by its light and warmth, welcomed visiting parishioners before it, and let its radiance chase the twilight. Now the spirit of fire is peevish because of its fate. It storms in the stove like Dante's infernal trees. Society and even domestic life will become less convivial, but we can at least recall the open fireplaces of our youth. The ancient fought for altar and hearth. Would anyone say, "Fight for your stoves"?

(No named characters.)

"The First and Last Dinner," 1829.[5]

Twelve close friends, all of about the same age and living permanently in Richmond, decide to dine together on the first and last day of the year, and further to save part of the first bottle of wine and recork it for the last surviving member. He

[5] For details, see Louise Hastings, "An Origin for 'Dr. Heidegger's Experiment,'" *American Literature,* IX (January, 1938), 403-410; see also Adkins, "Notes on the Hawthorne Canon," p. 366.

will drink it and then sit quietly, in remembrance. Thirty years pass and ten are left to dine. They are losing their hair, worry about the cold, and sing and riot little. The fiftieth anniversary comes, and only four wrinkled old men assemble. At length comes the last dinner, to be celebrated by one man, who is a ninety-year-old bachelor. He uncorks the old bottle and drinks to the others — now dead. He then sits quietly, in accordance with the original plan of the group. Confusing images pass through his mind. He slips into a apoplectic fit and dies next day.

(No characters named.)

"Footprints on the Seashore," 1838.

The narrator yearns one September morning for seclusion and therefore walks and muses all day by the seashore. He presses his footprints into the sand, sees a trio of girls, follows a flock of beach birds, returns to his own tracks and thus recaptures his thoughts, examines objects on the shore line such as shells and seaweed and jellyfish, writes verses and his name and draws huge pictures in the sand, and then climbs over the crags. He watches the waves roar into a weather-worn avenue in the rocks. He remembers previous rambles along the beach. He sees the girls again and then a boat offshore with fishermen. He scrambles into a nook he knows and has had some thoughts in. He eats some sea-soaked biscuit and an apple, then basks in the sunshine and conjures up story-plots. He tries out his eloquence, only to see the three girls peeping down at him from a cliff. The sunshine fades, but he is self-sufficient. The sun is setting, and the sea grows melancholy. Now the fishermen are cooking their catch, and the girls have joined them. When they call for him to come too, he does so.

(No named characters.)

"Fragments from the Journal of a Solitary Man," 1837.

I. The narrator's friend Oberon asked that his papers be burned at his death and then started to talk about his disconnected journal, but then died. Oberon was original, averse to society, and frustrated by having no part in common toils and troubles. The narrator religiously burns the papers but keeps the journal and offers selections from it. Oberon longed to travel but rarely went far. He hated the thought of losing his youth and preferred the idea of dying young, at about the age of twenty-five. He once dreamed that he was walking down Broadway and frightened everyone and everything there because he was in his shroud! He went in September once to Niagara and spent a short time in the ferry-house with some rough provincials, their dogs, a pet fox, and the drunken ferryman. Oberon knew that he should have paid more attention to the marriage of sublimity and beauty at the Falls. On Goat Island between the two cataracts he saw three lovely young girls, about whom he afterwards had only the purest and most pleasant thoughts. The narrator will conclude by offering Oberon's description of his return to his native village after being sick.

II. "My Return Home." Oberon walks from the top of the hill into his hometown. Nature's September garb is spring-like, but the setting sun reminds the young man of his grave sickness. The engine company is practicing in front of the meetinghouse. He sees the changed faces of old acquaintances. Some of the buildings are different. But the years seem to drop away. He wonders whether his friends will laugh or hiss at him but decides that they will not and that he will tell them, simply enough, that when one grows sick he thinks of home and the old burial-ground and his parents' tomb. He will encourage some youth in the village to take warning by his example, and to adopt a serious aim and remain a part of sympathetic humanity. Now the narrator interrupts to say that what comes next is the final passage of writing from Oberon's journal. Until lately the young man, only twenty-four years old, could not believe that he was fatally sick and had daydreams of marriage even. But now he knows; yet, taking a quiet interest and achieving a sense of brotherhood, he is not sad. Toward the world he is more generous, merciful, and hopeful.

Nightingale, Oberon, Dominicus Pike.

"The Gentle Boy," 1832.

In 1659 the harsh governor of Massachusetts Bay orders two Quakers hanged one autumn day. That evening Tobias Pearson, a former soldier under Cromwell, is walking to his home outside Boston when he encounters a frail, wide-eyed little boy about six years old weeping on the grave of the Quakers, one of whom, he explains, was his father. When pitiful little Ilbrahim adds that his only home is at the grave, Pearson, although repulsed at the thought of helping a Quaker, gathers him in his arms and carries him to his house. His wife Dorothy welcomes and warms and feeds Ilbrahim, who explains that the Puritan authorities took his mother from prison and exposed her to perish in the wilderness. Vowing to be his mother now, Dorothy puts him in the bed of her children, who have died. Soon the Pearsons' neighbors make known their disapproval by hissing at and then avoiding the couple. But such treatment only turns Pearson's heart slowly toward the gentle boy. A few Sundays later, the Pearsons take mild Ilbrahim to church and sit through a two-hour sermon on the dangers of trying to convert the misguided. Then a disheveled woman, recognized earlier by Ilbrahim and now revealed as his proscribed mother, goes to the pulpit and delivers a moving harangue in which deranged imagination is tangled with reason. She urges the chosen ones to raise their voices against the iniquitous. Ilbrahim goes to her, and she embraces him, but her duty requires her to follow her fanatic mission. So when Dorothy volunteers to continue to care for the boy, and Pearson after a delay identifies himself, Ilbrahim's mother — who calls herself Catharine — gives her son to them and walks over the hill unmolested by the pitying crowd. Before the end of winter, Ilbrahim becomes a child again, and he is joyful in the Pearson home, especially when a neighbor boy — an ugly child — falls from a tree and is nursed to health by the Pearsons. Ilbrahim lavishes an almost Oriental attention upon him. But one summer day, when well again, the wretch joins a group of Puritan children who pounce on Ilbrahim and almost kill him with blows and kicks. Then the gentle boy begins to brood, and in his sleep he calls for his mother. To match this change, Pearson slowly changes, until he has less contempt for the creed of the Quakers, who are still persecuted although Charles II is now on the throne of England. Then one snowy winter evening, while Pearson, now a thoroughgoing Quaker, sits in his house listening to a hoary old Quaker read the Bible and tell of leaving his own dying daughter to answer God's call, Ilbrahim's mother enters and goes to the little boy. In spite of Dorothy's loving care, Ilbrahim dies in his own mother's arms, saying that he is happy now. Gradually the New England Puritans treat Catharine with more respect, and when she dies they bury her beside the gentle boy.

Catharine, Ilbrahim, Mrs. Dorothy Pearson, Tobias Pearson.

"The Ghost of Doctor Harris," 1900.

The narrator, a member of the old Boston Athenaeum, occasionally sees a sprightly old man sitting in the reading room with a copy of the Boston *Post*. He learns from a friend that the white-haired old fellow is the Rev. Dr. Harris of Dorchester. One day, after seeing him, he learns that Dr. Harris has died earlier. But the narrator continues to see the ghost, sitting there silently reading his paper. They never speak, since silence should be observed in the library and the two have not formally met. The other members notice nothing. Once, the ghost appeals wistfully and helplessly out of bleary eyes to the narrator, who, however, resists doing anything. Finally the ghost is no longer there. The whole affair is very odd.

Rev. Dr. Harris.

"The Golden Fleece" (VI. in *Tanglewood Tales, for Girls and Boys*), 1853.

Jason, the son of Aeson, the King of Iolchos dethroned by King Pelias, has been nicely educated by Chiron the centaur and now resolves to seek his fortune. He takes a leopard skin, his father's sandals, and two spears, and is walking toward Iolchos when he is obliged to help an old crone with beautiful brown eyes and a peacock across a raging stream. When he loses a sandal in the process, the old woman is delighted because the Speaking Oak of Dodona told her about a one-sandaled man. Arriving at Iolchos, Jason causes quite a stir: it seems that the Oak has predicted that King Pelias will be dethroned by a one-sandaled man. So when Jason presents himself to the king, he is tricked by the crafty monarch, who promises to give him the throne if he can bring back the Golden Fleece from the region of Colchis. The Oak first tells Jason to go to Argus and ask that ship-builder to make him a fifty-oar galley, the Argo, and then offers an oak branch for his figurehead — in the shape of a beautiful maiden — which periodically speaks more advice later to the adventurer, including the sensible suggestion that he should summon forty-nine Greek heroes to become Argonauts and accompany him on his quest. They include strong Hercules, brave Castor and Pollux, the Minotaur-killing Theseus, sharp-eyed Lynceus, the singer Orpheus, Tiphys the star-gazing helmsman, and Atalanta the fierce mountain-woman. Off they go, and on their way they kill some six-armed giants for King Cyzicus, drive the Harpies away from the blind Thracian Phineus's dinner, defeat some birds whose feathers fall like steel-tipped arrows, and get help toward Colchis. Aeetes, the king there, hypocritically welcomes Jason and his fellow Argonauts, and tells him that he can go after the dragon-guarded Golden Fleece if he first yokes the two royal bulls, which are made of brass and spit fire, plows the grove of Mars with them, and sows the area with some dragon teeth left over by Cadmus. These difficult feats Jason is able to perform with the assistance of the odd enchantress Medea, King Aeetes's daughter and Circe's niece. So the king must let him try for the Golden Fleece. Medea tosses a sleeping potion down the throat of the dragon guarding the prize, which Jason then snatches and takes to his waiting vessel. The Argonauts row for their lives, homeward bound.

Achilles, King Aeetes, Aesculapius, King Aeson, Argus, Atalanta, Cadmus, Castor, Chiron, Circe, King Cyzicus, Helle, Hercules, Jason, Lynceus, Medea, Orpheus, King Pelias, Philoctetes, Phineus, Phrixus, Pollux, Theseus, Tiphys, Vulcan.

"The Golden Touch" (II. in *A Wonder-Book for Girls and Boys*),
    1852.

King Midas is very rich and yet is more fond of gold than of
anything else. One day, while fondling his hoard of gold, he sees
a sunny-smiling stranger who offers him anything he wants.
Midas asks for the power to transmute anything he touches into
gold. It is granted, but then Midas cannot eat, because his food
turns to gold as he touches it. In addition, his lovely little
daughter Marygold runs to accept his kiss, only to turn into a
glittering golden statue in his embrace. When the stranger returns,
Midas asks him to remove the curse, which can be done if Midas
bathes in the river and then sprinkles any golden object with its
water. Midas flings water on his daughter and returns her to life.
Years pass, and the wise king hates the sight of all gold except
the rich ringlets of his daughter's precious children.

Marygold, King Midas.

"A Good Man's Miracle," 1844.[6]

Walking through the muddy slums of London one day, Robert
Raikes encounters a swarm of ragged children playing and
swearing. A kind woman nearby tells him that conditions are
worse on Sundays when the children are even more idle. Raikes
decides to establish Sunday schools. Dead now, he meets in
heaven persons who go there after death because of his immeas-
urably good deed.

Robert Raikes.

"The Gorgon's Head" (I. in *A Wonder-Book for Girls and Boys*),
    1852.

Perseus, the son of Danae, is ordered by wicked King Polydectes, of the Island of Seriphus, to bring him the head of
Medusa, with its snaky locks. In this way, Polydectes hopes to be
rid of Perseus and then do some mischief to Danae. But Perseus,
aided by Quicksilver, the Three Gray Women, the Nymphs, and

[6]See Norman Holmes Pearson, "A Sketch by Hawthorne," *New England
Quarterly,* VI (March, 1933), 136-144.

Quicksilver's wise but invisible sister, speeds with flying slippers and a helmet of darkness to the Gorgons. Using his polished shield for a mirror — to avoid the petrifying gaze of Medusa — and Quicksilver's short sword for a weapon, he cuts off her head, which he puts into a magic wallet, and returns to Polydectes, whom he turns to stone, along with his wicked counsellors and people, by holding up the severed head when they demand to see it.

Danae, Princess Hippodamia, Medusa, Sister Nightmare, the Nymphs, Perseus, King Polydectes, Quicksilver, Sister Scarecrow, Sister Shakejoint.

Grandfather's Chair — see *The Whole History of Grandfather's Chair.*

"Graves and Goblins," 1835.

The speaker is a ghost, that of a youth who died before he could be a lover and was buried in a town cemetery rather than in a sweet spot of shade and glimmering sunshine which he had picked for his gravesite. He explains that the spirit of each dead person must haunt the region of his human activity until the stains left by earthly acts are gone. He knows a certain miser's ghost which must haunt the place where he buried his sinfully acquired gold until it is disinterred and does some good. A certain patriot has after death been chained to his country, instead of ascending to the sky, because of the deep yearning of his soul; he sadly haunts the bedchambers of guilty politicians to search their selfish motives. Mere earthly passion does not survive death; but when souls have loved, that love is immortal. Authors who in life yearned for fame are troubled after death, because they feed on the impure breath of mortals. The speaker is puzzled once when he watches the spirit of a dead maiden hovering about, until he hears her sigh for her mother. He talks to her, but one day when he calls at her tomb she is gone; he knows that the angels have rushed her away, or she would have whispered goodbye. He is growing purer and soon will vanish upward. He recently called upon an obscure, lonely author and whispered ideas to him while he dreamed. But the ghost will leave soon now, since the writer's mind is growing too hard and cold. At the end, the high-souled ghost longs for the call of some holy maiden, whose thoughts he might hallow and whose spirit might later meet him among the upper stars.

(No named characters.)

"The Gray Champion," 1835.

One afternoon in April, 1689, Sir Edmund Andros, the vicious governor of Massachusetts under King James II of England, is about to make a show of military strength before the oppressed people of Boston, when a venerable old man appears apparently out of the hoary past. This gray champion of the people sternly orders the royalist group to stand back and then announces that Popish James is no longer king and that Andros's power is ended. The Governor quails and orders his men back. Next day news comes, and he is indeed stripped of all authority. Where is the Gray Champion? Who is he? Stories vary. He seems the embodiment of New England liberty.

Sir Edmund Andros, [Simon] Bradstreet, [Dr.] Bullivant, [Thomas] Dudley, the Gray Champion, Edward Randolph.

"The Great Carbuncle: A Mystery of the White Mountains," 1837.

Long ago in the Crystal Hills eight persons try to find the famed great carbuncle, often seen glowing through the mountain mists. The Seeker has devoted a despairing lifetime to the search. Dr. Cacaphodel wants to find the gem to analyze it chemically and publish the results throughout the scientific world. The wealthy merchant Ichabod Pigsnort wants to make money on it. The bespectacled Cynic hopes not to find it. The bright-eyed Poet wants to put it in his attic and write about it for fame. Lord de Vere wants to take the jewel back to his ancestral halls.

And the newly married couple Matthew and Hannah hope to use it to light their humble abode. The eight camp together one night, and the next morning when Matthew and Hannah awaken they are alone. They happily help each other to the mountain, past the tree line and into heavy clouds, through which they finally see the sun-like carbuncle, gloriously flashing above a mysterious lake. At the base of the cliff beneath the jewel is the Seeker, his arms flung out in death. Next they see the Cynic, who takes off his sunglasses only to be permanently blinded by the ruby glow of the gem. Matthew and Hannah decide to leave the carbuncle where it is. They lead the Cynic down the mountain. It seems that Pigsnort was kidnapped by Indians and held for a huge ransom. Dr. Cacaphodel contented himself with taking a piece of granite for alchemical experiment. The Poet found a chunk of ice about which he wrote a cold poem. Lord de Vere contented himself with a big chandelier in his halls. The blind and wandering Cynic, vainly seeking light, finally perished in the great fire of London. When Matthew and his bride told and retold their story, some denied it, affirming instead that the gem became dim when once seen by mortal eyes; other pilgrims to the area found only bits of mica glittering on an opaque stone; still others say that when the married couple left the mountain the carbuncle fell into the lake beside the Seeker's form; but others affirm that the great carbuncle still flashes into the valley of Saco like summer lightning.

Dr. Cacaphodel, the Cynic, Hannah, Matthew, Ichabod Pigsnort, the Poet, the Seeker, Lord de Vere.

"The Great Stone Face," 1850.

Over a big valley populated by a variety of people presides a gigantic stone face. One afternoon a mother tells her little boy, Ernest, that there is an old legend in the valley that a child will be born hereabouts destined to grow great and noble, and with a face resembling the Great Stone Face. Ernest is thrilled and hopes that he will live to see the illustrious man. Soon Mr. Gathergold, an immensely rich old man, decides to return to his native valley and build a huge palace of marble and glass. Rumor has it that he resembles the stone face. Some say so when they see the yellow-skinned old miser come home in his huge carriage, but Ernest denies it. He turns to the Great Stone Face, which seems to say that the boy should be patient, that the man will come. Years pass. Ernest is now an industrious, kind, neighborly, dutiful young man. Mr. Gathergold, ruined in business, is now dead and his palace has been made into a hotel, and people concede that he never did really look like the Great Stone Face. Now Old Blood-and-Thunder, a war-weary general, returns to the valley. During the colossal sylvan banquet held in his honor, many people say that his energetic face is like the Great Stone Face. Ernest denies it and turns to the original, which seems to smile and urge continued patience. More years pass, and Ernest is now a middle-aged laborer and a part-time, informal preacher of profound natural wisdom. News comes that a thunder-tongued old statesman, later a candidate for President, is returning home to the valley. He is called Old Stony Phiz, because of his massive brow and gloomy eyes. Though some insist that at last the prophecy concerning the Great Stone Face is fulfilled, Ernest bluntly denies it. When he looks for comfort to the western rock, the Face again benignantly urges patience. Years pass, and Ernest is now an old man with cloudy white hair. Many wise men now visit him in his rustic home, because of his great wisdom. One day a poet, once a native in the valley, seeks him out, stays with him instead of at Mr. Gathergold's palace turned hotel, and tells him sadly that people who, like Ernest, look for a resemblance between the Great Stone Face and the poet are wrong, that he is unworthy. At sunset, accompanied by the poet, Ernest goes to a pulpit-like niche in the hills and preaches powerfully, because his words, thoughts, and life make a unit. In the golden light of evening, the clouds around the Great Stone Face resembles the white hair around Ernest's brow. The poet shouts that Ernest is himself the living likeness. And the people agree. But Ernest walks home, still hoping that a better man will return to the valley and bear the resemblance.

Rev. Dr. Battleblast, Ernest, Gathergold, Old Blood-and-Thunder, Old Stony Phiz.

"The Hall of Fantasy," 1843.

The narrator occasionally finds himself in a fantastic edifice, which is Moorish, Arabian, Gothic, and nondescript, with the light of heaven falling into it through stained glass. He and a nearby friend wander about and discuss it all. There are marble statues and busts of great writers, including Homer, Dante, Bunyan, and [Charles Brockden Brown,] the author of *Arthur Mervyn*. There is a wonderful fountain which spouts new shapes in varied colors, perhaps fed by the Castalian spring and the Fountain of Youth. The two wanderers observe drinkers at the fountain, some of whom are talking together humorously and others gravely. They are all a generous brotherhood, although the world does not think so. As for some of the individuals, there are those who fancy cities in the forest, streets in the sea, machines to distill heat from moonshine, lenses to make sunshine out of ladies' smiles, and so on. This palace is a place of refuge too, for sick men, exiles, and those in mourning. The narrator wants to test in the actual daylight all the things seen or imagined in the fantastic light streaming through the windows; until then, he will doubt them all. Next they see reformers, some of whom look at the world through little fragments of truth. True reformers must understand the sphere in which their lot is cast and not merely look at it through pictured windows. Father Miller is there, announcing the end of the world, a prospect which the narrator cannot bear to hear about, since — as he says — he loves many aspects of reality. Others object too — lovers, parents, poets, inventors, and little boys. The narrator's friend says that man's disembodied spirit can rebuild time and the world for itself. But the narrator prefers the firm old globe itself, peopled by the kindly race of man. Those who linger in the Hall of Fantasy have in a sense already destroyed the solid earth.

Professr Espy, Father [William] Miller.

"The Haunted Mind," 1835.

The narrator awakens with a start from midnight slumber. The clock has struck two. Yesterday is gone, and tomorrow has not yet arrived. All is still. He looks through the frosty window at the steeple and stars beyond. He is tempted to wish that he might lie thus throughout his whole life. Then he thinks of the dead. His gloomy heart opens, and out comes a procession including sorrows, lost hopes, fatality, shame, and remorse. The narrator sits up and looks through the gloom for familiar things on his table. Then he timidly thinks of his joy if a wife were near. Dazzlingly joyful images follow, of children, rainbows, birds, ships, and dancing. Finally he calmly wanders back into the wilderness of sleep, wondering if the final change will be as undisturbed.

(No named characters.)

"The Haunted Quack: A Tale of a Canal Boat," 1831.

The narrator is going from Schenectady by canal boat to Utica, on his way to Niagara one summer. Since his fellow passengers are mostly dull fellows, he whiles away the time at night by reading Glanville's book about witches. Suddenly a sleeping passenger mutters something about having poisoned a person and intending to give himself up now. He awakens and tells the narrator his story. He is Hippocrates Jenkins, once an apprentice cobbler near the canal and later a student under Dr. Ephraim Ramshorne, who before he died taught him how to mix quack medicines. Jenkins carried on in his master's line. He usually tested his worthless nostrums on animals, but once he gave a new concoction to sick old Granny Gordon, wife of the blacksmith, who threatened to kill the quack if she died. The patient turned purple, promised to haunt Jenkins, and then apparently gave up the ghost. Jenkins escaped to New York but was haunted nightly by Granny Gordon's ghost and therefore resolved to return and surrender to the authorities. The narrator tries to comfort Jenkins, who feels better after confessing. Next morning a crowd of people greet him as he disembarks. They explain that Granny Gordon did not die but that when Jenkins disappeared the authorities arrested her husband because he had threatened the quack's life. Thanking the narrator for his sympathy, Jenkins goes off with his old friends.

Judge Bates, Dickson, Squire Gobbledown, Bill Gordon, Mrs. Granny Gordon, Sheriff Graham, Hippocrates "Hippy" "Doctor" Jenkins, Dr. Ephraim Ramshorne, Mrs. Ephraim Ramshorne, Miss Ramshorne, Van Pelt, Betsey Wilkins.

"Hints to Young Ambition," 1832 (may not be by Hawthorne).[7]

One day when he was a child the narrator caught a fish and ran home to show it off. But it was greeted with indifference. Many pretentious young people are similarly impatient to parade their accomplishments. Instead, they should prepare for life slowly, carefully, and laboriously. Do not be like the gourd, which grows in the night but soon withers in the sun. Do not rush away from your elders too fast. Do not feel that the public cannot do without your services. Only by industry and perseverance can you find the temple of fame.

(No named characters.)

"The Hollow of the Three Hills," 1830.

Beside a pool in a circular hollow amid three hills, a lady meets with a withered, decrepit old woman, just as an autumn sunset is gilding the peaks above them. Kneeling, the lady asks for tidings of persons left behind. The old woman puts the other's head on her knees, draws her cloak about it, and muttering a prayer summons voices. An aged couple speak of a daughter who has dishonored them. Next chains and scourges are heard, and a man's voice laments a wife's perfidy. Finally a funeral bell announces the burial service of a child. The kneeling lady does not stir as the withered woman chuckles.

(No named characters.)

[7]See Browne, *Bibliography of Hawthorne*, p. 40.

The House of Seven Gables, 1851.

On the side street of a New England town stands a house with seven gables and an enormous elm tree beside its door. It is the ancestral Pyncheon house, owned by a family with a long tradition. It was built on the site of the home of Matthew Maule, whom Colonel Pyncheon — envious of the fine location — helped convict of witchcraft and helped cause to be hanged, though not before the wizard cursed his enemy's family. "God will give him blood to drink!" he said from the gallows. The day the colonel opened his seven-gabled mansion, a hundred and sixty years ago, he was found by his guests dead in his study, his ruff and beard red with blood. Generations come and go, and the family suffers vicissitudes: a claim to lands in Maine remains unsubstantiated, a Pyncheon turns Tory but repents in time to save the house from confiscation, a cousin of the present leading Pyncheon — the big man being Judge Pyncheon — is convicted of murdering his bachelor uncle and sent to prison, and the present inhabitant of the house — named Miss Hepzibah Pyncheon — has reopened its dusty little cent-shop. Descendants of Maule seem to have disappeared, though one, his son Thomas, superintended the building of the Pyncheon house, which has a brow-like second story, a brackish well, a weedy garden, mossy windows, and flowers in a nook near the chimney.

Early one morning, Hepzibah, who according to the previous owner's will can live there as long as she wishes, arises, gazes at the miniature portrait of a delicate young man, and goes into a paneled old room with a faded carpet, tables, a high-backed chair, and the portrait of old Colonel Pyncheon, to which she presents her habitual near-sighted scowl. With a deep sigh, the old spinster opens the cent-shop, now filled with flour, apples, soap, candles, vegetables, candy, gingerbread men, lead soldiers, matches, and the like. Unable to sew or teach school, she must now earn her food here. The town stirs. The old woman is ludicrous and pathetic at once. Her first customer is Holgrave, the daguerrotypist who rents a room in her vast old house. When she breaks down and cries, he comforts her by telling her that she is now a heroic part of the great working public, and then asks for some biscuits — which she gives him without letting him pay. Then a boy (Ned Higgins) comes for a Jim Crow cookie, which she does not charge him for; but when he returns for another, she demands his penny. It is done. She is now a tradeswoman. She feels a curious thrill almost of joy. But her day is mixed. Pessimistic and curious customers loiter or enter to observe her. When a rich woman passes, Hepzibah is momentarily tempted to curse her, repents, and scowls instead. The day continues. Hepzibah's rich cousin, Judge Jaffrey Pyncheon, walks by, well dressed, with an unpleasantly sunny smile, no longer handsome, and looks disapprovingly at her shop but then smiles when he sees her. Hepzibah notes that he resembles the portrait of their Puritan ancestor hanging in the back room, which she now visits. She begins to think of her brother (Clifford), persecuted because of traits in him from their soft mother. Returning to her shop, she sees old Uncle Venner, a kindly fellow with a fund of wisdom and much talk of his ultimate retirement to "his farm" — the workhouse. He advises Hepzibah to smile at her customers and cautiously asks when "he" (Clifford) is expected home. When Uncle Venner leaves, Hepzibah is sad and confused, gives wrong change, and finally welcomes the end of her first commercial day, even though her profit amounts to only a few coppers.

Suddenly an omnibus pulls up before the old house and her country cousin alights. She is Phoebe Pyncheon, a dancing ray of sunshine. At dawn, the girl awakens in her east bedroom, prays, and visits the rose garden. She then prepares breakfast, and she and Hepzibah talk of Clifford, whose miniature they look at together. When the grim old woman starts to open her shop again, young Phoebe offers to tend it for today, does well, and is praised as a veritable angel by Uncle Venner. Hepzibah says that Phoebe's practicality must come from her mother, certainly not from the Pyncheon side. She shows the girl Alice Pyncheon's harpsichord and describes their roomer, Holgrave, as a practitioner of mesmerism and a fellow with rowdy reformer friends. Phoebe enters the Pyncheon garden, with its rich old soil and its many plants, all apparently well tended, its bees and birds, and its diminutive rooster with his two wives and lone chick. Suddenly Holgrave, who has tended the garden, enters and commends Phoebe's ability to feed the chickens. He introduces himself as a daguerrotypist and shows her a picture of Judge Pyncheon which Phoebe with a shudder mistakes for a photograph of old dead Colonel Pyncheon's portrait. Holgrave bitterly criticizes the judge and comments that a heliograph does not lie. He offers to take her likeness, yields control of the garden to her for a flower now and then, and warns her against the bewitched water of Maule's well. When she goes into Hepzibah's parlor, she senses the presence of another person in a shadowy, withdrawn chair. The shadow of a voice asks her most kindly to keep the lamp away. She goes to the kitchen for matches, and Hepzibah follows, kisses her most gently, and suggests that she retire early. The girl's sleep is troubled.

In the morning, Phoebe helps tenderly uneasy Hepzibah prepare an unusually fine breakfast for Clifford, who now appears in a faded damask gown. This soft, gray-white man is sensually delighted with the food and the flowers which Phoebe gracefully presents him. Since grief for him has made generous Hepzibah unpleasant in his beauty-hungry eyes, Clifford now prefers young Phoebe. He demands that they cover the grim portrait of the ancestral colonel. The shop-bell is offensive to him, until his sister gently explains that they must now earn their living, unless they wish to accept charity from a certain offensive hand (the judge's). The prison-ruined man bursts into tears, then turns sly, and next falls asleep. Hepzibah gazes at him fondly and then hastens away. Phoebe learns the relationship between Hepzibah and Clifford when Ned comes for another cookie and identifies the guest as the old woman's brother. Next in comes Judge Pyncheon, with his gold-headed cane and gurgling voice and sultry smile. He offers to kiss his country cousin Phoebe, who backs away and thus temporarily annoys the unctuous man. She sees an uncanny resemblance between the heavily sensual man and their colonel ancestor whose portrait so frightened Clifford. On learning that Clifford is now in the house, the judge pushes past Phoebe to go see him, but Hepzibah enters and refuses him admittance, even though he offers all kinds of luxuries from his country home. He storms, smiles, speaks hypocritically, and then leaves. Hepzibah explains to Phoebe that the man is an absolute horror, and the girl sadly begins to believe that evil can roost in high places.

Since Clifford dislikes her ugliness, rustiness, and scowl, Hepzibah soon quits reading to him and playing the harpsichord for him, and sadly resigns to Phoebe the task of pleasing him. The pretty girl, who is really without intellectual or moral depth, sings appropriately sad songs to him and feeds his hunger for beauty. She is like a daughter to him, and yet he is keenly aware of her virginal bloom. Gradually, however, she grows somewhat more pensive, wondering as she must at the cause of his dementia. Soon a routine is established: while Clifford naps after breakfast, Hepzibah watches him and Phoebe tends the shop; later, the girl entertains him while his sister turns to business. Time passes. In the garden is an old summer-house, which Holgrave and Uncle Venner repair. In it Phoebe reads to Clifford, who prefers poetry to romantic fiction. There are also murmuring bees, red-blossomed beans, and humming-birds to delight Clifford. Hepzibah watches him with tears in her near-sighted eyes. When one hen produces a diminutive egg, she seizes it for his breakfast. The rooster and his hens make up a little rivulet of life. Clifford is frightened by a dark face which he sees amid the mosaic-work of pebbles in the well. After church on Sunday, the group often gathers in the old arbor. Clifford enjoys the plebeian company of philosophical Venner and hints that he has mysterious plans for the old man. Holgrave, looking rather sinister but still admired by Hepzibah for his pleasant manner, smilingly accuses Venner of Fourierism. Clifford is gay in the sunlight but at twilight weeps for his lost happiness. He enjoys watching the sweeping tide of humanity passing beneath an arched window and balcony of the house. Children, vehicles, peddlers, scissors-grinders, and parades — he is attracted by the sounds of all. Once he seems about to jump from the balcony into the midst of a noisy political procession, until he is restrained. He also wants to attend church. Phoebe has gone on ahead; so he and

Hepzibah dress and emerge from their dark door — only to stop, realizing that it is too late, that they are ghosts. Once, when Clifford is blowing soap-bubbles into the street below the arched window, Judge Pyncheon comes by, frowns when a bubble bursts on his nose, then sees his cringing cousin and smiles with a dog-day sultriness.

Clifford, who becomes fatigued easily, is now in the habit of retiring early, which is fortunate for Phoebe, who thus has a good deal of time to herself. Even so, she is changing: her eyes are larger, darker, and deeper, and she is less girlish. In the summer-house, she is occasionally thrown into the company of Holgrave, who tells her about his varied career as schoolmaster, salesman, country editor, peddler, sailor, communal farmer, mesmerist, and now daguerrotypist. He has retained his good conscience always but seems to obey strange rules. He is calm, cool, more intellectual than emotional. He asks Phoebe about Clifford and seems surprised that she does not wish to try fathoming the man's nature. Holgrave rants about the dead weight of the past, says that houses should last only twenty years, and mentions Maule's curse, which he says he accepts as real. He fancies himself quite a thinker, but one might well wonder whether he will amount to anything. He tells Phoebe that he is a publishing author and begins to read her the story of Alice Pyncheon. It seems that thirty-seven years after the Pyncheon house was built, the owner, Gervayse Pyncheon, grandson of the old colonel, summoned carpenter Matthew Maule, the only son of Thomas Maule, who had built the mansion, to ask him about the missing documents relative to the lands eastward. Matthew took offense at Gervayse's Europeanized manners and for revenge against the Pyncheons in general hypnotized his proud, beautiful, pure daughter Alice Pyncheon, who immediately thereafter described her vision of Wizard Maule and his carpenter grandson preventing blood-soaked Colonel Pyncheon from releasing a parchment document to his heirs. Later Alice, still a mesmerized slave, kissed Matthew's bride, then caught cold, and died, at which the carpenter gnashed his teeth, since he sought only to humble Alice, not destroy her. Phoebe is half-hypnotized by the exciting story of Alice, and Holgrave admirably resists a terrible temptation to say something to his auditor to make her his slave forever. In the darkening garden the two talk of Holgrave's unusual happiness here, of Phoebe's feeling of maturity because of her help to Hepzibah and Clifford — she has given them some of her sunshine — and of youth which swiftly passes. Phoebe explains that she must go home again, for a few days, but that she will be back soon. Holgrave says that he enjoys watching the drama of two centuries drawing to its close about the place now. Phoebe calls him heartless, but he explains that he has only a mystical feeling, that he really knows nothing of consequence concerning the place. Two mornings later, Phoebe takes the train bound for home. Hepzibah notes her growing sadness. Clifford calls her a bud now blooming. Uncle Venner urges her to return fast, since otherwise he may be at the workhouse, and calls her an angel essential to the well-being of her old cousins.

Four sunless, stormy days pass after Phoebe's departure. Then the next morning Judge Pyncheon ponderously enters the shop and responds to Hepzibah's scowl with his usual sultry smile. He wants to see Clifford, which Hepzibah refuses to permit, accusing her dark visitor of hounding her nearly demented brother. The judge gushes forth his protests. He is eminently respectable, in position, public service, church work, avocations, appearance, and manners; but it should be noted that sometimes a costly marble edifice is built over a stagnant pool containing a corpse which diffuses its foul scent through the whole place. The judge tells Hepzibah that he set Clifford free, that he is convinced that the perverse man knows where their rich dead uncle's treasure may be located, and that if he does not reveal the facts he will have him shut up for life in an insane asylum. Terrified, Hepzibah agrees to call Clifford and warns her frowning adversary that God is watching. The judge goes into the parlor and flings himself impatiently into the old, ancestral chair. Going for Clifford, Hepzibah looks uneasily out at the rainy street, wishing that Uncle Venner, limping along, would bring aid. Then she wonders whether Clifford does know something about the location of the alleged family treasure but decides that he does not. With Phoebe gone, Hepzibah can turn only to Holgrave, who, however, is also absent; when she looks into his chambers, she sees only a frowning daguerrotype of the hated judge. Her attempt at a prayer from the arched window falls back on her heart like lead. Finally she knocks at Clifford's room, but it too is empty. Screaming to Judge Pyncheon that her brother has disappeared, she finds the ponderous man still silently seated and Clifford now beside him bowing in mock obeisance and laughing. Saying that the weight is lifted, her brother then orders her to get some money and a cloak, escape with him, and leave the house to the judge. She follows her brother's lead, and they leave the mansion with the judge inside, like a dead nightmare.

The two dash out through the summer rain, soon find themselves at a railroad station, and board a train. Clifford sounds gay, like a cracked musical instrument, but Hepzibah views the passengers about them as though they were figures in a dream. Clifford strikes up a wild conversation with a gimlet-eyed old man across the aisle and speaks of the efficacy of railroads in creating a new order of nomads, of the need to tear down all houses — particularly those with blood-stained corpses in them — and of the value of mesmerism, spiritualism, electricity, and the telegraph — except when it is used to apprehend bank-robbers and murderers. To his awestruck neighbor, he repeatedly describes a certain seven-gabled house presided over by a corpse. Suddenly Clifford wants off the train, and he and his prayerful sister alight at a way-station under gloomy clouds.

Meanwhile, Judge Pyncheon remains seated back in the fore-boding house, heedless of time. This is odd, because he is burdened with engagements — he should see Clifford and then his broker, attend an auction to add a parcel of land to the Pyncheon holdings, buy a horse, check into the fallen tombstone of one of his wives, give generously to his political party and a trifle to a needy widow, and consult with his doctor about his throbbing and kicking heart. He also has a private political dinner to attend, with all manner of luxurious foods and wines. Will he be nominated for governor? But there is blood on his shirt front. Darkness falls, and his watch ticks on. The wind rises. One might imagine before the seated figure a procession of Pyncheon ghosts — including those of the judge himself and his son. They all point toward the old colonel's picture-frame. The moon rises, and a mouse approaches the seated figure. Is that a cat outside or the devil watching for a soul? Finally dawn breaks. The watch has stopped ticking. A brave fly crawls toward the staring eyes of the judge.

The morning is gloriously sunny. The house seems alive and happy, and Alice Pyncheon's posies glow red in the mossy eaves. Uncle Venner tries to obtain some slops for his pig, but no one answers his rap at the Pyncheon house, although Holgrave yells a greeting to him. Various neighbors and potential customers of the shop gossip that Hepzibah and her brother have gone to Judge Pyncheon's country estate. The passing butcher is annoyed when Hepzibah fails to emerge and buy some choice cuts. The Italian hurdy-gurdy player and his monkey give a performance but fail to elicit any coins. The rumor starts that the judge has been murdered, and the city marshal is consulted. Crowds avoid the house, but brave boys race each other past its gloomy confines. Then Phoebe returns from the country; observing the untidy garden, she senses a change. As she tries a door near the garden, it opens from the inside. Holgrave gently leads the anxious girl to a big, empty room, where, worried but smiling at her return, he asks for her wisdom and strength as he shows her a picture of Judge Pyncheon sitting in death. Worried about Hepzibah and Clifford, he explains that for certain reasons he is connected with these events. Probably the colonel, the uncle, and the judge all died because of a similar hereditary weakness, he explains. He adds that in his opinion the natural death of the bachelor Pyncheon uncle was staged by the judge to look like murder, for which Clifford was unjustly imprisoned. Holgrave and Phoebe forget the presence of death and exchange tender vows of love, in spite of her brief objection that she is too simple for his pathless ways.

Then, before he can act on her advice to throw open the doors of the house and admit social forces, Hepzibah and Clifford enter and embrace Phoebe, happily returned to them.

After what is soon called his natural death, Judge Pyncheon is quickly forgotten. A theory is advanced that as a youth he was surprised by his uncle while ransacking his desk. The old man had a seizure and died, and his would-be robber found two wills, one favoring him and another of later date favoring Clifford. Destroying the latter, he planted evidence pointing the finger of suspicion at Clifford, who was accordingly soon imprisoned for murder. The son of the judge predeceased him; so Clifford and Hepzibah inherit his wealth and country estate, to which they decide to move. Clifford is easier in his mind and happier now but still is not well. No great mistake can ever really be set right. Holgrave tells Phoebe that he is a Maule and laughingly expresses the non-reformer's sorrow that their country estate is built of wood rather than permanent stone. He finds a spring — which Clifford now vaguely remembers — in the ancestral portrait and reveals behind it the now useless deed to Indian lands. When they all decide in September to move into the country, they take with them Uncle Venner, who fancies that he hears the shade of Alice Pyncheon playing sweet music over the house of the seven gables.

The Duke of Devonshire, Dixey, Gubbins, Mrs. Gubbins, Ned Higgins, Rev. Mr. Higginson, Holgrave, [Edward Greene] Malbone, Cotton Mather, Matthew Maule, Matthew Maule, Mrs. Matthew Maule, Thomas Maule, Maule, Sir William Phipps, Moll Pitcher, Alice Pyncheon, Arthur Pyncheon, Mrs. Arthur Pyncheon, Clifford Pyncheon, Gervayse Pyncheon, Mrs. Gervayse Pyncheon, Hepzibah "Old Maid" Pyncheon, Jaffrey Pyncheon, Judge Jaffrey Pyncheon, Mrs. Jaffrey Pyncheon, Jaffrey Pyncheon, Phoebe Pyncheon, Colonel Pyncheon, Mrs. Pyncheon, Mrs. Pyncheon, Mrs. Pyncheon, Rev. Mr. Pyncheon, Pyncheon, Pyncheon, Pyncheon, Pyncheon, Pyncheon, Pyncheon, Pyncheon, Pyncheon, Mrs. Pyncheon, Miss Pyncheon, Scipio, Smith, Dr. John Swinnerton, Uncle Venner, King William.

"Howe's Masquerade" (I. in "Legends of the Province House"), 1838.

One summer afternoon, the narrator leaves Washington Street in Boston to enter the old Province House, built about 1679. After the proprietor Thomas Waite mixes him a port sangaree, he inspects the place — staircase, cupola, garret, and balcony — and then reenters the barroom to listen to an old gentleman's reminiscence.

Toward the end of the siege of Boston, Sir William Howe, the royal governor, gives a fancy-dress ball. Doughty old Whig Colonel Joliffe attends with his granddaughter, and so do the Rev. Mr. Mather Byles, Lord Percy, and other Tories. Suddenly a funeral march is heard. Sir William orders Dighton, the drum-major, to silence it, but that man apologizes and says that he is not responsible for the disquieting music. Then down the dismal staircase comes a procession of figures disguised as regicide judges of King Charles I. Next comes a sequence of earlier New England rulers. Finally come figures of other provincial governors, shuffling along as though marching at a funeral; the last figure in this procession is muffled but dressed exactly like Sir William himself. That insulted ruler draws his sword and confronts his likeness but, evidently catching sight of its features, recoils. When Colonel Joliffe asks him if he would care to inquire further into the mystery, Sir William blusters but to no avail. The old colonel says that British rule in ancient Massachusetts is now at its last gasp. The figures in the pageant then vanish more completely than the Indians did at the Boston Tea Party.

The narrator is brought back to the present time when he smells cigar smoke and hears a spoon rattling in a glass of whiskey punch. It is hard to imagine the past when the living present intrudes so. He goes back out to Washington Street.

Sir Edmund Andros, Governor [Jonathan] Belcher, the Earl of Bellamont, Governor [Richard] Bellingham, Sir Francis Bernard, Governor [Simon] Bradstreet, Governor [William] Burnet, Rev. Mr. Mather Byles, Dighton, Governor [Thomas] Dudley, Governor [John] Endicott, General [Thomas] Gage, Governor [John] Haynes, Sir William

Howe, Susan Huggins, Governor [Thomas] Hutchinson, Colonel Joliffe, Miss Joliffe, Governor [Sir John] Leverett, Lord Percy, Sir William Phipps, Governor [Thomas] Pownall, Governor [William] Shirley, Governor [Samuel] Shute, Sir Henry Vane, Thomas Waite, Governor [John] Winthrop.

"The Intelligence Office," 1844.

In the Intelligence Office, in which the Intelligencer records the wishes of mankind in his Book of Wishes, come many persons looking for a variety of things, including items they have lost. Some seek housing, a place to eat, lost beauty, yesterday's sunshine, and the like. One frenzied man, with everything about him awry including his eyes, asks for a place, any place so long as it is definitely his own. A young man comes in and offers to exchange his heart for that of another; when a slender maiden immediately follows, the Intelligencer makes the transaction easily. Why do some want to exchange a diamond for an earthy pearl or to pour pure liquid into a base pot? A woe-begone man wants a lost, precious jewel returned to him. The Intelligencer rummages among ivory tablets and ruby hearts with golden arrows, and finally finds the Pearl of Great Price, which, however, he then cannot give back. A worldly man enters and offers his huge estate, once a castle in the air, to anyone who will take its accompanying encumbrance. The Intelligencer refuses to make the transaction, and the man departs with his evil conscience. Many others enter in need of things; some succeed in exchanging vice for virtue. Human character is revealed best by a study of wishes rather than acts. An old man wants to find tomorrow but cannot. A little boy is looking for a lost butterfly. A vigorous but warm-hearted man finally enters and announces that he is looking for the Truth. The Intelligencer says that such a pursuit is most rare and that he cannot be of assistance; he does add, however, that his folio of recorded wishes is delusive because he is not a minister of action but only a recording spirit: the desire of man's heart does for man what the Intelligencer seems to do.

The Intelligencer, Peter Schlemihl.

"John Inglefield's Thanksgiving," 1840.

On the evening of the first Thanksgiving Day after his beloved wife died, the rugged blacksmith John Inglefield is sitting at dinner. Beside him are his son, who is a theology student, his sixteen-year-old daughter Mary, and his former apprentice Robert Moore, who is now a journeyman blacksmith. Absent, in addition to his wife, for whom a place has been set, is Mary's twin sister Prudence, who has strayed sinfully from home. But suddenly she appears, in demure cloak and hood, greets her father modestly, says that she has come to spend the evening at home, and is welcomed. Her father lets her sit where the mother's place was and in the flickering firelight almost mistakes her for his wife. Her brother shakes her hand affectionately and tells her it is providential that she returned when she did, because in a few weeks he will go as a missionary to the islands of the Pacific, never to return home again. When Mary offers to embrace her, grief-stricken and shamed Prudence shrinks away and says that she should not. Moore, however, takes her hand and holds it to his heart. The family seems reunited. Inglefield even laughs gaily, and the others seem to forget that Prudence fell and was trampled in the dust. As she is pouring her father a cup of herb tea, the hour for domestic prayer arrives. Suddenly Prudence puts on her cloak and hood, waves farewell to the group from the door, and smiles mockingly from a face twisted with sin and evil. Inglefield, between wrath and sorrow, tells her to stay and be his blessing or leave with his curse. She seems momentarily to be struggling with the fiend; then she is gone into the darkness. That same evening, at the theater in a nearby city, one among the painted beauties is dissolute and mirthful. She is Prudence, whose visit home was a waking dream during which her guilty soul strayed back to innocence. But the dark power of sin drew her away again.

John Inglefield, Mary Inglefield, Prudence Inglefield, Inglefield, Robert Moore.

"Lady Eleanore's Mantle" (III. in "Legends of the Province

House"), 1838.

One night the narrator is invited to the Province House by Thomas Waite, the host, to have an oyster supper with [Bela] Tiffany, the tale-teller. An old loyalist listens as they pause and talk over a bottle of Madeira.

Lady Eleanore Rochcliffe, the ward of Colonel Shute, Governor of Massachusetts Bay, arrives from England. She is intensely proud, and as her mounted escorts, including Captain Langford, bring her to Boston she wraps herself regally in her curiously embroidered mantle. A funeral bell happens to toll as the party comes to the Province House; and Dr. Clarke, a champion of the common people, remarks wryly that the lowliest corpse takes precedence over the most impatient of living aristocrats. Suddenly Jervase Helwyse, a demented young man who was in love with Lady Eleanore in London, kneels and begs her to alight from her carriage by walking on him. She does so, haughtily. Dr. Clarke opines that she is in for trouble. A few days later the Governor gives a splendid ball for his ward, who attends but seems scornful, graceful, wildly unnatural, and tired by turns. Helwyse again approaches her, this time to beg her to sip wine from his goblet and then pass it around, and also to cast her accursed mantle into the fire. As the young man is being thrown out, he warns her that her face will wear another aspect in due time. Meanwhile Dr. Clarke whispers something to the Governor, who calls a premature end to the ball. In a short time the dread smallpox descends upon the city, first smiting the high-born, including Captain Langford, but then all ranks. The plague is traced to Lady Eleanore and her mantle, which was embroidered by a stricken old woman in England. Helwyse returns to the Province House and makes his way past Governor Shute and Dr. Clarke, since he wants to see Lady Eleanore ruling with Death on a single throne. The blasted woman is begging for water and hiding her features behind her bed curtains. She tells him that since she wrapped herself in pride as in a mantle, Heaven has cursed her. Helwyse seizes her mantle and sees to it that it is burned along with an effigy of the once haughty beauty. The plague suddenly ends.

The narrator and his friends linger at the Province House. The old loyalist will tell the next story.

Dr. Clarke, Jervase Helwyse, Captain Langford, Lady Eleanore Rochcliffe, Governor Colonel [Samuel] Shute, [Bela] Tiffany, Thomas Waite.

"Legends of the Province House" — see "Howe's Masquerade," "Edward Randolph's Portrait," "Lady Eleanore's Mantle," and "Old Esther Dudley."

"The Lily's Quest: An Apologue," 1839.

Adam Forrester and his beloved, Lilias Fay, whom he calls Lily because she is so delicately beautiful, want to build a Temple of Happiness. But whenever they choose a lovely spot, a dark and gloomy relative of Lily's named Walter Gascoigne shakes his head and tells them something sad about the place: it might be the scene of a ruined home, the locale of a murder, or the like. Finally Adam and Lily decide to build where they chance to pause in their quest. Walter smiles inscrutably. As their graceful temple rises, Lily grows slimmer and weaker, and finally she is found dead within its unfinished portals. When Adam begins to realize that on this afflicted place his hope for eternal bliss is erected, Walter slinks away, knowing that the darkest riddle of mankind has now been read.

Lilias "Lily" Fay, Adam Forrester, Walter Gascoigne.

"Little Annie's Ramble," 1835.

The town crier rings his bell to announce the approach of a circus caravan. The narrator takes sweet and smiling little Annie by the hand for a little walk. They look at the carts in the street, hear the music of an organ-grinder, go past some dress shops and pastry shops and candy stores, then see a book store (the narrator is tempted to put Annie into a gift book) and a toy shop and a place with caged birds. A dog and a cat come by, and then there is the noisy circus. They visit all the animals. On the street again, they hear more noises, including that of the town crier again, this time announcing that Annie, aged five years, is missing and that her mother is looking for her. The narrator takes her home again, philosophizing on the beneficent influence of innocent childhood on people no longer young themselves.

Annie.

"Little Daffydowndilly," 1843.

Little Daffydowndilly looks like a flower, delights only in what is beautiful and pleasant, and dislikes work. His mother places him in the school of Mr. Toil, who is severe and ugly, and makes his charges work so hard that the boy runs away. He encounters a man of experience who agrees to go with him and avoid Mr. Toil. But wherever they look they see what appears to be Mr. Toil, whether among farmers making hay or carpenters or soldiers. The man of experience explains that the people who seem to be Mr. Toil are really a series of brothers of the toilsome man. One, a French-bred fiddler, calls himself Monsieur le Plaisir, but his real name is Toil. An Italian-bred idler, who calls himself Signore Far Niente, is another brother. Finally Daffydowndilly decides to return to school. He finds it nearby, since he and his companion have been walking in a circle. In time, the boy begins to like school, realizing the important lesson that diligence is not more toilsome than sport or idleness.

Daffydowndilly, Signore Far Niente, Monsieur le Plaisir, Mr. Toil.

"Main Street," 1849.

A showman presents a pictorial exhibition of the various changes in the course of many years along Main Street [Salem]. At first it is a leaf-strewn Indian path along which the Squaw Sachem and Wappacowet, her second husband, walk. Next the showman presents Roger Conant, the first settler in Naumkeag, and some early domestic scenes. The redman is beginning to vanish. Endicott enters. Next the area is a village street, with a rude meetinghouse — quite a contrast to English cathedrals far away. John Massey, the firstborn of the town, is now a toddler. Nathaniel Ward and Morton of Merrymount, among many other people, are observable. More years pass, and quaint but sturdy houses are now visible. It is time for the Thursday Lecture, and various sinners are paraded and punished. John Massey is now twenty years old. Quakers are exposed under Major Hawthorne's order. Captain Gardner marches off to fight at the outbreak of King Philip's War. More years roll on, and new scenes come into view. It is now time for the witchcraft trials, involving John Proctor and his wife Elizabeth, Chief-Justice Sewell, and the Rev. Mr. George Burroughs. More years speed by, and Goodman Massey is nearly eighty. Next we see the effects of the Great Snow of 1717, which buried the houses along Main Street as though they had never been. The showman tries to present more scenes, but a wire breaks and thus prevents the sunny present and the hidden future from rolling into view. At almost every new pictorial representation of times along Main Street, one critic in the audience objects because the tiny figures are only pasteboard and he sees things precisely as they are. At the end, he demands the return of his quarter.

Lady Arabella, Balch, Governor [Simon] Bradstreet, Mrs. Bradstreet, Joshua Buffum, Rev. Mr. George Burroughs, Martha Carrier, Ann Coleman, Roger Conant, Mrs. Conant, Captain Curwen, Emanuel Downing, George Downing, Governor [John] Endicott, Mrs. Anna Gower Endicott, Daniel Fairfield, Goody Foster, Captain Gardner, Major [William] Hawthorne [Hathorne], Ann Hutchinson, George Jacobs, Jeffrey Massey, Goodwife Massey, Goodman John Massey, Cotton Mather, [Thomas] Morton, Norman, Norris, Rev. Mr. Noyes, Peter Palfrey, Mercy Parris, Hugh Peters, Mrs. Elizabeth Proctor, Goodman John Proctor, Sir Richard Saltenstall, Chief-Justice [Samuel] Sewell [Sewall], Cassandra Southwick, the Squaw Sachem, Dorothy Talby, Tibula, the Tidy Man, Wappacowet, Nathaniel Ward, John Willard, Roger Williams, Governor [John] Winthrop, Woodbury.

"The Man of Adamant: An Apologue," 1837.

In the intolerant days of long ago, Richard Digby fancies himself to be uniquely chosen for salvation. So he leaves his village and walks into the dark forest until he finds a sepulchral cave, dripping with lime water which converts to stone whatever it touches. He spurns the water from a bubbling fountain nearby and refreshes himself with a drop or two of moisture from the cave roof, which is hung with stony icicles. He already has a weakened and hardening heart, caused by a circulatory obstruction. He talks to himself, reads his Bible to himself, and — one might add — prays to himself. One evening, after three days in the cave, Digby is misreading his Bible by the fading light when the form of Mary Goffe, radiant though disheveled, appears before him. She was a convert to his preaching in England and has apparently followed him to America impelled by faith and love. She urges him to return to the village, but in vain. When she brings some water to him in a birch bark cup, he smites it from her hand, saying that she is an accursed temptress who can have nothing to do with his Bible, his prayers, or his heaven. At that moment his hard heart stops beating and Mary Goffe — in reality only a spirit, because she is really dead and buried in England — melts into the sunshine. More than a century later some children are playing in the area of Digby's cave, now surrounded by settlements and farms, when they find what seems a repulsive statue of a repellent man. The children's father explores the cave, finds it hideous, and blocks up its entrance with stones and dirt.

Richard Digby, Mary Goffe.

The Marble Faun: or, the Romance of Monte Beni, 1860.

In the sculpture gallery of the Capitol in Rome, four young people — Kenyon, Miriam Schaefer, Hilda, and Donatello — notice that the marble faun of Praxiteles resembles Donatello. It is pleasant, amoral, and unheroic in appearance, and perhaps might be educated to the virtues. Miriam makes mischievous remarks, and Hilda seems timid. When Miriam asks to see whether his ears are pointed like those in the statue, Donatello refuses and then seems contrite, after she wishes that she were a guiltless faun herself. Kenyon discusses sculpture, his profession, while Miriam and Hilda contrast it to their work, which is painting. Donatello follows Miriam like a slightly savage dog. Her wild, bushy-bearded model (Brother Antonio) is seen lurking by a pillar as the group leaves the museum.

It is rumored that Miriam, who is dark, beautiful, and mysterious, is the wayward daughter of a Jewish banker, a German princess, the partly Negro offspring of an American planter, the lady of an English nobleman, the daughter of a ruined merchant, and so on. Some months earlier, she became lost in the catacomb of St. Calixtus, which she was exploring with Kenyon and with timid Donatello and Hilda, who shuddered when their guide told of a pagan lost for fifteen centuries after trying to spy on proscribed Christians there. When Miriam emerged, she was accompanied by a shaggy man. Was he a beggar, pilgrim, thief, political offender, murderer, or lunatic? He began to dog her steps and became her model. Miriam joked that he would teach her the lost art of Roman fresco-painting in return for her eventual eternal companionship in darkness with him. She seems sadder now, and Donatello hates the model with an animal-like instinct.

One morning he walks past a Roman courtyard with a fountain and some broken-nosed old statues and up a stairway to Miriam's studio. He finds the pensive girl mending a pair of gloves. She talks so sadly to the faun that he grows sad. She shows him her paintings – of vengeful Biblical women, of sentimental things, of figures in isolation, and finally of her beautiful but unsmiling self. Although she says that she is not good for him, he vows to follow her always. When he leaves, Miriam goes to visit Hilda, who lives high in a medieval tower, rare in Rome, which has a shrine honoring the Virgin and a lamp which must be kept burning, or else the Church will inherit the property. Doves hover about the windows of Hilda, who is herself a dove. She is a New England orphan with a little property and came to Rome to study art but has become a marvelously skillful and respected copyist of the rare paintings of masters. The two girls discuss a copy of Guido's "Beatrice Cenci" which Hilda has faultlessly copied from memory. Hilda calls Beatrice a fallen though sinless angel until Miriam reminds her of the deed for which she was punished; then the younger girl says that Beatrice's doom was just — at which Miriam compares her companion's innocence to a sharp sword and calls her judgment severe. She then gives Hilda a packet of letters to be delivered precisely four months hence to a person in the Palazzo Cenci.

Meanwhile, Donatello walks to the grounds of the Villa Borghese to meet Miriam. The beautiful gardens abound in trees, lawns, fountains, old statues, and altars — and malaria. The faun runs along happily, embraces a tree trunk, kisses some flowers, and then climbs a tree — for a fine view — until he spies Miriam, then alights beside her. She wonders whether he is a man or an animal, and asks him to summon nymphs and satyrs, at which he smiles and says that he loves her. Perhaps his character needs her dark element for contrast. But she seriously warns him that she will bring him only evil. When he says he fears nothing, she resignedly determines to love him for a time. They run races, weave garlands, and then walk toward some music in a grove, where a vagrant band is playing. Donatello seizes a tambourine and dances ecstatically, frenziedly. Joining him, Miriam resembles a nymph. The entire varied group looks like a sculptured procession on a sarcophagus. Suddenly the model appears. Donatello offers to throttle him, but Miriam tells her faun to leave now. He does so but vows to make her path his forever. Miriam and the model stand in such chilly remoteness that only fragmentary sentences float from them. When he says that an evil bond unites them, that it is usless to try to avoid their common fate, she says that he should seek absolution, that their relationship may well end in death. He hints that she might be thinking of killing him, to which she replies that he has no right to think her a murderess. He seizes her hand and in the fading light pretends to examine it for blood-stains. She counters by saying that it was pure until he first touched it. They leave the gardens and enter the swarm of people beyond the Porta del Popolo.

Meanwhile, Kenyon waits on the Pincian Hill where he knows Hilda walks. She comes by, and the two stroll past many Roman scenes and before innumerable fine vistas. Rome seems like a classical corpse with a dusty veneer. They see Donatello and discuss his sadness, his love for Miriam, and his faun-like qualities, then Miriam's mysteriousness. Kenyon then sees Miriam kneel before her stern model, whom Kenyon soon thereafter tries unsuccessfully to follow. One morning Miriam visits Kenyon's studio near the Corso, to inspect his statue of a dead young pearl-fisher tangled in seaweed, his busts of Milton and of certain illustrious contemporary Americans, and a delicate copy of Hilda's slender hand. His visitor wishes him luck with the possessor of the original hand, but they agree that the little copyist is probably devoted exclusively to the old masters. Then they discuss nudity and excessive petty realism in modern statues. When Kenyon shows Miriam his large clay model of Cleopatra, she praises the rapturous, wicked figure and adds that Hilda could never have inspired it. Then she thinks of herself and starts to confess a burning secret which makes her lonely. But Kenyon, reserved and alarmed, is tardy in offering sympathy, and Miriam storms out of his studio, well aware that her secret cannot be revealed and also that her relationship with cold Kenyon must now inevitably change.

The jealous camaraderie of Anglo-Saxon sculptors and painters in Rome results in many social gatherings, one of which Miriam, Hilda, and Kenyon – with Donatello following along – attend. The host has a portfolio of old drawings. One of them Hilda fancies is an original sketch by Guido for his painting of the archangel Michael defeating the devil, in the Church of the Cappuccini. Her friends examine the sketch, and all but Miriam agree that the devil's face resembles that of Miriam's model. Then they all go on a moonlit ramble through part of Rome, accompanied by several other artists. They visit the Trevi Fountain, from which Miriam drinks and takes water to fling in the face of her model, who turns up there and refuses to leave. Donatello asks whether he should drown the hated spectre, but Miriam soothes him as one might a faithful hound. The group walks on, past Trajan's Forum and several old temples, to the Coliseum, where, like other pilgrims seeking remission of their sins, Miriam kneels at a cross in the center of the floor. Conversing about activities in the Coliseum in times gone by, Kenyon and Hilda see Miriam retreat to an obscure arch and there dance madly in anguish. Donatello offers his sympathy, but she rebukes him for spying and eloquently begs him to leave her forever, since evil overwhelms her. He refuses. Soon the group walks on past the Forum to the Capitoline Hill and then the Tarpeian Rock, from which traitors were formerly hurled to their deaths. The four talk of ancient Roman patriotism, the beneficent tyrant Marcus Aurelius — a bronze equestrian statue of whom is nearby — fatalism, and free will. Miriam tells Donatello that it was right for evil men to be killed here, to save innocent persons. Kenyon and Hilda begin to walk down, and then Hilda returns to be with Miriam; but before she can join her she hears a deadly scream quiver down through the air. Donatello has flung the bearded model over the cliff to his death. When Donatello queries her, Miriam admits that her eyes ordered the deed. As they embrace, they realize that they are knotted together in sin; and as they walk back home, they have an ecstatic sense of freedom and then a sense of being part of the fellowship of sinners. Seeing Hilda at her high window praying toward the sky, Miriam asks her to pray for them, but Hilda does not hear and soon goes back into her room.

Next morning, Miriam and Donatello, who looks sick, go as planned to the Capuchin Church and meet Kenyon, who is worried when Hilda does not join them and tells his other two friends that she returned toward them as they were leaving the Tarpeian Rock. They consult Guido's painting of Michael and the devil, and Miriam scornfully says that the angel looks too tidy after putting down evil. Then she encourages Donatello, who has been hanging back, to go with her and look directly at a dead monk lying in state on the main floor of the untidy church, through which oozes a lugubrious burial chant. But when they approach the purplish face of the corpse, they shudder. It is Miriam's murdered model. Kenyon notes everything but with fine discretion says nothing, resolving to let Miriam speak first to explain the riddle if she wishes. She is dumbfounded. She bids Donatello wait and returns for a closer look. Then she visits the basement cemetery, where each Capuchin monk is buried for twenty years in holy soil from Jerusalem and then is dug up again to contribute his bones to wall and ceiling decorations. Miriam pays the sacristan to have masses offered for Brother Antonio (as the model is called here). Then she takes Donatello away to the Medici gardens and offers to do anything in her power to console the apathetic fellow. She urges him to go to his home in the Apennines and regard everything in the immediate past as a dream. If he has need of her, she will respond. Then she departs, and he lies down in a stupor. Miriam finds her steps leading her to Hilda's tower. She encounters the girl sitting listlessly beside her copy of Guido's "Beatrice." She refuses to touch Miriam and permanently withholds her friendship from the lonely woman. Miriam describes her as hard and in need of a sin to soften her. Hilda tells what she saw the previous night at the rock, including Miriam's look of hate turning to the joy of relief, then confesses that she needs relief now but cannot confide in Kenyon, and finally accuses Miriam of darkening the sky. The two part unhappily.

In June, Kenyon takes a horseback trip to Tuscany to visit Donatello. The young count greets him hospitably but looks older, thinner, pale, and sad. He tells Kenyon that he often gazes at the stars from the top of his massive tower. In a stone-floored and heavily pilastered room, Donatello serves his guest the pride of Monte Beni, its famous pale yellow wine, which they call Sunshine, once drunk by a Pope. Kenyon notes that the room has peeling frescoes which portray the vicissitudes of an individual who resembles Donatello. The sculptor has permission to do a bust of his host, who agrees but says that he hates to be stared at for long. Chancing to mention Miriam, Kenyon explains that she has also left Rome. Beginning the next morning, Kenyon soon learns from mouldy documents and — more pleasantly — from a kindly old servant that the pedigree of Monte Beni goes back to pre-Roman times, earlier even than Etrurian and

Pelasgic people, to the era of satyrs and sylvan nymphs. The servant laments that Donatello, once a rosy, carefree boy, is now sad. He refuses the diversion of wandering musicians, improvvisatori, jugglers, and paupers.

One day Donatello takes Kenyon to a secluded spot with a lovely fountain and a statue of a moss-clothed maiden. He recounts a family myth: the maiden loved a knight and gave him dewy kisses until he tried once to wash a blood-stain in the pure water. The knight saw her one final time after that, and she had blood on her brow. While in the woods, Donatello tries to call the furry and feathered people to him; but when only a poisonous lizard answers, he grovels beside the fountain and fails to respond to Kenyon's ineffectual attempts at comfort. One day the sculptor persuades sulky Donatello to show him his tower. They climb past a prison cell in it to an owl roost and then to the count's small room, fitted with religious items and also an alabaster skull — to remind life-loving Monte Beni noblemen of death. The two talk of secret sin and of death; then Kenyon notes with delight the wondrous view of Umbria from the summit of the tower. Donatello voices a terrible fear of falling to death from a height. Suddenly Kenyon feels his heart tugged back toward Rome by a sensitive cord. Then the two fancy resemblances to those they love in one of the clouds produced by a sudden thunder-storm. At twilight Donatello tells his guest to descend, adding that he will keep a vigil on the battlement of his tower. When he says that he is tempted to become a monk, anti-Catholic Kenyon, sensing that some unknown sorrow in Rome has humanized his faun-like friend and given him a troubled soul, begs him instead to make the world his cell and good deeds his prayers.

Kenyon begins a clay bust of Donatello but accidentally keeps making it look fierce and bestial. Its Cain-like appearance so pleases Donatello that his guest rebukes him for lingering unduly in the valley of remorse. Later Kenyon watches Tuscan winemaking operations but prefers his memories of New England cider-pressing scenes. Suddenly the old servant tells him that a woman is awaiting him in a room beyond the chapel. It is

Miriam. During their long talk in the magnificent, marble-floored saloon, stiff but helpful Kenyon tells listless Miriam that Donatello loves her, is more perceptive intellectually, is in danger of lapsing into deeper lethargy, and therefore needs to travel a little. She agrees to meet Donatello at noon exactly two weeks hence under the statue of Pope Julius [III] in the great square of Perugia, if Kenyon can take them there in the course of their proposed ramble. Miriam explains that she is now less womanly because she has been rejected by Hilda, whose purity, however, the two agree is properly undefiled.

Before he is quite aware of doing so, Donatello is accompanying the now restless sculptor through rural scenes, walled towns heavy with a sense of the past and picturesque decay, along wayside shrines and fortresses, and into Gothic churches ablaze with stained-glass windows. They speak of the oppressive past and of the weight of sin, and of Dante and Milton. All along their journey, Kenyon senses that a muffled figure is near them, following or preceding them. Finally, one sunny morning the two travelers reach the hill city of Perugia, wander through its colorful streets, crowded with people selling fruit and vegetables. Kenyon approaches the statue of the Pope, which Donatello, now looking healthier, feels may be blessing him. The cathedral clock strikes noon. A crowd of Italian admirers stares approvingly at Miriam, while she looks up at the bronze papal face as to a needed father. Kenyon welcomes her and offers to lead her to Donatello, but she refuses, preferring to await her lover's summons. He calls, she goes to him, and in a voice of infinite sadness he apologizes for his inevitable coldness, then rejects her offer to be flung aside, saying that they share a common lot. Kenyon approaches, speaks of their mutual need, yet warns them that since their love is apparently twined with black threads it can hardly result in marriage. They instantly agree. Since Miriam has told Kenyon that Hilda is depressed and needs him, he adds a few words about spiritual duty and then leaves for Rome.

Torpid Hilda has been spending the summer in languid, deserted Rome. She goes to galleries but is idle. At such times, the realism of the Dutch masters is preferable to tiresome religious paintings and the sensual nudes of the Italians. An artist, spying on her once, paints her staring in shocked surprise at a spot of blood on her white dress. Her doves are listless, and she seeks sympathy at her shrine of the Virgin. For the first time she experiences the exile's pain. She wishes that Kenyon were with her. She visits church after church. If their altar pictures were painted better, she might have become a convert. One day she enters St. Peter's, that vast jewel casket and the Mecca of numberless devout pilgrims. Kneeling at the mosaic of the archangel Michael, she notes the relief on the face of a woman leaving a confessional and then disburdens herself of her weighty secret in another confessional, marked English. But before she emerges, immensely relieved, the priest, New England born, has stepped out to tell her that he feels free to reveal her secret to the authorities, since she is heretic and hence is not entitled to the privilege of the confessional. They argue briefly, he fails to persuade her to become a convert, but in the end the head-shaking father blesses her, saying that the authorities probably already have all necessary details of the murder. The priest's benedictory gesture is witnessed by someone standing near the high altar — Kenyon. He approaches the happy girl, and they talk of Catholicism, St. Peter's, and Hilda's blessed relief. Kenyon is rather sarcastic until he is assured that his friend has not become a convert. Talking about the sights along the way, they walk back to Hilda's tower, and then the girl leaves him for her faithful doves.

Soon cheerless winter descends on Rome, during which Hilda deserts the icy galleries and visits Kenyon in his studio. He is delighted by her professional approval of his Cleopatra, now struggling out of her marble case. Hilda also praises his un-finished bust of Donatello, rightly noting that it shows the subject's growing intellectual power. When Kenyon says that the count has sadly changed, Hilda turns pale and hints that he has good reason to do so. Kenyon is surprised and says that Miriam wanted the two of them to discuss her case frankly. This only gains Miriam a profound rebuke from Hilda, who brands her absent former friend as lacking in pride for talking loosely about herself. Kenyon then says that Hilda is so pure that she neither needs nor ever gives mercy. They part. Back in her tower, Hilda is troubled for failing Miriam, who loved and needed her. Suddenly she thinks of the packet of letters, which should be delivered this very day. She takes them through a fetid quarter of Rome to the Palazzo Cenci.

Kenyon goes the next day to the Vatican galleries to meet Hilda, to whom he now intends to propose. But she is absent; so the statues mean nothing to him. Only the Laocoon pleases him. In the Corso a masked penitent, who speaks to him, seems to resemble Donatello. In the evening, after attending an unsatisfactory comedy, Kenyon sees Miriam in a carriage with a sallow-faced Italian. She tells the sculptor not to despair when the lamp goes out. He rushes to Hilda's tower and sees its immemorial lamp flicker and die. He rushes to her door, but she does not answer his thunderous knocking. In the morning he questions her neighbors and examines Hilda's room in the inscrutable landlady's presence. The girl's little writing-desk is missing. Kenyon continues his investigation for a week, even going to the inefficient Roman police, but to no avail. Once Hilda's light is extinguished and her doves begin to fly away, Kenyon, formerly cool man of marble, is intensely worried and wanders the streets of dreary Rome comfortless. He is inwardly critical of priests, the nobility, soldiers, and the whole Roman population. Happening to encounter the kind-looking priest to whom Hilda confessed, Kenyon asks about Hilda but learns nothing. Has she been swallowed by an abyss? Is she a prisoner of religious authorities bent on converting her?

In response to an anonymous letter, Kenyon walks along the Appian Way in the beautifully mild and caressing weather — it is February now — and out to the Campagna, to keep an appointment. He goes past unknown tombs and pyramids to an excavation site in which he sees a partly unearthed Greek statue in fragments. Then Miriam and Donatello appear, dressed as peasant and contadina. Donatello discovered the statue only a few days before. Kenyon is gloomy until Miriam assures him that Hilda is safe and will rejoin him in two days. Miriam also tells him

something of her background: partly English, Jewish, and southern Italian, she refused to be forced by her family into a
marriage with an older man whose evil could be explained only
on the grounds of insanity. So she fled to Rome and a new life,
only to be followed by the creature from the catacomb. She
wonders if Donatello's mysterious crime, which has wedded him
to her, is a blessing since it has emotionally and intellectually
elevated him, just as Adam was changed by his fall; but Kenyon
shies away from such theorizing and leaves the two.

Two afternoons later, following Miriam's instructions, Kenyon
goes to the Corso at the height of the carnival, which to him is a
dreamy mixture of costumed revelers, carriages, flowers, confetti,
watchful soldiers, sportive fights, and other rather forced gaiety.
Suddenly he sees Donatello and Miriam, disguised and masked,
and follows them through the wild crowd. When he begs Miriam
for more information, she tenderly rebukes him for interrupting
her sacred farewell to Donatello, at which Kenyon solemnly
apologizes, and the three part. Kenyon goes to a balcony which
Miriam told him about earlier and then suddenly sees Hilda there
with an English group and in addition the priest who heard her
confession. She throws him a rose-bud. That night Hilda's lamp is
tended again, and soon the doves begin to return to her
window-sill. Where has the girl been? Wandering in picture land,
hand in hand with Claude, Guido, and Raphael? We cannot
retrace her steps, which led her out of a secret place to this
balcony overhanging the noisy street in carnival. Surely the
reader will not ask for details. Was Hilda in the grip of a wily
religious power or a despotic government? Since she remains
quiet on the subject, her release continues to be perplexing.

One day Kenyon and Hilda wander through the streets of
Rome and happen to enter the Pantheon. He suggests first that
Donatello's character is unsuitable in the sadly serious world of
today, and second that perhaps sin, like sorrow, is so educative
that Donatello like Adam has been elevated by it. When Hilda
voices her terrified objection, Kenyon begs forgiveness and asks
for her guidance home. They see Miriam; she is kneeling in
prayer and then silently puts her hands out toward them in a

kind of blessing from the verge of an abyss. Thus the sculptor wins shy Hilda's love and consent to marry him. Miriam sends an immensely costly bracelet of Etruscan gems.

Some time later, the author interviews Kenyon and Hilda at St. Peter's, and learns a few more details. When Hilda took Miriam's packet of letters to the Palazzo Cenci, she was detained in a pleasant convent and the authorities soon connected her with the murdered monk, since Miriam was politically suspicious. Her Italian companion in the carriage which passed Kenyon on the street was an influential relative. Donatello returned to Rome because his conscience prompted him to deliver himself to the authorities. He now languishes in a dungeon. If her real name were revealed, everyone could connect Miriam with one of the century's most dreadful events. Does Donatello have furry, pointed ears, like a faun?

> Brother Antonio, Prince Barberini, Luca Barboni, [Thomas] Crawford, Emperor Diocletian, Donatello the Count of Monte Beni, [John] Gibson, Girolamo, the Grand Duke of Florence, the Grand Duke of Tuscany, [Horatio] Greenough, Hilda, Harriet Hosmer, Kenyon, Memmius, Panini, Pietro, [Hiram] Powers, Miriam Schaefer, Stella, [Cephas Giovanni] Thompson, Tomaso.

"The May-Pole of Merry Mount," 1836.

In New England two hundred years ago, "Jollity and gloom were contending for an empire." Some of the founders of Merry Mount are having a gay maypole dance, during which Edgar and Edith, the Lord and the Lady of the May, are married by a gay, flower-decked priest. The lovers sense that this golden, Comus-like moment, will be followed by something less bright. Into the riotous scene intrude stern John Endicott, his lieutenant Peter Palfrey, and several other heavily armed Puritans. They cut down the colorful maypole, arrest Edgar and Edith and their humorously disguised cohorts, shoot their dancing bear, and thus break up Merry Mount. But Endicott cannot help admiring Edgar, who since he is unable to fight for Edith entreats his captors to spare her. And the Puritan leader admires brave Edith as well. So with his gauntleted hand he tosses a wreath of roses over them as they trudge away, toward life and its burdensome responsibilities, with no more thoughts about the vanities of Merry Mount.

Rev. Mr. [William] Blackstone, Edgar, Edith, John Endicott, Peter Palfrey.

"The Mermaid" — see "The Village Uncle."

"The Minister's Black Veil," 1836.

One Sunday the congregation of the Milford church is surprised to see the Rev. Mr. Hooper ascend his pulpit with a black crepe veil over his face and down to his mouth. His sermon has no more than its usual gentle gloom, but at the end of the service the people rush out in some consternation and gossip about the veil. Squire Saunders fails to invite the minister to Sunday dinner. In the afternoon Mr. Hooper preaches a funeral sermon, and when he bends over the corpse — that of a young lady — it seems to shudder, or so one witness says. That night Mr. Hooper is about to marry a young couple, when he sees his veiled face in a mirror, spills the untasted wedding wine, and rushes out. Next day his fiancee Elizabeth begs him to put aside the veil. He refuses and explains that he is hiding his face either for sorrow or for a secret sin. When he refuses even to look her directly in the face, Elizabeth bids him farewell. Years pass. He becomes an efficient minister, winning many converts and sympathizing wonderfully with sinners. At last, on his deathbed, attended by Elizabeth, he is asked by a neighboring minister to put aside the ever-present veil. But the old man refuses, saying that he will not do so until friends show each other their true natures and until men shrink not from the eye of God. He falls back dead and is buried veiled.

Governor [Jonathan] Belcher, Rev. Mr. Clark, Elizabeth, Goodman Gray, Rev. Mr. Hooper, Squire Saunders.

"The Minotaur" (I. in *Tanglewood Tales, for Girls and Boys*), 1853.

Young Theseus lives with his mother Aethra and his grandfather, King Pittheus of Troezene, until he is old enough to lift a heavy stone and take from beneath it the sword and sandals left by Theseus's father, old King Aegeus of Attica. Then the young man goes to Athens to be acknowledged by his royal father, who, however, is viciously advised by the wicked enchantress Medea and some troublemaking nephews. Medea, now the king's wife, wants her son Medus and not Aethra's son Theseus to have the throne. So she tries to poison Theseus but fails when the king recognizes his sword. The evil woman then flies away in a flaming chariot. When Theseus learns that Athens must pay an annual tribute of seven youths and seven maidens to King Minos of Crete, who feeds the victims to his Minotaur, he volunteers to be one of the sacrificial party, sails with black sails past Talus, the Man of Brass, and puts up a bold front before King Minos. During his supposedly final night of life, Theseus is led by King Minos's beautiful, tender daughter Ariadne to Daedalus's labyrinth, finds the roaring Minotaur — with the horned head of a bull and a man's body — and kills it. Then he makes his way out again by following a silken cord given him and held by Ariadne, who now bids him farewell. Theseus forgets to hoist sunshine sails as a signal to his watching father that he is safe. When the old man sees black sails, he tumbles himself into the sea. Theseus becomes an excellent monarch.

King Aegus, Aethra, Ariadne, Daedalus, Medea, Medus, King Minos, the Minotaur, King Pittheus, Procrustes, Scinis, Talus the Man of Brass, Vulcan.

"The Miraculous Pitcher" (V. in *A Wonder-Book for Girls and Boys*), 1852.

One evening old Philemon and his old wife Baucis are sitting by the door of their humble cottage beside their small garden, when the customary uproar from the village in the valley nearby alerts them to the approach of a pair of travelers, whom the inhospitable, selfish villagers are stoning and attacking with dogs. Simple, kind-hearted Philemon and Baucis offer the travelers a welcome, in spite of the strange nimbleness of the younger guest, who carries a snake-entwined staff which hops as though alive, and in spite of the darkly frowning, thunder-voiced older guest. The humble farm couple offer a simple meal of milk, bread, honey, and grapes; miraculously their empty pitcher flows with more milk, of a divine fragrance. The guests retire for the night to the bedroom of the old couple, leaving them to sleep on the floor. In the morning, the younger guest, whose name is Quicksilver, points out a shimmering lake where the cold village used to be, explains that the hospitality of Philemon and Baucis converted the pitcher into an inexhaustable fount of Olympian nectar, and tells them to ask any favor they wish. They ask to be allowed to grow old together and to die at the same instant. The wish is granted, and after years of offering hospitality to wayfarers in their home, now a tall edifice of marble, they are converted into an oak tree and a linden tree with intermingling boughs and whispering leaves.

Baucis, Philemon, Quicksilver.

"Monsieur du Miroir," 1837.

I have studied Monsieur du Miroir more than I have anyone else in the circle of my acquaintance; yet I have little real knowledge of him. Let me tell you about this object of grave reflection. He is a mystery. We never disagree. He resembles me and wears mourning at funerals in my family. I have seen him move his lips, but he never speaks. Is he dumb, or is the world deaf? Sympathy is between us, and he copies my fashion in dress. We sometimes seem like twins of fate destined to live, enjoy, suffer, and die in unison. Once I had a toothache, and his face was swollen. When my mistress discarded me, he looked lackadaisical. He takes up my quarrels but has never actually struck a blow for me. I have seen him in the ball room and at the theater. I do not like to notice him, especially in public. He is fond of water, not to drink but to souse himself in, like a merman. I have seen him in a horse pond, in mud puddles, and in the bottoms of wells. Once, I saw him in a virgin fountain, making the place all the more solitary. His clothes always seem dry, however. He must be a magician, so speedily can he follow me, even through locked doors. If I look up while writing, he is there in the globe of the brass andiron. I once saw him in a lady's eye, but the years have so changed him that he need not hope for the position again. He is standoffish; when I advance to shake his hand, he too advances, but we never clasp hands. I should prefer the company of a young lady to his, but our fates are interwined. When my coffin lid is lowered, what will become of him? What terror if he should then haunt our old frequented paths! I loved him well in my youth and even called him handsome, but now when we met we glance sadly at our wrinkles and thin hair. He is wasted by toil and now seems disappointed. Has my fate assumed this image of myself, which thus haunts me and originates every act which it appears only to imitate, thereby deluding me by pretending to share events which it really predicts? No, I ought to continue to like this being, to hope that he has treasures in reserve, and to bestir myself to kindle genial warmth in him; if I cause his locks to whiten, my intellect and benevolence may also beautify his features. Let us turn to the spiritual world. Perhaps there are innumerable creatures like him near all of us. Is he himself only a wanderer from the land of shades? Here he is now, returning my gaze with as much awe as though he too muses through a whole evening of solitude. He counterfeits me. Which of us is real? Speak! Listen! I wish that he could answer my vain questions. Farewell, Monsieur du Miroir. Perhaps you are not wise, even though your business is reflection.

Monsieur du Miroir.

"Mr. Higginbotham's Catastrophe," 1834.
The gossipy young tobacco peddler Dominicus Pike is going toward Parker's Falls with his cart and mare on Tuesday morning when he encounters a rough-looking man who tells him that

Squire Higginbotham of Kimballton, past Parker's Falls, was hanged from his pear tree the night before by an Irishman and a Negro. Pike repeats the story outside Parker's Falls that evening, but it is denied by an elderly farmer who claims to have seen Higginbotham that morning. On Wednesday Pike goes on toward town and learns from a mulatto on the road that Higginbotham was hanged from his pear tree by an Irishman the night before. Pike spreads the story again, this time in Parker's Falls, until the mail coach arrives and Higginbotham's pretty niece gets off and counters the story. This time Pike is almost tarred and feathered. On the Kimballton turnpike, the peddler mulls over the odd story and because of insatiable curiosity determines to go see Higginbotham, who the tollman says has just ridden on ahead toward his garden. Pike rushes after him, just in time to rescue him from his Irish servant, who is in the act of trying to hang him from the pear tree. It seems that three men plotted to hang and rob the rich squire, but two of them successively lost courage and thus kept delaying the crime one night each. In gratitude, Higginbotham helps Dominicus Pike, who eventually marries the pretty niece.

Miss Higginbotham, Squire Higginbotham, Dominicus Pike.

"Mrs. Bullfrog," 1837.

The narrator, Thomas Bullfrog, an effeminate little drygoods store worker, begins by saying that some men act like fools in choosing their wives. With certain exceptions, any male and female may be happy enough in marriage. On his marriage morning, he and his pearly-toothed bride Laura take a coach toward his place of business. He offers to kiss her and stroke her ringlets. She disapproves. He fiddles with her lunch basket and finds a bottle of brandy. Their driver goes through a pile of gravel, upsets them, and gets boxed on the ears and nose by a bald, sunken-cheeked witch dressed like Mrs. Bullfrog, who, when the coach is righted, lapses back into her formerly apparently charming self. Bullfrog takes the newspaper, dislodged from the lunch basket by the accident, and reads that one Laura energetically sued a former lover for breach of promise. When he asks her why she has concealed her "imperfections" and dragged her former love affair through the courts, she says that it was for the five thousand dollars with which Bullfrog is now going to stock his drygoods store. He gushes with tenderness and overlooks all defects.

Mrs. Laura Bullfrog, Thomas Bullfrog, Jehu.

"My Kinsman, Major Molineux," 1832.

When the kings of England begin to appoint colonial governors, the native American people soon respond with inflamed acts of popular jealousy against the Tories. One moonlit summer evening the ferryman deposits a single passenger at the edge of town. He is a vigorous, handsome youth of nearly eighteen years, dressed in country clothes, with a stout cudgel and a lean wallet. His name is Robin Molineux, and he seeks his kinsman Major Molineux, who has promised the boy's father, a country clergyman and the major's cousin, a start in life in the city. But whenever the boy asks where his kinsman lives — he curiously neglected to appeal for directions to the ferryman — he is met with rebuffs. When he inquires of a periwigged aristocrat who keeps muttering sepulchral hem-hems, the proud old fellow warns him away authoritatively with a threat to have him thrown into the stocks. Robin wanders into narrow and crooked streets, is enticed into a tavern partly by the fragrance of good cheer; but when the initially obsequious inkeeper of French extraction learns the nature of his inquiry, he knowingly reads from a wanted poster and tells the lad to move along. Robin is tempted to use his cudgel and force someone to tell him where his high-born kinsman resides. The bell announces the hour of nine, and Robin peers into various shop-windows until he finds himself in a mean-looking street. A bright-eyed girl, with round arms, a slender waist, and a scarlet petticoat tells him laughingly that his kinsman is asleep inside. Robin at first regards her as his kinsman's housekeeper but then — good and also shrewd as he is — backs off. Little parties of men sweep noisily by, ask him incomprehensible questions, and when unanswered curse him roundly. When he is near the town church, dreamy in the moonlight, Robin accosts a bulky man with bulging forehead, bushy eyebrows, fiery eyes, and a face painted half red and half black, as if he were the product of a fiend of fire and a fiend of darkness. Resisting the offensive man with his cudgel, Robin wrings a reluctant statement from him that if the lad waits by the church for an hour he will see his kinsman come by. So Robin, soon growing weary after his thirty-mile walk without much food, rests near the sleeping church, hears distance-muffled sounds as of a town snoring, and muses in utter loneliness. What is his father doing now? Does his mother avert her face in thought of him? Each evening his devout family joins in sunset domestic worship. With a start, the boy wonders where he is, and the pillars of the church seem to resemble the pines about his old home. A stranger comes by, and Robin asks him about his kinsman. The stranger is a genuinely kindly man who listens to the shrewd lad's story and decides to wait by the church with him for the promised appearance of Major Molineux. Soon the shouting increases; and a torch-lit mob, led by the red-and-black man with the bulging forehead, appears, with the long-sought kinsman being dragged along in an open cart in tar-and-feathery dignity. Major Molineux recognizes Robin at once, and his ghastly agony is only increased. But Robin, who hears in the wild uproar the voices of the sleepy watchman, the courteous innkeeper, the girl with the scarlet petticoat, and the aristocrat who says hem-hem, is himself affected with a sort of mental inebriety and also laughs convulsively at his kinsman. The procession quickly winds out of sight. The helpful gentleman, still beside Robin, asks him whether he is dreaming; and the lad replies that he would like now only to be shown the way back to the ferry. But the gentleman says that since he is shrewd he should stay in town for a while, for he might be able to rise in the world without the help of his kinsman.

Robin Molineux, Major Molineux, Hezekiah Mudge.

"My Visit to Niagara," 1835.

The author approaches Niagara with great enthusiasm, but when he arrives with its roar in his ears at Manchester, the village near the falls, he grows apathetic, has dinner, smokes, delays, and then finally walks toward Goat Island and sees the radiant rainbow vapor. He goes along the path to the Horseshoe, goes out on the bridge, and feels the rushing river shake the very earth. He is sorry that he ever read and heard about the famous falls, because now he must adapt his false conceptions of Niagara to reality. He is momentarily disappointed. That night he dreams of storm and whirlwind. He awakens at midnight and finds his awe and enthusiasm reviving. The beholder must cast aside preconceived notions and respond to the falls with a simple heart. On his last day there, he goes to the Table Rock. The waters seem to descend to the falls like the march of destiny. He sees a guide and two adventurers walking behind the falls. He takes pleasure in watching a variety of fellow spectators. His contemplation of the scene is unwearied. He walks by a devious footpath down to the ferry. At one point he is in glorious solitude, in a spot famous throughout the world.

(No named characters.)

"Nature of Sleep," 1836.

Following an English authority named Dr. Philip, Hawthorne briefly discusses the difference between the sensitive system, which requires periodic sleep to renew its excitability, and the vital system, which falls asleep only at death. He then considers the irony of our longing for sleep, since it only brings us closer to death.

(No named characters.)

"The New Adam and Eve," 1843.

We cannot distinguish between the natural and the artificial. Only through imagination can we loosen the hold of truth and reality, and realize how unnatural we are. Let us imagine the

entire world swept clear of all men and women, but with
evidence of their existence left behind. Now imagine — half
sportively and half seriously — a new Adam and Eve, mature in
mind and heart, entering the scene. Such a pair would distinguish
between art and nature. It is dawn. They wander into a modern
city [Boston]. Eve wants to stay close to Adam, who, however,
wants to explore. They find buildings, streets, signs, loneliness,
and desolation. Eve happily finds a tuft of grass and then looks
at the sky adoringly. They wander through many open doorways,
finally into a clothing shop, where Eve bewitchingly throws a
robe over her shoulders and Adam follows by donning a mantle.
A church spire pleases them by pointing heavenward, but the
snug interior of the place leaves them cold. The court of justice
is a complete puzzle since they have no notion of sin and crime.
It is the same with a legislative hall and then a prison. If man tried
to cure sin by love, there would be no need of jails. The sight of
gallows — symbol of mankind's unsuccessful system of fear and
vengeance — causes an unaccountable shudder in Adam and Eve.
They walk into a Beacon Street mansion. The sound of an
Aeolian harp intrigues them, but not the sight of family portraits. The marble statue of a child impresses them strangely,
especially Eve. Adam guesses that perhaps they are treading in
the footsteps of beings like themselves but now gone. Eve tries
on a thimble and strikes chords on the piano. The table, lavishly
set for a dinner party, leaves them indifferent, but they try an
apple, are frightened by the wine, and drink some wonderful
water. Adam opines that their task is to find a path to the sky.
They leave the mansion and stroll into a bank, and are momentarily amused by glittering gold coins. At a jeweler's shop Adam
bedecks Eve with pearls, but she drops them for some roses in a
vase. By now they guess that all these buildings are man-made,
but never do they understand why some of them are magnificent
and others are squalid. In the suburbs they see the obelisk at
Bunker Hill but mistake it for a kind of prayer. They fling books
about in the Harvard Library, although Adam fancies that one
tome seems about to speak to him. At dusk they wander into
Mount Auburn Cemetery but do not make any distinction

between body and soul yet. One statue there is of a child, beside which Adam suggests that they sleep. Eve voices her happiness at the prospect of being always at Adam's side.

Adam, Eve.

"The New England Village," 1831 (may not be by Hawthorne).[8]

The narrator decides to reside in the New England village of N - - - , near the Merrimack River. He meets the pleasant clergyman, a bachelor fifty-five years of age, who shows him a decayed old farmhouse, which is about to be purchased by a lawyer named Forester. Ten years pass, and the narrator visits his friend again and wonders if he has married. But the minister reveals only that Forester, his charming wife, and their two children greatly improved the farm and their residence there. Then, however, a stranger came by while the Foresters were celebrating their fifth wedding anniversary, and soon thereafter they seemed to decline in health and means, and moved away. The clergyman continues by reporting that about a year after receiving a rather sad letter from Mrs. Forester, whose husband had started a law practice in the West, he met the man, sadly wasted, in Montreal. The minister persuaded him to return to his abandoned farm home in N - - - , but shortly after he did so the same stranger reappeared, after which Forester became mortally sick. On his deathbed, he confessed to his wife and the minister that he had been imprisoned for theft and that the stranger was a fellow ex-convict who was blackmailing him with the threat of exposing him to his wife and community if he did not pay up. Forester died commending to the minister the care of his wife and children. The narrator remarks that the good man has undoubtedly been dutiful in this respect. The minister blushes, says that he has been, and reports that he has married the Forester widow and now resides with her and her children in the farm house.

[8]See Blanck, *Bibliography of American Literature,* IV, 1.

Ellen Forester, Mrs. Mary Forester, William Forester, Forester, Keziah Spinney.

"Night Sketches Beneath an Umbrella," 1838.

The narrator reads travel books one rainy winter day and then that night goes out for a walk under an umbrella. Everything is so black that he can see no sky. A lamp is near, and a snow-bank, and a deep stream of mud, in which he would surely hate to die. More lamps twinkle down the street. He sees a woman buffeted by the impudent wind. At the center of town are rows of bright shops. He sees a retired sea-captain going off to spin yarns at the insurance office, then a man in quest of a doctor, and a happy, rain-splashed urchin. Next a happy couple whose warm love no rain can chill. The narrator passes dwellings of the rich and the poor, but into each will come the dark guests of sorrow and death. A subterranean cataract roars. The laden mail-coach passes. Finally a lonely figure with a lamp appropriately points a moral: fear not to tread the dreary path, because our lantern of Faith will lead us home.

(No named characters.)

"The Old Apple Dealer," 1843.

The narrator describes and ponders on an old, thin, hueless man in the railroad depot who sells apples, cakes, and candy. He is too utterly negative to be considered desperate. He takes his poverty and discomfort as a matter of course and without dignity. He shivers quietly and folds his thin arms across his chest. He is unobtrusive when a customer approaches. He pockets an occasional silver coin with a sigh. His life has probably been all of a piece, and he seems too underdeveloped to have known either joy or grief. He is a contrast to the energetic ten-year-old boy who also sells food in the depot, but the man is a more complete contrast to the steam engine of the train as it bursts in. Doubtless there is a region for him where he will shiver and sigh no more.

(No named characters.)

"Old Esther Dudley" (IV. in "Legends of the Province House"),
1839.

The narrator, Bela Tiffany, and their host listen to an old
loyalist, who cackles out a tale which is slight but may still cast
an influence.

The hour comes when defeated loyalist Sir William Howe
must leave the Province House. In his loneliness and shame he
wishes that he might die in the King's cause. An old woman's
voice tells him to trust to heaven. The woman is old Esther
Dudley, a supernumerary who is fabled to have served all the
royal Governors and who now vows to stay until Sir William
returns to triumph. He weeps, gives her some gold, urges her to
go to Halifax with him, and when she refuses gives her the huge
Province House key. She stays on and on. It is rumored that
from her tarnished mirror she can summon shades of overthrown
notables. She is unharmed, because of fear and pity. Years pass.
She occasionally drinks royal old wine with a few old Tories. She
spins wonderful tales of yore to the entranced children of the
town. Whenever news comes of a victory by Washington or one
of his generals, she transmutes it into a Tory success. One night
she dresses up in mildewed velvets and brocades to celebrate the
King's birthday. She climbs to the cupola to look out for the
return of his troops. Finally she hears or dreams that a new royal
Governor is coming to the Province House. She unlocks the door
and crosses the threshold to meet the richly dressed, gouty
personage, saying, "God save King George." Replying that he
hopes the lands prosper which still acknowledge the royal
sceptre, Governor Hancock supports the collapsing old woman,
who voices her fear that she has welcomed a traitor and hopes
that death will rescue her. Hancock gently tells her that she
symbolizes the past while he and his escort represent the present
and future. Faithful old Esther drops her key and dies.

The old loyalist finishes his tale with his face quivering. The
lamp dies down. The clock of the Old South tolls. And the
narrator resolves not to return to the Province House for a long
while, if ever.

Esther Dudley, Republican Governor [John] Hancock, Sir William Howe, Bela Tiffany.

"The Old Maid in the Winding Sheet" — see "The White Old Maid."

"The Old Manse," 1846.

Hawthorne begins by describing the pleasant old parsonage, of which he is the first lay occupant. He has a delightful little study in the rear, with pictures, flowers, and his few books. He enjoys boating on the nearby Concord River, which has fragrant pond-lilies and near which the famous battleground is located. The Manse has a pleasant orchard and garden, with apples, squashes, and cabbages, among other items. When it rains, the place is gloomy and Hawthorne retreats to the old garret with its ghosts, musty books, and old magazines and newspapers. But on a pleasant day he goes boating with Ellery Channing from the Concord into the lovely Assabeth River, which has lilies (praised by Thoreau) and ducks. The two men build a fire, cook their noonday meal, talk happily, and listen to the river as it calls them to freedom. They return home, all the same, through the golden sunset. Autumn is the most tender season, with its crickets, cardinal flowers, and blessed breezes. October brings frost, and then the Manse is lonely. The place is being renovated now by the owner — a hint that he wants to return. Hawthorne must leave for work in the Custom House. He closes with an apology that he has written here nothing more substantial than little fictive flowers. Nonetheless, he invites the reader to be his guest at the Old Manse.

Zechariah Brown, [Dr. William] Ellery Channing, Thomas Davis, [Ralph Waldo] Emerson, [George Stillman] Hillard, [James Russell] Lowell, [Henry David] Thoreau.

"Old News." 1835.

I. ["The Colonial Newspaper."] The narrator peruses a

volume of old newspapers (to be dated about 1740) and imagines a merchant in a high-backed chair and wig reading his news, with its comments on religious controversy, availability of bond-servants and slaves, weather, foreboding in the sky, sicknesses, payments of claims following the witchcraft delusion in 1692, funerals, dancing classes, a horse race, Election Week pleasures, and celebrations of the King's birthday. The old merchant is then imagined as sallying forth through various streets on a shopping tour.

II. "The Old French War." Twenty years later (about 1760) the newspapers are somewhat larger and more aristocratic. They now include war bulletins, witty essays, evidence that the colonists more nearly resemble their British brethren than they formerly did, reports of an essentially martial people stirred by the exciting Old French War, letters from provincial officers, accounts of Indian atrocities, columns of curious military adver-tisements, domestic news of great variety, and accounts of a growing though still small native literature. The narrator offers the reader his arm for a walk through the streets, to see old buildings, bewigged gentlemen, gorgeously dressed ladies, British troops, and much else. The Boston fire of 1760 changed the city considerably. Imagine the tragedy as a given family emptied its blazing home! But only the antiquarian would prefer the old city to the new.

III. "The Old Tory." It is now twenty years later (about 1780). The mood of the newspapers has changed, to one most displeasing to a gray, withered old Tory, whose reading of the Revolutionary War news makes him conscious of a stigma but for no crime. He was a provincial captain who proudly fought on the Plains of Abraham, stayed in Boston when the British army evacuated the city, and now idolizes King George in secret. He was almost tarred and feathered. He is treated scornfully. He hates the modern rebel newspaper, with its disloyal figurehead, its rough and knobby paper, and its wretched print. New items: lands at auction, complaints against "traitors," prize vessels offered for sale, Washington's army activities, the formation by women of a society to clothe the Continental troops, disloyal and irreligious acts, crimes such as horse-stealing and rape and murder, desertion, and the proclamation of a fast. The miserable old Tory and all like him who honorably cling to the losing side should be pitied and sympathized with. They could go to a cold reception in England or stay behind in America and endure public opprobrium. They misinterpreted temporary evils during transitional revolutionary times for permanent diseases of the democratic system being established. Revolutionary times encourage both individual virtues and pernicious general immorality. The old newspapers were undeniably more picturesque than revolutionary ones.

Anna Adams, Sir Jeffrey Amherst, Deacon Beautineau, Governor [Jonathan] Belcher, Governor [Sir Francis] Bernard, Captain Bulfinch, Caesar, Mrs. Henrietta Maria Caine, Dr. Caner, Michael Cario, Rev. Mr. Peter Clarke, Rev. Mr. Colman, Dipper, Jonathan Furness, Green, Captain Hallowell, Robert Hewes, Abigail Hiller, Mary Jackson, Robert Jenkins, Daniel Jones, Juba, Kneeland, John Lucas, Miriam, Sarah Morehead, Harriet Pain, Pompey, Governor [Thomas] Pownall, Alice Quick, Mary Salmon. Scipio, Captain Scut, Timothy Sheaffe, Samuel Waldo, Weatherwise, [Acting] President [Edward] Wigglesworth [of Harvard College].

"Old Ticonderoga: A Picture of the Past," 1836.

The author visits the old fortress at Ticonderoga. The whole scene is disappointing except for the ruined interior. A young lieutenant fresh from West Point guides him around, lecturing unpoetically about the geometrical design of the fort. The author would prefer a hoary veteran for a guide; such a man might summon the wraiths of dead comrades at arms to march through the gateway. The author sits in one of the roofless barracks, overrun with weeds and spicy herbs. Nature is tranquil all around. He closes his eyes to the ruins and lets his fancy roam back to the past when the woods about the place were uninhabited, when the first Indian penetrated them, when the

French established the fort, and finally when during the Old French War Ethan Allen and General Burgoyne fought over the region. Then present-day sounds recall the author to the present, and his dreams from the twilight past vanish.

(No fictional characters named.)

"An Old Woman's Tale," 1830.

The narrator explains that in the house where he was born an old woman used to crouch by the fire, knit, and tell him stories from a store of memories spanning almost a century. Usually they concerned her birthplace, a Connecticut Valley village, whose inhabitants were periodically subject to a simultaneous slumber. Here is one such story. On a moonlit summer evening David and Esther are walking in an open grove by a delightful spring. They speak of the beauty and stillness of the night. Perhaps they fall asleep and share a dream, in which through a misty autumn-like night a crowd of villagers yawn and walk. They are neighbors and acquaintances and yet are individually unknown to David and Esther. They gather in little groups, talk — though their words do not reach the young couple observing them — and seem to be renewing friendships after half a century. An old fellow sits in front of the tavern, with an Indian fighter near him, and a sailor; also present are a thin young man and a pale maiden, a hunter, an elderly Squire in a blue coat, and some religious men. A lame old woman appears, magnificently dressed, takes a shovel, and roots in the stubborn earth near the fountain. Esther dreamily asks David to go and help her; but the Squire approaches the old woman first, and they embrace. They seem to be discussing the shovel. But then his coat seems to become the sky, and her red petticoat a part of the dawn. He consults his watch, and then all of the dream folk flee as the wind rises and moans. David and Esther awaken and realize that they have had the same dream. They find a shovel and dig by the spring. David soon strikes something.

David, Esther, the Squire.

"An Ontario Steamboat," 1836.

Going first class from Ogdensburg on a Lake Ontario steam-boat, the narrator takes the occasion to observe the three classes of passengers. He is especially struck by the mob of emigrants from Ireland and England, deplores their poverty, but hopes that morality will win and that these aliens will promote our coun-try's welfare.

(No named characters.)

"P.'s Correspondence," 1845.

The narrator's friend, P., mentally disordered, confined to a small room in New England, but well-traveled in imagination, writes a letter from "London, February 29, 1845."

Here I sit in London listening to the noise of the streets coming through my windows. I have been with Lord Byron, now sixty years of age, fat, gouty, religious, and reconciled to Lady Byron. When will his bones, now returned from Greece, be interred in Westminster Abbey? Robert Burns is now eighty-seven years old, a patriarch with floating white hair and a crickety liveliness; he is embalmed in many biographies. Sir Walter Scott is paralytic and dictates tales to an imaginary secretary, although his fame is long dead. Dickens gave promise of literary greatness but died after beginning his *Pickwick Papers.* Napoleon Bona-parte nervously walks the streets of Pall Mall between two policemen; he is decrepit and rheumy-eyed. Shelley is reconciled to the Church of England — has even taken orders — and assures me that there is a logic in his works, from the earliest chaotic ones to his latest conservative ones. How could the rumor be correct that he drowned twenty-three years ago, if I saw him only yesterday in London? Coleridge, now not talkative, has just finished "Christabel." Keats was out walking on the crowded street, and I watched him fade away; he is writing an epic, a Miltonic poem on man — and woman — just within reach of perfection. Canning recently spoke at the House of Lords, and Cobbett spoke in the lower house, looking — the way many of my acquaintances do — as if just disinterred. The elder Kean did

Hamlet's ghost at the Drury Lane Theatre, and I saw many old celebrities there. What about our promising American writers? — Bryant dead after "Thanatopsis," Whittier hanged in South Carolina ten years ago. It is sad that fate kills early some of our hopeful mortals while mocking the world by letting others live. Many departed poets visit me in spirit, perhaps wanting me to be the amanuensis of their posthumous work. Give my respects to Brockden Brown. Is Joel Barlow still alive?

> Joel Barlow, Napoleon Bonaparte, [Charles] Brockden Brown, [William Cullen] Bryant, Robert Burns, Lady Byron, Lord Byron, [Thomas] Campbell, [George] Canning, Dr. [William Ellery] Channing, [William] Cobbett, [Samuel Taylor] Coleridge, Allan Cunningham, [Charles] Dickens, [William] Gifford, [Fitz-Greene] Halleck, Dr. Reginald Heber, [Edmund] Kean the elder, [John] Keats, John Kemble, [Henry Wadsworth] Longfellow, James Russell Lowell, Charles Matthews, [Thomas] Moore, John Murray, John Neal, P., Sir Walter Scott, [Percy Bysshe] Shelley, Mrs. [Sarah] Siddons, [Robert] Southey, [John Greenleaf] Whittier, [Nathaniel Parker] Willis, [William] Wordsworth.

"Pansie: A Fragment" — see "The Dolliver Romance" (of which it is the first chapter).

"The Paradise of Children" (III. in *A Wonder-Book for Girls and Boys*), 1852.

The world is young and gay, but the young orphan boy Epimetheus has no playmate in his home; so a little girl named Pandora is sent to him. They play happily in spite of her curiosity as to the contents of an intricately carved box, tied with an elaborate knot of gold cord. The messenger Quicksilver has ordered it to remain closed. One day the two children argue about it; and while the boy is out alone gathering figs and grapes, Pandora begins to fancy that a carved face on the lid of the box urges her to open it. She undoes the knot; then, fearing the Epimetheus will never believe that she has not also looked inside, she resolves to have one peek. Inside, creatures seem to beg to be released. Meanwhile Epimetheus repents of his argument, gathers some flowers for his friend, and returns home, just as a huge cloud gathers. As he enters, he sees Pandora about to lift the box lid. He wants to see too; so he fails to try to prevent the girl from releasing what proves to be a swarm of bat-winged, stinging troubles, passions, cares, sorrows, diseases, and naughtinesses, which bite both children and then fly throughout the formerly happy world. Flowers droop. Children age. And pain comes. One day Pandora hears another voice within the box. She and sulking Epimetheus open it together. Out flies a sunny, smiling, rainbow-winged creature called Hope, who promises to lighten their burdens in this world and the next, if they will only trust her. They promise. It is fortunate, in a way, that troubles have come, because Hope spiritualizes the earth.

Epimetheus, Hope, Pandora, Quicksilver.

"Passages from a Relinquished Work," 1834.

"At Home." The narrator is the ward of Parson Thumpcushion, so called because of his vigorous pulpit delivery. The narrator likes the stern old Puritan but finds his methods of rearing sons — though successful with his three real sons — unpalatable. So he gaily undertakes a piece of light-hearted desperation, suggested by his notion to become a wandering storyteller with a merry band of vagabonds.

"A Flight in the Fog." The narrator leaves home one foggy June morning, looks back on his native village, where Mr. Nightingale has his drygoods store and Dominicus Pike manufactures tobacco products, and decides to change his name and become an itinerant storyteller once he gets a hundred miles from home.

"A Fellow-Traveller." One noon, after a week or two, the narrator stops beside a delightful brook for a drink and sees a Bible-reading fellow-traveler, who rather somberly offers him some bread and cheese. The two decide to walk along together, and they do so day after day. When the narrator first tries telling stories before an audience, he is hissed so loudly that he refunds their money.

"The Village Theatre." In September the two stop at a village tavern, converted into a theater. While the narrator, now more confident and known as the Story Teller, prepares to tell the tale of "Mr. Higginbotham's Catastrophe," his religious friend, whose name is Eliakim Abbott, conducts a prayer meeting in the schoolhouse, with indifferent success. The Story Teller is a great hit. Then the landlord, who is also the village postmaster, hands him a letter from Parson Thumpcushion. The Story Teller goes quietly to his room, pictures his stern but also perhaps apologetic former guardian in his mind's eye, and burns the undoubtedly wise and conciliatory letter unread. Then the Story Teller, now rather disturbed, leaves town with Eliakim at his side.

Eliakim Abbott, Little Pickle, Nightingale, Dominicus Pike, the Story Teller, Parson Thumpcushion.

"Peter Goldthwaite's Treasure," 1838.

One chilly November day, Peter Goldthwaite, an impoverished failure of a get-rich-quick schemer, refuses an offer from solid, practical John Brown, his former partner, to buy his rickety old house. Instead, Peter chats away with Tabitha Porter, an old maid of more than sixty years, whom his grandfather took in from the almshouse a half century ago and who is now Peter's companion and domestic servant. Peter reminds her that his great-grand-uncle, also named Peter Goldthwaite, is rumored to have hoarded a quantity of metal in the walls of the old homestead. The present owner and occupant now resolves to tear its inner walls apart and find the treasure. Tabby wryly urges him to ransack the kitchen last of all. That night Peter dreams of gold coins, precious dishes, and jewels, and confuses himself with his own rich ancestor. In the morning he seizes his axe, hammer, and saw, and begins to demolish the garret, in which are stored musty account books, garments, canes, shoes, and the like, and even a mirror in which Peter sees what looks like the former Peter Goldthwaite. For warmth, Tabitha economically burns the rubbish which Peter makes splinters of, in their wide kitchen fireplace. Days pass, without success; but every evening Peter, who has an ever-gay and aspiring soul, talks of their inevitably bright future. He bangs his way down to the second story, but still no treasure. He does find a valueless chunk of dusty parchment and a time-blackened old lamp. One bright and sunny January day, during a sparkling thaw, Peter looks out the window at a passing throng of various pleasure seekers. John Brown happens by, but Peter refuses his renewed offer to buy the old place. When Peter withdraws his head and looks about his dismal and half-wrecked house, however, he has grave doubts. But they are only momentary, and he digs on, now finding a rusty old key and a bottle of precious old wine, along with some useless little coins and a medal. Finally everything is gutted but the kitchen. On the eve of the advent of spring, a terrible storm comes up. Peter serves the old wine to himself and Tabby, feeling that the old key must fit an old chest in the kitchen. At this moment, John Brown happens to think tolerantly of Peter and so makes his way to the Goldthwaite mansion to see if he needs any comforting. Brown arrives as Peter is opening the chest, which contains nothing but old provincial bills of credit, purchased long ago by his ancestor before they became completely valueless. Brown again offers Peter a handsome price for his house and even an apartment for himself and Tabby. Peter accepts, with reviving spirits, saying that he has a fine plan for investing his profits.

John Brown, Peter Goldthwaite, Tabitha Porter.

"The Pomegranate Seeds" (V. in *Tanglewood Tales, for Girls and Boys*) 1853.

While Mother Ceres, who supervises all crops, is busy one day with her work, her daughter Proserpina leaves the sea-nymphs with whom she has been playing and strays into the fields to pick flowers. She finds a curious shrub, uproots it, and sees a rumbling black chariot with four horses and a noble but sullen driver emerge from the huge hole beneath it. He seizes Proserpina and carries her off from the vale of Enna to his underground kingdom. He is Pluto, and his thousand-room palace is built of gold and lit with gems; but the girl is frightened, refuses a drink of forgetful Lethe or any bite of food, and remains disconsolate. Meanwhile, Ceres, up above ground, has heard some sounds like her daughter's scream, goes home only to find the place empty, and starts a long search for the girl, during which she asks nymphs and Pan and finally dog-headed old Hecate for information. Hecate advises her to give up and enjoy a life of misery, but Ceres takes her ever-burning torch and consults sunny Phoebus, who tells her that he saw Proserpina being abducted by the king of the Underworld. Ceres wanders on and on in search of her daughter, then pauses to nurse Prince Demophoon, the son of King Celeus and Queen Metanira of Eleusis. Experienced old Mother Ceres improves the prince's health by bathing the lad in a fragrant liquid and then putting him to rest in a bed of red-hot coals. When the secretly watching queen shrieks out her objections, Ceres says that the boy will now not be immortal, then leaves to continue her search. She decides that all crops on earth will fail until she is reunited with her daughter. Finally Quicksilver, the nimble fellow with the winged shoes and the snaky staff, assists by paying a visit to Pluto. Meanwhile, Proserpina keeps on with her hunger strike, which has already lasted six months. But just as Quicksilver begins his persuasive appeal to Pluto, the girl, who has gradually thought somewhat more highly of her somber host and his dismally magnificent palace, which her presence has brightened, succumbs and starts to eat a withered old pomegranate, brought her because she cannot stand the unnatural pastries and spiced meats proffered by Pluto's fancy cook. Pluto releases the girl, who leaves him with a shade of reluctance but who goes above ground with Quicksilver all the same, leaving a trail of freshly blooming flowers and happy cattle along her path. Ceres is sitting morosely at home, sees her torch flicker and die, then looks up to see her daughter returning to her happy arms. When questioned, Proserpina admits that six of the pomegranate's seeds remained in her mouth, at which Ceres tells her that she must therefore spend six months annually underground with Pluto. The happy girl does not really mind.

> King Celeus, Mother Ceres, Prince Demophoon, Hecate,
> Queen Metanira, Pan, Phoebus, King Pluto, Proserpina,
> Quicksilver.

"The Procession of Life," 1843.

Life is like a festal or a funereal procession, directed by the
Chief Marshal. It is wrong, however, for the marchers to group
themselves according to external circumstances, such as wealth.
Let us call by trumpet our groups more sensibly. First, all people
who are similar because of sickness; rich, gouty people will thus
march with sickly urban sufferers and sedentary tailors and
shoemakers and pale students and authors. Another trumpet blast
calls all men and women of intellect, surely a noble group; peer
and ploughman (for example, Byron and Burns) thus join hands.
Another trumpet call: all those united by sorrow can march
together; grief is a leveler. But the so-called broken-
hearted – frustrated bachelors and disappointed artists and politicians – are excluded. Now the trumpet bids all sinners band
together, into a brotherhood of crime; rich financier is thus
linked with petty forger, and harlot with prudish matron. Let us
call together all who are good. No one answers the trumpet,
because even the worthiest is conscious of error and imperfection. So let us summon all those who love; this call embraces
all the truly good, even though one type of good person is often
intolerant of a different type of good (for example, Christian and
pagan). Hereafter, supposed antagonists will reason that they
have both been good. Now the sun is setting. Call into one group
all those who lost or never found their proper place in life:
Quakers who should have been soldiers, authors who wrote
diligently but lacked genius, and so on. This group should
include those who delayed doing anything because they thought
they were apt for something but knew not what. Now here
comes the Chief Marshal, on his pale horse. He is Death, the
guide of all. At the very end he deserts us; but God, who made
us, will not leave us on the toilsome march or let us perish by

the way.

The Chief Marshal.

"The Prophetic Pictures," 1837.

Walter Ludlow persuades Elinor, his bride-to-be, to pose with him for companion portraits by a certain eminent and intelligent artist in Boston. Walter explains that the European-born artist is uncanny in his ability to capture the secret passions of his subjects. The couple go to his studio, see marvelous portraits there, and begin their sittings. Walter reports that some say the painter can capture his subjects' features and make the resulting pictures prophetic. The girl is unworried. At one point, while they study their likenesses, the artist busies himself with a crayon sketch. Elinor suddenly regards her picture as expressive of grief and terror. Walter sees his as showing a lively expression, as though a bright thought were flashing forth. The painter explains that he cannot help portraying what he regards as their hidden selves. When he shows Elinor his sketch, she stifles a shriek, wonders whether Walter saw the sketch, but tells the artist to alter nothing. The two are married, hang their portraits side by side – hers showing melancholy and his showing wild passion – and gradually become sad. The artist wanders far into New England, in isolation from society for a long while. When he returns, he goes to the Ludlows' home to see his portraits. He sees Elinor and Walter standing before them. The girl's sad face needs only fear to make it exactly like her portrait. Walter becomes evil-looking, like his picture. Elinor looks terrified, as Walter draws a knife to stab her, calling it all their fate. Their postures now resemble those of the crayon sketch. But the artist steps between them, as though he were a magician controlling the phantoms he evoked. Walter lapses into gloom. The painter reminds Elinor that he tried to warn her (by the crayon sketch). She admits it but says that she loves Walter. The moral is that even if we could see our fate, some of us would rush toward it and others be swept toward it, while none would be turned aside by prophetic pictures.

Elinor Ludlow, Walter Ludlow.

"The Pygmies" (II. in *Tanglewood Tales, for Girls and Boys*), 1853.

The earth-born giant Antaeus lives in friendship and inter-dependence with millions of earth-born pygmies. He is as tall as a mountain, with a gigantic pine tree for a stick. They are scant inches tall. But he is like their big brother, and when they war with the cranes and are getting the worst of it he aids by flourishing his club aloft. One day, while Antaeus is sleeping and his pygmy brethren are swinging in his hair and jumping on his lip, mighty Hercules approaches, on his way to the garden of the Hesperides. The pygmies arouse Antaeus, and he makes the mistake of challenging Hercules, who exchanges club blows with him, wrestles with him, hoists him into the air away from the earth – the source of his strength – and finally hurls him a mile away, a hill of dead bones. The pygmies become so furious that they soon attack Hercules while he is asleep and snoring, by setting his hair on fire and shooting ineffectual arrows at him. Highly amused, Hercules sues for peace and retreats out of the pygmy kingdom in six strides.

Antaeus, King Eurystheus, Hercules.

"Rappaccini's Daughter," 1844.

Up from Naples, long ago, comes passionate, shallow Giovanni Guasconti to study at the University of Padua. His new landlady, Dame Lisabetta, opens the window and shows him a gorgeous garden, which she says is cultivated by the learned Dr. Giacomo Rappaccini. Giovanni looks down at the luxurious botanical specimens growing there, and especially at one rank purple plant near a shattered fountain. Soon a tall, emaciated, sickly man walks through the garden, tending the plants with thick gloves and then calling his daughter Beatrice. When she enters, Giovanni is dazzled by her vivid and flower-like radiance and beauty. She handles the blossoms confidently, even calling the vivid purple one her sister. That night Giovanni dreams of a rich flower and a beautiful maiden. Next day he has dinner with Professor Pietro Baglioni, a learned friend of his father; Professor Baglioni is most genial and hospitable, and over some Tuscan wine warns Giovanni about Dr. Rappaccini and his deeply learned daughter Beatrice. He adds that Beatrice may have her eye on his own professorial chair. Back in his room again, Giovanni looks out at the lush garden and again sees Beatrice, but now he notes that an orange reptile dies when a drop of dew from the purple flower hits it, and that an insect flies near Beatrice and then also falls dead. All the same, Giovanni tosses the lovely-looking girl a bouquet he bought; she accepts the gift courteously. But does it quickly wither in her grasp? Days pass. Giovanni is not exactly in love now with Beatrice but instead senses an emotion which seems the offspring of love and horror both. One day when he is rapidly walking through the streets of Padua, Professor Baglioni accosts him, says that he looks bad, and warns him that Dr. Rappaccini, who happens to be hovering near at this very moment, has begun to make the young man the subject of an infernal experiment. Giovanni breaks away at the mention of the name Beatrice, but Professor Baglioni says to himself that perchance he will yet foil the learned Dr. Rappaccini. When Giovanni gets home again, Lisabetta tells him that she knows a secret passage into the garden and for a gold coin leads him to a tendril-covered entrance. Once inside, Giovanni is strangely calm, but he is shocked by the flowers, which seem to be the product of a kind of vegetable adultery. Beatrice enters, and the two begin a pleasant conversation, during which she tells him to believe only what he sees — better, only what she tells him, for she is truthful. Giovanni seems to grow faint, but he delights in her presence and her simultaneously gay and profound talk. When he tries to touch her purple flower, however, she seizes his hand and warns him that its touch is fatal. He is now in love, and when next morning his wrist pains him — it bears purple marks — he dismisses the matter lightly. Soon the two are meeting daily in their Eden of poisonous flowers, but they never kiss or even touch one another. Weeks pass; then Professor Baglioni calls on Giovanni, telling him that Beatrice is poisonous and that her father is conducting an experiment. Then he leaves the anguished young man a vial containing an antidote to make the worst poisons innocuous. Giovanni grasps some flowers, and they droop; he breathes on a spider, and it dies in convulsions. His love turns to hate, and he wishes that Beatrice were dead. But when he is with her again, she seems heavenly and his rage turns sullen. She talks for a while about her father and her sense of estrangement from society, at which Giovanni bursts out and calls her an accursed horror. She prays to the Virgin Mary, admits her monstrousness, tells Giovanni that he can simply retreat to society, breathes upon an insect to verify her suspicions, and then says that although her body is poisonous her spirit is from God and hence craves love. Even though Giovanni has blighted their relationship, he tenderly offers her the antidote, saying that they should drink it together to recover. But she insists on drinking part of it first, just as her father suddenly appears and looks at the young couple with a proud and potent smile. He tells his daughter that she — together with her lover — is proof against all mankind. She replies that she would rather be loved than feared, tells Giovanni that perhaps there is more poison in his nature than in hers, and then dies. Poison was her food; therefore its antidote is her death. At this moment, Professor Baglioni looks down from the window above the garden with an expression of triumph and horror.

Professor Pietro Baglioni, Giovanni Guasconti, Dame Lisabetta, Beatrice Rappaccini, Dr. Giacomo Rappaccini.

"A Rill from the Town Pump," 1835.

At the corner of two main streets in Salem, the town pump notes the noon hour and then begins to comment on the downright manner in which it discharges its duty. The pump aids all comers. It provides a drink which is better than alcohol, helps the schoolboy clean his blooming face, and gives tottering age a drink. The pump can remember the time when Indian sagamores drank from its source, then when Endicott, Winthrop, and Higginson did so too. Later the spring was covered with the refuse of new-built cellars, but then the town pump was sunk into it. Now it loves to watch oxen lower its water level. Water is virtuous: it washes, puts out fires, restores health, eliminates sin even, and might do away with war eventually. Perhaps a marble fountain will mark this spot some day. Its message is a moral one: it is good to cool fevers and cleanse stains.

[John] Endicott, Rev. Mr. [Francis] Higginson, Governor [John] Winthrop.

"Roger Malvin's Burial," 1832.

After the frontier Indian battle known as Lovell's Fight, in 1725, two wounded men try to get to their settlement again but cannot. Old Roger Malvin is dying. Reuben Bourne wants to stay and help him, but Roger tells him to make it back home again and marry Dorcas Malvin, the old man's daughter, to whom the younger man is betrothed. The dying man also urges Reuben to return and bury him; rather slyly, he adds that perhaps he will not be dead if help can be sent fast. Reuben reluctantly agrees. Tying his blood-stained handkerchief to the branch of an oak sapling beside a huge granite rock against which he props the fatally wounded man and vowing to return, he abandons Dorcas's father, makes his way with difficulty to a group looking for remnants of the Indian fighters, is taken to his village, and passes several days in delirium. When Dorcas is permitted to question him about her father, Reuben finds it impossible to tell the truth and hints that he buried the man by saying that he did what he could and that a noble tombstone stands above the corpse. Becoming a hero, he regrets his words but finds that pride and fear combine to prevent his remedying a story about behavior in the oak forest which none can brand a sin. He marries Dorcas. They do not prosper. He grows sad, downcast, and irritable. Years pass, and finally they decide to move into the virgin wilderness. Their handsome son Cyrus, aged fifteeen years and giving promise of glorious manhood, accompanies them joyously. Day after day the little family push west. Cyrus, already an adept woodsman and hunter, sees that his father is veering slightly north, in spite of the boy's comments on the matter. Reuben seems to be called by a voice. One day just before sunset, they make camp, and Dorcas with a song on her lips starts preparing supper while her two men go in quest of game. Cyrus bounds off in one direction, while his father in a muttering daze circles in the opposite direction. Hearing a sound beside some oak trees and beneath a huge granite rock, Reuben fires. Just before Dorcas rushes up in hope of venison, he sees that he has expiated his rankling sin by sacrificing a life dearer to him than his own, that of his boy, now lying asleep but dreamless. Dorcas shrieks. Tears gush from Reuben, and a prayer — the first in years — ascends from his lips.

Cyrus Bourne, Mrs. Dorcas Malvin Bourne, Reuben Bourne, Roger Malvin.

The Scarlet Letter, 1850. (See also "The Custom House.")

Near the Boston cemetery stands a weather-stained wooden jail, beside the door of which is a lovely rose-bush. The beadle brings Hester Prynne out, with a scarlet letter A on her dress. She must stand on the scaffold in the market-place with her illegitimate child in her arms. Repaying the rigid crowd with a haughty smile, the beautiful woman begins to reminisce: in her mind's eye she sees her father, with beard and ruff, her remonstrating mother, now dead, and a dim-eyed, deformed scholar. Her clutched child's cry brings her back to the present. Amid the crowd stands a small, wrinkled, intelligent-looking man, with one shoulder higher than the other. When Hester sees him, she starts convulsively; when he sees her, his features writhe. Then he tells a townsman that he has been a captive of the Indians and learns from him that Mistress Prynne has had an illegitimate child whose father she refuses to name, and further that she might have been executed for her transgression but for the probability that the learned Master Prynne, who sent her on ahead to Massachusetts, has been drowned following her from Europe. So she is to be punished by having to wear the scarlet letter. The wizened stranger mutters that the name of Hester's lover will be known. On the balcony above the scaffold sit Governor Bellingham, John Wilson the old clergyman, and the Rev. Mr. Arthur Dimmesdale, all of whom urge the exposed sinner to name her guilty partner. Dimmesdale, who is pale and has a lofty brow, is especially eloquent, telling Hester not to be silent through pity and tenderness, and adding that perhaps her lover lacks the courage to confess for himself. But she steadfastly refuses. Her baby wails at the sound of the minister's tremulous voice. In time Hester's ordeal on the scaffold ends, and mother and child return to their prison room, there to become highly frenzied. The jailer brings in the wrinkled scholar, who was recently the captive of the Indians, and introduces him as a physician named Roger Chillingworth. He examines the baby first and mixes it some medicine as carefully, he tells Hester, as though the child were theirs, not hers. When he gives the mother some medicine, she wonders whether it is poison, to which he replies that his purpose is not shallow revenge. So she drinks it. Then Chillingworth blames himself, a foolish, misshapen, decayed man of thought, for leading Hester, a beautiful but weak young woman, to the marriage altar, simply because he hoped to warm his cold heart by her warmth. She says that she wronged him. He calls it quits between them, adding that he seeks no revenge against her but rather against her lover, whom Hester still refuses to name. Chillingworth arrogantly says that although the man wears no letter on his garments he will read a secret one on his heart; then he forces her to swear not to reveal that her husband lives.

When Hester is released from prison, she makes an ascetic home for herself and her baby in an abandoned cottage on the outskirts of town, near the water and the forest, and supports herself by sewing expertly for all sorts of customers except brides. She decides not to leave the area of her sin, in spite of being reviled, since she feels rooted and linked to this town because of her past — and perchance because of continuing love. She sews also for the poor and gives of her slight subsistence to wretches who repay her with insults. She often feels a curious sympathetic throb in her letter, which some say is hell-lit, even

when apparently sinless persons pass by — for example, a clergyman, a chilly matron, a timid girl. She tries to avoid concluding
that others are as corrupt as she. Hester worries about her child,
whom she has named Pearl and who is a healthy, graceful, deep,
and wildly disordered little sprite. Since she is a wildly garbed
outcast like her mother, Pearl must make playfellows out of
elements in nature — a pine tree becomes a Puritan elder, and
ugly weeds become children to be uprooted. But Pearl's favorite
toy is her mother's scarlet letter, which the child handles with a
mocking smile and occasionally pelts with flowers. Hester
wonders what her child is, and Pearl doubts whether she has a
heavenly father. Hearing that Governor Bellingham may try to
take Pearl away from her to have her reared in a more Christian
fashion, Hester waiks one day with her daughter, dressed fantastically in red, past a crowd of vicious little children, whom
Pearl scatters as though she were a scarlet fever, to the Governor's
sunny mansion. They enter a long hall, with a cushioned seat
under a bow-window, gilded books, a pewter tankard, stern-
looking portraits, and armor, into the mirror-like surface of
which Pearl peeps impishly. When the austere Governor comes up
and starts to catechize Pearl by asking her who made her, the girl
says that she was plucked from the rosebush by the prison.
Bellingham is shocked and threatens to take her from Hester,
until the young minister Dimmesdale, at the hysterical demand
of the distraught mother, speaks most eloquently for the child,
saying that she is God's work, simultaneously a blessing and a
torture to her mother, and the means to keep that fallen
woman's soul alive. The Governor agrees to let mother and child
remain together. Chillingworth, standing nearby with a crafty
smile, and darker and more misshapen than ever, watches as Pearl
with unaccustomed gentleness lays her cheek tenderly against the
tremulous minister's hand. Chillingworth then tells old Rev. Mr.
Wilson that one can easily see the mother in the scarlet-clad child
but that it would take a philosopher to analyze her so as to
identify her father. Wilson suggests instead that the mystery
might better be left unresolved and that thus every Christian man
in town could be a kind of father to Pearl. Hester walks out

triumphantly with Pearl and tells Mistress Hibbins, the Governor's witch-like sister, that she now will not accompany the old crone to see the Black Man in the forest.

For about three years now, Chillingworth has been in the village, studying and practicing his art of medicine. He has chosen for his spiritual guide young Arthur Dimmesdale, whose health is now deteriorating. Some say that he is too pure for this world. He is melancholy, and his hand at his heart seems to indicate pain there. Some say that it is little short of a miracle that the learned leech should have arrived in time to care for their minister. The two men walk together and talk together, the conservative Dimmesdale being fascinated by Chillingworth's liberal views. They now live together in the home of a pious widow, since the minister is unmarried. Chillingworth burrows into his friend's heart, believing that there must be some relationship between its secret and the man's apparent malady. Gradually some of the townspeople develop an irrational, heartfelt prejudice against ugly Chillingworth; they regard him as evil and see the minister as locked in a spiritual battle with him. One day they talk of secret and open guilt. Dimmesdale says that Hester, who happens to be walking nearby with Pearl, may be less miserable than sinners who are still unexposed. When Chillingworth hints that his patient has a malady which no doctor can cure without knowing what is wrong with his inner being, Dimmesdale replies by saying that a secret sinner can still do God's work and then rudely rush away. He soon apologizes to his friend. Not long thereafter, while Dimmesdale sits one noon in unusally heavy slumber, his leech approaches and thrusts his vestments aside. What he sees causes him to dance in satanic wonder, joy, and horror! When he first began to live with the minister, Chillingworth was a truth-seeker. Then he began to dig into his patient's heart, like a sexton rooting in a grave. Now he pitilessly plans a malicious revenge. Meanwhile, Dimmesdale is only unconsciously aware of the wretchedly evil nature of his physician and therefore blames himself for abhorring him. Dimmesdale has achieved immense popularity, since only he among scholars in the region is able to preach with the tongue of flame. Sinner that he is, he sympathizes with all mankind. He longs to tell his congregation that he is a polluted pastor. He scourges himself, fasts, stares at himself in his mirror, has visions of angels and demons — and of Hester and little Pearl — occasionally regards the whole world as impalpable, and keeps vigils.

One night in May, while most of the town is asleep, Dimmesdale like a sleepwalker mounts the scaffold on which Hester and Pearl were exposed to ignominy seven years earlier. He shrieks aloud in an agony of vain repentance, then fears discovery — but no one comes. He sees lights at the Governor's mansion. He grows calm and then gradually becomes stiff with the cold. Hester and Pearl come by, having watched by old Governor Winthrop, who has just died. Dimmesdale calls them up to stand beside him. Pearl holds his hand but laughs mockingly when he refuses to agree to stand in public with them there on the morrow. Suddenly a meteor illuminates the cloudy sky, and Dimmesdale notices old Chillingworth smiling and scowling in the distance. He comes forward and soon leads his now dazed patient home. In the morning, Dimmesdale preaches a magnificent sermon, at the end of which the sexton tells him that a meteor wrote the letter A — meaning Angel for the late Governor, doubtless — and then gives Dimmesdale his glove, found at the scaffold and undoubtedly left there by Satan.

Hester has been changing. The public, aware of her deeds of mercy, thinks more kindly of her; some say that her scarlet A means Able. But her vernal nature is withered, and she is growing hard. Her luxuriant hair is hidden beneath an unlovely cap. Isolated from society, she has become a free-thinker and wanders clueless. Seeing Dimmesdale close to lunacy, she resolves to rescue him from Chillingworth, who is now lower than she is and whom she finds on the shore, collecting herbs. While Pearl plays in the water, Hester observes the change in Chillingworth: once wise and just, he is now a fierce-looking, red-eyed, darkly smiling fiend. She asks him to forgive poor, tormented Dimmesdale and leave him to God's punishment. But Chillingworth, painfully recognizing his diabolical qualities, refusing to stop torturing his victim, blames it all on fate, and tells her to reveal anything she

pleases to her minister. Watching Chillingworth walk away, she
wonders why the grass does not flame beneath his feet and soon
says to herself that she hates the man, that he wronged her more
than she did him. Seven years now, and the scarlet letter has
produced misery but no repentance! Hester calls her daughter
from the beach. The girl has fashioned a letter A of seaweed for
her dress, and she now asks her mother why she wears the red A
and why the minister keeps his hand over his heart. Hester is
tempted to confide in bewildered little Pearl but rejects the
temptation as involving too great a price for the child's sympathy. It is not until several days later that Hester has an
opportunity to meet Dimmesdale in the primeval forest, on his
return from a visit to some Indian converts. She prefers the
outdoors to his study for such an interview, because of her sense
of guilt. When he walks by, listlessly, she tells Pearl to go play
near a babbling brook, and the vivacious, griefless little girl
dances off elfishly. Hester calls Dimmesdale, and they clasp each
other's chill hands. They agree that they are miserable, and when
she tells him that at least his work should be satisfying, he
replies that he is surrounded by personal falsehood and
emptiness. He longs for a friend to know him truly, or even an
enemy. Hester then tells him that Chillingworth, surely an
enemy, is her husband. Dimmesdale is stunned at the ugly
indelicacy of such a situation and says that he cannot forgive her
concealment. But she forces him to do so, and they agree that a
vengeful violator of the human heart is worse than they ever
were. He turns listless again and asks her to think for him. When
she urges him to leave his present false life and start anew
— back in England or on the Continent -- he says that he lacks
the necessary strength to venture into the wide world again,
alone. She replies passionately that he would not be alone! It is
not surprising that Hester, taught — but taught amiss — by shame
and desperate loneliness, should be freely critical of society and
now indifferent to its dictates. But what if Dimmesdale, sensitive,
hemmed in by a social system of which he is a spiritual leader,
should fall again? One might excuse him only on the grounds
that his mind has been darkened by seven years of remorse. He

now feels an unusual joy. Hester flings her scarlet letter toward the brook, unpins her lovely hair, and smiles radiantly. They call Pearl, who has been playing unaffectedly in the tangled wilderness, full of berries, birds, and animals — including a wolf, which, it is said, let the gentle child pat its savage head. Together Hester and Arthur admire little Pearl, who, however, refuses to answer her mother's call until the poor woman puts her letter back on and pins up her hair. Even then the child must be dragged toward the embarrassed minister; and when he awkwardly impresses a kiss upon her brow, she runs to the brook and washes it off. The dell grows dark, and the melancholy stream murmurs on. Dimmesdale leaves ahead of the others, sees in the harbor the semi-piratical ship on which they plan to escape back to Europe, and thinks of his last professional act here — delivering the Election Sermon. He feels energetic. As he approaches town, all of its familiar features seem changed. He strangely longs to sin — to whisper blasphemies, irreligious comments, and impure words into the ears of his innocent parishioners. He feels confused. Did he sign away his soul in the forest? Cackling old Mistress Hibbins laughs at him and seems to think so. He has freely chosen a path of known sin. He returns home, enters his study, and soon is interrupted by old Chillingworth, whose services he now says gratefully he can dispense with. The physician knows and takes his leave. Suddenly the minister flings his half-written sermon into the fire and scribbles a new one all through the night.

On the morning of the new Governor's inauguration, the occasion for a gay public holiday, Hester walks through the streets in a freer fashion, as though to say that the people may have one last look at her hated letter, for she will soon be far away. Pearl flits brightly at her side. The townspeople seem relaxed, and there is muted splendor in the festive scene. Indians appear, as do swashbuckling, ferocious sailors. Chillingworth is seen talking to the captain of the ship now in port; then that showily garbed man comes and tells Hester that the crooked old physician plans to accompany her party to Europe. Hester answers calmly but with inner consternation. The official procession then begins, with military persons first, then civilian authorities, and finally the minister, now energetically purposeful. Seeing him, Hester feels dreary, perhaps because he seems so beyond her reach. Pearl too is uneasy at the sight of him. Mistress Hibbins comes by, elaborately dressed, taunts Hester with questions about the forest, and tells Pearl that they might ride through the air some night and learn about the child's father. Soon Dimmesdale's musically modulated voice drifts from the meetinghouse to Hester, once again an object of curiosity on the street because of her letter. Pearl darts here and there, as wild as the Indians and sailors she dances around. Dimmesdale speaks of God and human communities, especially those now springing up in New England. Through his generally optimistic remarks is an undercurrent of sadness, seemingly in prophecy of his own imminent death. Once the speech ends and the officials emerge from the church, the crowd roars its praise of their young divine, who, however, is now pale and feeble. He pauses in his march and then calls Hester and Pearl to ascend the nearby scaffold with him, where — he says — he should have stood seven years before. In spite of thwarted Chillingworth's warning whispers, Dimmesdale tears off his vestments and reveals to the horror-stricken crowd a scarlet letter on his chest. He then asks Pearl for a kiss, which she places on her father's lips while her tears fall on his cheeks. Hester wonders whether their mutual woe has ransomed their souls, so that they can share life in the next world. But Dimmesdale, voicing uncertainty because of their act of spiritual violation, is content to praise merciful God and die.

Various theories emerge as to the minister's letter. Was it the product of self-torture, the magic of Chillingworth, the gnawing tooth of remorse? Some witnesses of Dimmesdale's death absolutely denied that there was any mark on his chest. The moral emerges: be true and be frank in showing your real nature to others. Chillingworth soon shrivels up and dies, leaving Pearl his property. Later she and Hester disappear. Much later Hester, still wearing her scarlet letter, returns to her secluded cottage, which in time becomes the respository of rich but unwanted gifts; in addition, she receives letters with foreign armorial seals. Hester at one time is seen embroidering lavish baby garments. And so she lives out her lonely days in the region of her sin, sorrow, and penitence. She is often a comfort to wretched women, who seek her out for counsel. When she dies, she is buried beside her minister. Over them is a slate with a red letter on a dark field.

Bacon, Governor [Richard] Bellingham, the Black Man, Rev. Mr. [William] Blackstone, Brackett, Governor [Simon] Bradstreet, Roger Chillingworth, Coke, Sir Kenelm Digby, Rev. Mr. Arthur Dimmesdale, Governor [Thomas] Dudley, Apostle [John] Eliot, Governor [John Endicott], Finch, Doctor Forman, Hibbins, Mistress Hibbins, Anne Hutchinson, King James, Isaac Johnson, Increase Mather, Noye, Sir Thomas Overbury, Hester Prynne, Pearl Prynne, Mr. Surveyor Pue, Ann Turner, Rev. Mr. John Wilson, Governor [John] Winthrop.

"A Select Party," 1844.

One autumn day a Man of Fancy has a party in one of his castles in the air, a magnificently iridescent cloud palace lighted by meteor lamps. He invites many guests, the first of whom is the Oldest Inhabitant, famous for recalling forgotten men and things. Also we have an unselfish, humble person, capable of squaring the circle, making water run uphill, jumping down his own throat, and so on; his name is Nobody. Monsieur On-Dit is there too, constantly gossiping; and the Clerk of the Weather, the Wandering Jew (rather common now and so out of place that he soon left for Oregon), and an incredibly lovely woman called Dream. Then frightening horrors appear, next to many other creatures of fancy: an incorruptible Patriot, a Scholar without pedantry, and the like. A young, brilliant-eyed stranger comes: the Master Genius for whom our country prays. Many others arrive, including Posterity, about whom a throng of fellow guests gathers. Taking the huge group on a tour of his castle, the Man of Fancy shows them a hall with ideal statues and a library full of such unwritten items as the rest of Chaucer's *Canterbury Tales* and the end of Coleridge's "Christabel." One noble saloon has curtains of sunrise, and rainbows are scattered about. It is time for refreshments, which include a phoenix and ice cream from the Milky Way. Many guests go home on will-o'-the-wisps, lighted by the Man in the Moon with his lantern.

> A Beautiful Woman, Mother Cary, the Child Unborn, the Clerk of the Weather, Davy Jones, Joel Doe, the Dream, Counsellor Gill, the Man in the Moon, the Man of Fancy, a Man of Straw, a Married Pair, the Master Genius, Nobody, Old Harry, the Oldest Inhabitant, Monsieur On-Dit, a Patriot, a Poet, Posterity, a Priest, a Reformer, Richard Roe, a Scholar, [Charles] Sealsfield [K. A. Postl], the Wandering Jew.

Septimius Felton: or, the Elixir of Life, 1872.

One early spring day on the road between Lexington and Concord, three young people are talking. They are pretty Rose Garfield, tanned and freckled; ruddy young Robert Hagburn, strong and tall; and scholarly Septimius Felton, who is a dark combination of Puritan and Indian blood and is studying for the ministry. Septimius, who loves sunny Rose unhopefully, remarks sadly that life is too short to worry about the coming of war. After debating courteously with the minister who passes by, the young man goes home to dinner, prepared by his old Aunt Keziah; then he turns to his studies, feeling a curious sense of immortality so long as he keeps active, pure, and strong. In the morning, a horseman tears by to warn the inhabitants of the area that the redcoats are coming. Septimius goes out, soon sees Rose kissed by an aristocratic British officer who is marching by with his detachment, challenges him but is interrupted, and then returns to his books — but restlessly now. So be takes his gun, watches the first volleys of shots from some woods, and soon encounters again the handsome Britisher, who suggests that they exchange shots at the command to fire. Septimius is grazed, but the unknown soldier falls, mortally wounded. He forgives

Septimius, gives him his military and personal effects – including a shattered miniature and a wallet with a mysterious, blood-soaked manuscript, which is the legacy of a learned uncle – and asks to be secretly buried at once in the woods. Then he dies. As Septimius is burying the body, the minister passes by and participates in the rites. On the way back to town, Septimius meets Rose; both are agitated, and they kiss and plight an inexplicably reluctant troth. Continuing on his way, Septimius then meets Robert, who has been wounded slightly and who soon thereafter guesses that Rose is no longer a possibility for him and therefore enlists in the army.

Within a day or two, Septimius has begun to wear a path beside his unnamed victim's hillock, which Rose visits with Septimius without learning what is beneath. Their engagement grows melancholy. Septimius now begins to study the manuscript bequeathed to him uniquely and fatally by a dying hand, but it is illegible, a shimmering, blurred cipher. Petty daily events pester him: the demands of his old aunt, talk of the war, a wounded soldier, the advice of the inquisitive minister (that he become a soldier or at least an army chaplain), and Rose's love (which seems to delay his self-centered progress). Once, he fancies that the manuscript contains a mysterious recipe – how to extract rich juice from something rooted in a grave. When the summer is advanced, a pale thin, crazy-acting girl (later named Sibyl Dacy) comes to the hill-side grave looking unsuccessfully for something amid the little flowers growing there. To hospitable Septimius's questions, she says that she lives there, but Rose soon explains that the girl was released after the siege of Boston and now lives with the mother of Robert Hagburn, who soon is marching off toward Quebec with General Arnold. The girl asks Rose where she might find a flower called the *Sanguinea sanguinissima*. When Septimius tells Rose that the crazy girl is interrupting his intellectual walks on the hill, his fiancee begins to feel unneeded.

Through the winter Septimius broods on the manuscript. Then in the spring, Dr. Jabez Portsoaken appears by the grave, introduces himself to Septimius as a former British army surgeon and the uncle of Sibyl, hints that he can add something to the young man's incomplete knowledge, and advises him to study spiders and herbs. Septimius invites him to his house, where the old man sees the dead British officer's sword and identifies it as that of Cyril Norton. Aunt Keziah reluctantly serves Dr. Portsoaken an infernal-tasting drink of herbs and rum. Septimius shows his guest a list of flowers copied out from his old manuscript, but not the manuscript itself. The doctor hints that the ill-fated Norton family has a recipe going back to Friar Bacon and involving such ingredients as Septimius's list of flowers but also including the rare *Sanguinea sanguinissima* (which does not grow hereabouts); the recipe was supposed to have a life-giving potency. Branding as folly the search for such a recipe, Dr. Portsoaken puffs his vile pipe a final time and then leaves. Septimius is now aware that he must study further; so first he reads some scientific books at war-agitated Cambridge nearby and then flatters Aunt Keziah into telling him the recipe for her infernal drink. She not only does so but explains that it came down to her from certain long-lived Indian ancestors; unfortunately, however, she cannot recall a certain ingredient, for which she is content to substitute rum. Septimius then goes to his hill, where Rose and Sibyl are walking arm in arm. The three discuss death, which Sibyl says makes heroism (such as Robert's) possible in this uncertain life. Next she points out a curious purple-veined plant growing out of the little hillock and then tells them about - - - Hall in England, whose wise old lord, named Sir Forrester, sought the means to prolong his life indefinitely. He learned to do so by sacrificing what was closest to him. He destroyed a pure young orphan girl, his kinswoman, who, it is said, stabbed herself when he took her to the woods, so that he would not have to do so. He stepped in her blood and left bloody footsteps wherever he walked, including on his own threshold. He drank the juice of a crimson flower beside her grave and thus became immortal, though woeful and lonely. For the family recipe to be efficacious now, the seeds of the red flower must be planted in a fresh grave of someone who suffered a bloody death.

Septimius is impressed by Sibyl's legend, soon begins to feel

that life is all illusory, applies the stories of Sibyl and Dr.
Portsoaken and Aunt Keziah to himself, and renews his efforts to
decipher the manuscript, which he begins to see is a wise but icy
message on social morality written in Old English, Latin, and a
bit of Greek. It warns the reader to keep his heart calm, avoid all
stimulants including wine and love and hate and spiced meat,
stay clean, bask in the sun, smell the breath of healthy babies
and cows, and devote all thoughts to himself. Septimius next
finds gorgeous, dahlia-like flowers, crimson and with golden
centers, growing from the grave and spreading down the hill. One
day Sibyl tells Rose that it is the *Sanguinea sanguinissima*. When
Aunt Keziah grows sick and asks Septimius to pour her an herb
drink from her pot bubbling at the hearth, he throws in some of
the red flowers — since this is a chance to experiment — and
serves it to her. After a curious lecture on her frustrations as a
Christian woman who would have preferred being a witch, the
contorted old crone dies. Rose (now curiously represented to be
Septimius Felton's half-sister and living with him and their aunt)
is not in attendance, since she has returned after lunch to her
school-teaching duties. Septimius, pallid and with a wrinkle
deepening over his nose, bursts into tears and soon goes back to
his hill-top refuge, where he gradually begins to feel no sense of
guilt, then meets Sibyl, and learns that he should consult Dr.
Portsoaken about the flower. He goes into an old street in
Boston and finds the learned doctor surrounded with pipe,
brandy, and cobwebs, in the midst of one of which is a gigantic,
iridescent, seemingly intelligent spider named Orontes, who evidently takes a dislike to Septimius. Feeling like the fly in the
doctor's own web, he is advised that the red "flower," of which
he has brought some samples, is really a rare fungus. He is also
told to check into any coffer or chest Aunt Keziah left, to
ascertain whether he is the heir of a new defunct English family
and can therefore lay claim to ancestral halls and a fortune. He
abstractedly says that he will investigate when he has time. But
instead, he returns to his decoctions and distillations, always
aiming to make his medicine gold-colored, cold, and fragrant — in
accordance with the demands of his recipe — but without success.

He thinks of loving Sibyl but decides to remain secure in his loneliness. She tells him darkly that she has a mission and that when she has fulfilled it she will go.

One day Septimius happens to notice the silver key he took from the dying British soldier; fancying that it might unlock his dead aunt's coffer, he searches for it and finally finds it. Robert Hagburn, stalwart and polished now and home on leave, interrupts the opening of the chest by visiting Septimius and urging him to become a chaplain and thus be part of the exciting times. He also asks for Septimius's sister Rose's hand in marriage. Septimius is delighted but is glad to be alone later to turn to the chest. In it he finds some papers concerning his ancestors; one entry in Latin miraculously provides the solution to some stubbborn ciphers in the ecstatic young man's recipe. He immediately succeeds in brewing the potent elixir, stands it in the sun and then the moon, and watches it go through its mysterious self-digestive phases. Its color finally resembles that of moonlight, and it turns frosty to the touch. Feeling powerful, Septimius now dallies. He walks with lovely, smiling Sibyl; they discuss the way they will spend their eternity on earth: rule, observe, travel, learn why women lead such accursed lives, play, philosophize, write history, preach, and perhaps sin. But Septimius does not want Sibyl to do any sinning. Since death is a unique cure for some evils, Septimius is reconciled to not utterly conquering it but will welcome it, much later. He senses a certain doubt in Sibyl but decides to let her drink his draught too.

On the day of the wedding of Robert and Rose, haggard Septimius makes a rare appearance, feels superior and protective, chats superciliously with the worried minister about a preaching career at some much later date, and then tells Rose that once she is married he will be absolutely free to confront his destiny without any family ties. Sibyl, who gently refused to be a bridesmaid for Rose, telling her that no bride would want a grave flower like herself in that capacity, soon slips away with Septimius. Dr. Portsoaken arrives too late to see her but instead talks with some old crones about Felton family history. Finally we see wild-eyed Sibyl going to Septimius's study. The young man shows her his elixir, in a delicate, long-stemmed glass. She tells him that she was the original of the miniature shattered by his bullet, which killed her British fiancé Cyril Norton. She planned to haunt the hill-side grave and poison her lover's killer. But her purpose changed. So she now takes a long draught from the glass and then prevents Septimius from doing the same by dropping it on the hearth. Septimius is enraged until she explains that there were two recipes, that his elixir is a virulent poison because of the hill-side fungus – the product of seeds she sowed there with Dr. Portsoaken's help – that she loves Septimius, and that his quest for immortality is a joke which they will laugh at together in the next world. Then she dies. Septimius places her body on the hill-side grave and is later rumored to have gone to England, where he claims Smithell's Hall. Dr. Portsoaken is taken into custody for questioning; he acted as he did because he favored the claim of a Britisher to an estate in England left tenantless upon the death of Cyril Norton. The doctor is later released for lack of evidence and then disappears, leaving behind little but cobwebs and an empty spider skin.

> General [Benedict] Arnold, Friar Bacon, the Black Man, Goody Chickering, Sibyl Dacy, Martha Denton, Gaspar Felton, Septimius "Seppy" Felton, Sir Forrester, Rose Garfield, Robert Hagburn, Mrs. Hagburn, Aunt Keziah "Kezzy," Cyril Norton, Dr. Jabez Portsoaken, General [George] Washington.

"The Seven Vagabonds," 1833.

The narrator, an eighteen-year-old youth, is out walking when he comes upon a three-way branch in the road. He can go straight on to Boston, detour toward the sea, or turn right to Stamford, in Canada. Impending rain impels him toward a wagon in which he finds an old puppeteer, who for a silver coin shows him his ingenious demonstration. In the wagon also is a "bibliopolist," a neat, bespectacled man in his early twenties, who lectures the narrator on his stock of books and then sells him several. The narrator envies both strolling men their good and varied life. The rain beats down, and into the wagon come a tall, dark foreigner, who is carrying a mahogany diorama and who also plays the fiddle, and with him a beautiful, dancing damsel, who lets the narrator look into the peep-show and lectures him on its sights – Barcelona, Sicily, Venice, and so on. Now he envies the violinist and his attractive companion. The door opens and admits on his way also to the camp-meeting at Stamford a wandering conjurer, called the Straggler, who first begs money from the narrator and then rather diabolically tells him his fortune with a pack of greasy cards. The old showman and the bookseller propose that they all band together and go to Stamford in a group. Next in comes a somber Penobscot Indian, on his way to shoot arrows at the Stamford camp-meeting. The girl invites him along. More and more, the narrator envies these vagabonds their merry and varied life, which is a contrast to smoky city monotony. When the old showman remarks that the narrator cannot earn his way, that resourceful fellow offers to tell extemporaneous stories to various audiences for his keep. This will be his vocation, he vows, and he begs the girl, whom he calls Mirth, to sponsor his plea. She does, and he joins them. The sun breaks out, and the seven trip along merrily on the road to Canada, until a rigid and rusty old Methodist preacher rides by and tells them that the Stamford camp-meeting is broken up. So the vagabonds split up and go various ways. The Straggler goes toward Stamford; the old showman and his bookish friend, toward the seacoast; the fiddler and merry Mirth, east; and the narrator and the Indian, pensively toward Boston.

Mirth, the Straggler.

"The Shaker Bridal," 1838.

After forty years as presiding elder of the Shakers at Goshen, Father Ephraim, now old and infirm, has gathered other leading Shakers to tell them that he wishes to follow the primitive form of their order, as established by sainted Mother Ann, and name Adam Colburn and Martha Pierson as Father and Mother of the village. One of the visiting elders has some doubts, since Adam and Martha, once practically betrothed but then separated by years of misfortune, may still be subject to carnal temptations. So Father Ephraim asks Adam to speak. That calmly despairing man, possessing no second spring of hope, says sternly that he came to Goshen worn out with trouble and hopes now only to be a brother to Martha and to strive with her for the spiritual and temporal good of the place. When asked to speak in her turn, pale Martha at first says only that Adam has spoken well for her but then adds that she will try to do her best. The fanatics surround her. She and Adam join hands and receive Father Ephraim's order to teach the celibate Shaker faith until children shall be born no more and the sun will set forever on the world of sin and sorrow. Adam folds his arms resolutely. But Martha sinks like a corpse at the feet of that cold object of her earthly love.

Adam Colburn, Father Ephraim, Martha Pierson.

"Sights from a Steeple," 1831.

The narrator climbs toward heaven up the spire to view parts of the town beneath and also the sea beyond. He sees golden clouds, fields, villages, little rivers and lakes, and hills. He wishes that he could become a spiritual Paul Pry and strip the roofs off the houses and learn all the secrets, including the guilty ones, of the inhabitants beneath. Along one fine street ornamented with lofty trees he sees a young man walking, then two pretty girls. He looks at the busy wharf, then at a warehouse and a rich merchant with wig and powder nearby. The young man meets the two girls and walks along with them. There are three processions: a group of soldiers, some boys imitating them, and a funeral. A storm comes up, with lightning, thunder, and rivers of rain. The three young people scurry toward shelter but run into the limping merchant, who thrusts the youth aside and takes his two daughters home. The rain beats the roofs and rises again smokily. The sea boils under the storm. The hills are misty. But the clouds eventually give way to a patch of blue, and then a rainbow appears.

(No named characters.)

"The Sister Years . . . ," 1839.

Shortly before midnight on New Year's Eve, 1839, the Old Year might be observed to sit on Salem's new City Hall steps. She has a loaded bandbox and an annual-like book. Her sister the New Year approaches with her basket, and the two talk. The Old Year says that politics have vacillated and much energy has been wasted on pettiness. The New Year hopes that things will soon be perfect. The Old Year is doubtful, however, and says that her receptacle of things past includes outmoded patterns, lost beauty, dark hair, widows' tears, old love-letters, and disappointed hopes. The New Year says that in her basket she has sweet-smelling hopes, some gifts for children, and good resolutions. The Old Year warns her fresh-looking sister not to expect too much and then, as midnight tolls, fades away. When the watchman shouts happy New Year, she gives him a rose of hope. Drinkers toast her. Some people live just long enough for her to bury them. But let us all redeem the pledge of the New Year.

New Year, Old Year.

"Sketches from Memory," First Series, 1835.

"The Notch in the White Mountains." One September the author walks past Bartlett through the Saco Valley into the brilliantly crystal White Mountains and their famous Notch. A stagecoach loaded with passengers passes. They all approach the mountain house where they will spend the night.

"Our Evening among the Mountains." Ethan Crawford, the huge mountaineer landlord, blows his tin trumpet, and his various guests enter as the echoes ring from the mountains. Inside, a vast fire is blazing. Conversation and supper are pleasant. Someone tells the legend of "The Great Carbuncle," from which the author fancies he could fashion a moral tale. He regrets his inability to write about Indians. Most of the party, with the probable exception of two pairs of newlyweds, are to arise at three the following morning for their mountain-climb.

"The Canal Boat." One day the author embarks on a canal boat thirty miles below Utica and determines to voyage along the Erie Canal part way between the Hudson River and Lake Erie. He sees many curious vessels on the turbid canal, and a variety of passengers, including a curious British traveler whose frantic note-scribbling indicates that he is probably preparing a misinformed book on the odd Americans he is misjudging now. At night the various passengers, with the men divided from the women by a crimson curtain, prepare to retire. The wild snoring of a few disturbs the author; so, after falling out of his narrow berth, he goes out on deck, disembarks during a pause to examine a dismal, phosphorescent forest somewhere between Utica and Syracuse, and is left behind. He happily walks off toward Syracuse.

Ethan Crawford, Crawford.

"Sketches from Memory," Second Series, 1835.

I. "The Inland Port." The author disembarks from a Lake Champlain skiff at Burlington, which resembles a fishing-town on the seacoast, although there is a sickly, unbriny smell about. Numerous Irish emigrants show their lazy strength, merriment, and red-cheeked children. The square has a variety of buildings, including a brick custom house, since Burlington is a port of entry.

II. "Rochester." The author visits Rochester and is impressed by the Genesee River falls, over which Sam Patch took his last leap, for fame. The author could draw a moral: most people who pursue empty fame are as foolish as poor Sam! Rochester has grown fast and is now crowded with people, lottery offices, court-house activity, hotels, and drunken recruits for military posts in the West.

III. "A Night Scene." The author's steamboat on its way to Detroit puts in for repairs at the mouth of a river, and during the dark evening some wild Irishmen gather wood for the boat. While doing so, they build a huge fire on the bank, and in its picturesque light they look like devils feeding the flames of their own torment.

(No named characters.)

"Snow-Flakes," 1838.

When the December weather turns snowy, the author rejoices, because he is a New England nursling of the storm. As the cloud-spirits weave a white mantle for Mother Earth, he grows cheery and imaginative. The garden begins to fill with snow, black roofs turn gray and then white, and schoolboys have a Homeric snowball fight. The wind howls, and men's hearths become altars sending smoke to a chilly, tyrannical deity. The storm continues through the afternoon. A man outside pushes through the deeper snow. A sleigh and a sledge pass. Evening darkens early. Nature is in her shroud. Then a flock of snow-birds flits by, and the author's spirits are cheered.

(No named characters.)

"The Snow-Image: A Childish Miracle," 1850.

One cold winter afternoon, Violet Lindsey and her little brother Peony go out to play in the dazzling white snow, while their loving mother sits at the window sewing and watching. The two children talk imaginatively of making a snow-sister. If such a miracle could be wrought, childish hands should be the instruments. While Violet directs operations and executes the finer touches, Peony mainly brings loads of snow. The snow-image grows before them, almost – the watchful mother thinks – as though an angel-child had come to play invisibly with her darlings. A rose-colored cloud seems to tint the cheeks of the snow-image, and a cloud of gold seems to play about its head. Called by her gay children, the sensitive mother sees them in the twilight – or seems to see them – dancing with a strange child, with rosy cheeks, yellow hair, a white dress, and white slippers. A flock of snow-birds flies by and flutters about the snow-sister's head. When the mother asks who the strange child is, Violet and Peony insist that they created her for play. Then home comes

Mr. Lindsey, their father, a common-sensible, considerate hard-ware dealer. When he sees the strange child, he insists on bringing her into the house and placing her before the raging stove, since her hands are freezing to the touch. Violet and Peony, and even Mrs. Lindsey, beg the stubborn man not to do so. While the parents are looking for warm clothing for the childish visitor and are trying to find out from the neighbors who she is, Violet and Peony begin to cry: their drooping snow-sister has melted into a shapeless heap of snow and a pool of water. Mr. Lindsey meant well, but he should have inquired more carefully into the nature of the creature he sought to aid; his would-be kindness was mischief. He calls for the maid to come and sop up the mess which his children have brought into the house.

Dora, Peony Lindsey, Violet Lindsey, Lindsey, Mrs. Lindsey.

"Sunday at Home," 1837.

The narrator remains home on Sunday and watches the sun gild the steeple of the nearby church. He sees the children go to Sunday school and their elders make up the congregation later, spies on the pretty girls, watches the solemn minister enter, and hears the hymn and fragments of the sermon. Later the after-noon service lets out, and the narrator hears a little practice music after that.

(No named characters.)

"Sylph Etherege," 1838.

One summer evening Mrs. Grosvenor is spying on her deli-cately charming ward Sylvia Etherege. With the older woman is Edward Hamilton. They talk mysteriously of an experiment they are trying on Sylvia, to cure her of romantic nonsense. But Mrs. Grosvenor is afraid that Hamilton will ruin his chances with the girl by advancing the cause of a rival. It seems that Sylvia, an orphan, lived with a bachelor uncle and was betrothed to a cousin, named Edgar Vaughan, whom she had never seen because he was in Europe studying. Now Hamilton, an intimate of Vaughan's, reports to Mrs. Grosvenor and Sylvia with news of his friend, whose letters to Sylvia — so ethereal that he addresses her as Sylph — have evoked an image of a perfect lover. Hamilton seems the reverse — dark in features and with an evil smile though polished manners. Sylvia cannot like him. He gives her a miniature of Vaughan; it shows a face almost too perfect, and the romantic girl clasps it constantly and conjures up blissful fantasies. Toward the close of summer, the girl learns that Vaughan has arrived from France and will come to her this very evening. But when he appears, it is Hamilton, dark and smiling villainously. The girl faints. Mrs. Grosvenor is alarmed; although she agreed to let Vaughan — calling himself Hamilton — try this experiment to cure her ward of illusions, she now trembles at the consequences. Vaughan sneers and determines to win the now shaken girl to his heart. In time, their nuptials are announced. But one moonlit evening he calls on Sylph Etherege and finds her sitting in shadows. When he comments to Mrs. Grosvenor that the girl might fade into the moonlight or float away on the breeze, Sylph replies that she will do neither but that he cannot keep her there. His smile is both mocking and anguished. He thinks that she is going to heaven to seek the original of the miniature she clasped so lovingly.

Sylvia "Sylph" Etherege, Mrs. Grosvenor, Edward Vaughan.

Tanglewood Tales, for Girls and Boys: Being a Second Wonder-Book, 1853. (See also "The Minotaur," "The Pygmies," "The Dragon's Teeth," "Circe's Palace," "The Pomegranate Seeds," and "The Golden Fleece.")

The literary occupant of the Wayside, Concord, Massachusetts, welcomes Eustace Bright, now a senior on his winter vacation from Williams College. The two walk in the snow and visit a ruined summer-house behind the Wayside. Eustace describes the recent activities and sicknesses of the various children to whom he told his six stories, now published in *The Wonder-Book,* and reports that, ambitious as he is for literary fame, he has six new ones which he would like an opinion on. They are called *Tanglewood Tales* and include the following: "The Minotaur," "The Pygmies," "The Dragon's Teeth," "Circe's Palace," "The Pomegranate Seeds," and "The Golden Fleece."

Eustace Bright.

"The Threefold Destiny: A Fairy Legend," 1838.

Best read as an allegory is the story of tall, stately Ralph Cranfield, who after ten years of wandering in various foreign climes has returned home — for temporary rejuvenation, he thinks — to his widowed mother, who still lives in their same backward little village. He went away summoned by a threefold destiny: he was to be loved by a maiden who for a sign should point a finger at a heart-shaped jewel, he was to find a mighty treasure and dig for it where a mysterious hand pointed, and three sages should come to him with a wand and offer him colossal power. An acquaintance of his childhood, Faith Egerton, greets him as he enters his village at twilight one summer day, but he hurries on to his home. There he sees his old tree, in the trunk of which he sees the Latin word *effode*, meaning "dig," which he carved there and above which now grows a hand-like bump. His mother comes out and is overjoyed at having him home again to worry over. That night Ralph dreams again of the heart-shaped jewel, the hand pointing out the spot to dig for his treasure, and the sages offering him power. In the morning three venerable villagers, the sagest being Squire Hawkwood, come to welcome Ralph and offer him a position as village schoolmaster. Courteously promising to think it over, Ralph is inwardly struck by the similarity of these humble delegates and the three sages in his recurrent dream. Walking through the village the following morning, he is pleased by the fresh smell of the cows as they graze. When a child creeps near him, he lifts it back to its mother and realizes that children will be his charge. He calls on Faith Egerton, who greets him with comely grace. He sees that she is wearing — and then is pointing toward — a heart-shaped brooch which he fashioned for her out of an arrowhead before he left home. He clasps her in his arms. And his wealth he finds by tilling the earth around his mother's dwelling. Work, wealth, and joy are often near home.

Ralph Cranfield, Mrs. Cranfield, Faith Egerton, Squire Hawkwood.

"The Three Golden Apples" (IV. in *A Wonder-Book for Girls and Boys*), 1852.

Hercules must find the garden of the Hesperides and bring the three golden apples back from it to his cousin the king. He asks some pretty maidens for direction. They try to detain him; so he tells them the story of his previous tasks, after which they dance and sing before him. Then they explain that he must question the Old Man of the Sea, which Hercules does in spite of the monster's assumption of many different shapes. The Old Man tells Hercules to find Atlas, the giant who holds up the sky, and predicts that he will have many adventures on the way. After visiting Egypt and voyaging in a huge bowl, he finds the giant, who gives Hercules the sky to hold while he strides off to the garden of the Hesperides for the three golden apples. Hercules tires and is worried when Atlas returns with the apples but refuses to take the burdensome sky back again. So Hercules tricks him into holding it while he shifts his lion skin to make a cushion, and then picks up the apples and rushes off.

Antaeus, Atlas, Geryon, Hercules, Hippolyta, the Old Man of the Sea.

"Time's Portraiture . . . ," 1838.

The newspaper carrier identifies himself as Time's errand-boy and then addresses his generous patrons, in the hope of a tip. There are many misconceptions concerning Time, who really dresses in a modern, dapper manner, wanders everywhere and not merely among old ruins, watches out for mischief and inflicts injuries even on old friends, talks not only about wretched old days but also about novel things to come, and concerns himself with new literary works and business ventures and marriages and births and deaths. The Carrier rejoices that Time is not immortal but must be buried in the grave of eternity. Meanwhile, please realize that he is a tolerable fellow to be endured for a while.

The Carrier, Time.

"The Toll-Gatherer's Day: A Sketch of Transitory Life," 1837.

If one prefers contemplation to activity, he might choose to be a toll-gatherer and sit at a little house half-way across a bridge. A typical morning begins with the sound of a ponderous hay wagon. Then the mail-coach dashes past, then a family chaise, a carryall with pretty girls, a sulky with a sour-faced pickle manufacturer, a black-clad preacher, a butcher's cart and a vegetable wagon, a man with lobsters, a milk cart, a shining barouche with blushing bride and happy groom, and then a sick woman leaning against a sad man. The morning grows hot and dusty, but the toll-gatherer stays cool in his little house. After the noon lull, the draw is raised to let a schooner loaded with wood pass under; but it gets stuck, to the annoyance of two nearby sailors, some smart-looking people, a couple of peddlers, a shepherd with a flock of sheep, a circus caravan, and a company of soldiers. The schooner finally passes, as the sage old toll-gatherer knew it would. Toward sunset some people come out to fish along the bridge, and tired horses tramp by, thinking of their stalls. All should rest, for tomorrow will be wearisome too. The toll-gatherer regards the passersby as flitting phantoms.

(No named characters.)

"The Two Widows" — see "The Wives of the Dead."

"The Unpublished Allegories of the Heart" — see [I.] "Egotism: or, the Bosom Serpent" and [II.] "The Christmas Banquet."

"The Village Uncle: An Imaginary Retrospect," 1835.

The hearty old narrator calls for another log on the fire, as he remembers or imagines his past life. He asks his Susan and his dimly visible children to gather around and listen on this Thanksgiving night in their house on the bay across from Nahant. He hardly knows whether he has lived the glimmering events of these fifty years or only dreamed of living them. He asks Susan to stand by the blazing hearth, so that he can see her gray hair and spectacles. He recalls their fishing village, with its curious dwellings, sandy street, and stores. He remembers his expert fishing and the yarns that gnarled old Uncle Parker used to tell in Mr. Bartlett's store. He seems to see Susan, the mermaid, behind the counter of the shop. She was slim, then, and gay and innocent, like sunshine. He wooed her and shot wild fowl to feather their bridal bed. They lived in a cottage with a whale's jawbones for an arched gate. He read aloud from their Bible, and Susan sang evening psalms. Their children went to the solemn-phizzed pedagogue in the little schoolhouse. The father told them about God by discoursing on nature in the vast and in the minute. His life glided on until be became the uncle of the village and advanced to a happy old age. He smiles at everything now — at children playing in the surf, fish of all kinds, wheeling seagulls, the rocks on the hill. The sun is setting, but the ocean and sky remind him of eternity. What is left but to bless his children, all about him now on this Thanksgiving night, and then die? Should his moral be that since fancy can create such a happy dream, one ought to dream from youth to age? No, since dreams cannot preserve us from reality, his moral should be that one needs chaste and warm affections, humble wishes, and honest toil.

Bartlett, Uncle Parker, Susan.

"A Virtuoso's Collection," 1842.

The narrator steps into a new museum one day, pays half a dollar to an odd-looking doorkeeper, and walks up to the owner, who offers to show him his collection. It includes many stuffed animals, for example, the wolf which ate Little Red Riding-

Hood, and also Alexander's Bucephalus. Among the many stuffed birds are Noah's dove and Shelley's skylark. There are magic objects, like Aladdin's lamp and Prospero's broken wand. Some more nearly real things are also there — such as a rusty iron mask and the axe which beheaded King Charles — which appall the narrator, as do Brutus's bloody sword and Achilles's shield. There are many oddities, like Stuyvesant's false leg and a bit of the Golden Fleece. The owner begins to strike the narrator as hard, cold, unfeeling. They look at fabulous shoes, pipes, clothes, lamps, and cups. When the virtuoso offers a draught from Hebe's cup, the narrator is thrilled but declines, saying that he does not desire an earthly immortality and that one whose life is unduly protracted would lose his spiritual being. They look at lost books, magic flowers, bugs, paintings and sculpture, and furniture. Asking who the doorman is, the narrator learns that he is Peter Rugg, the missing man. Then the virtuoso takes up a rusty dart and says that it served Death for four thousand years but fell blunted from his chest. The narrator guesses that his guide is the Wandering Jew, for whose merciful death he volunteers to pray. The virtuoso smiles coldly, saying that only the world of physical sensation holds any meaning for him. The narrator, horrified but pitying, shakes the wanderer's icy hand and leaves.

Peter Rugg, the Wandering Jew.

"The Vision of the Fountain," 1837.

The narrator at fifteen years of age moves to a country village a hundred miles from his original home. One September morning he fancies that he sees a living creature in a spring in the woods — a lovely naiad clothed in moss and a rainbow. Then it is gone. As he walks to the clergyman's house where he is staying, he sees the vision again, on a tree-clothed hill. Again it disappears. Days and months pass. One January night, on the eve of his return home for a visit, he joins the clergyman's family, who are all sitting in semi-darkness in a ghostly group around a dim fire. Suddenly he sees his vision again, and someone pronounces the name Rachel. It seems that Rachel is a nearby squire's daughter who left for school the morning after the narrator arrived in the area and has just now returned home.

Rachel.

"A Visit to the Clerk of the Weather," 1836.[9]

When the narrator humorously tells a friend that he cannot say whether they will have an early spring, because he has not consulted the clerk of the weather, a bony-handed old crone suddenly seizes him and whirls him magically through the parting clouds, sets him down on green turf, and disappears. The narrator sees a gigantic, hollow pyramid made of rocks acres in height. He enters a lofty chamber and sees a huge, fierce-eyed creature writing with a pen made of a poplar tree. Lining his cavern are thunder-bolts, faded rainbows, hailstones, sacks of wind, and a portable tempest. The monster explains that he is seventy centuries old and then asks where his visitor comes from. The narrator says that he is from Boston, but the puzzled giant replies that he has heard of no planet by that name. The narrator explains that he is from earth, upon which his host voices his recollection of such a mud-ball, at present — he adds — given over to John Frost in payment of a debt. When the narrator asks that Frost be made to release his grip, the giant complains that certain people on earth pretend to be able to predict the weather. He is then interrupted by the entrance of two other guests — Frost himself, who has the appearance of an icy dwarf, and a lovely damsel. She is dressed in a colorful gown, has a green turban, and walks in moccasins which are bespangled with dew-drops. She is Spring and claims that Frost is preventing her return to earth because his wife has sent him on an icy journey to get her a polar bear for a lap dog. The narrator saunters about the massive hall, then suddenly is seized by the crone who brought him there, and flies with her back to the world.

The Clerk of the Weather, John "Jack" Frost, Mrs. John Frost, Spring.

[9] For details, see Adkins, "Notes on the Hawthorne Canon," p. 367.

"Wakefield," 1835.

To be read in an old magazine or newspaper is the story of a man — call him Wakefield — who left his wife in London one day, telling her that he was going on a brief journey but living instead in the next street for twenty years. Imagine the details. Wakefield is sluggish, passively intellectual, unimaginative, cold-hearted, selfish and vain and crafty and strange. One October evening he smiles at his wife, says that he will be gone three or four days, and escapes around the corner. He imagines prying eyes, little realizing how insignificant he is and how quickly chasms in human affections close. He disguises himself, watches a physician call upon his "widow," and lets time pass. Now Wakefield is caught by fate. After ten years, he chances to bump into his wife on the street but moves away at once. Is he mad? He retains his original small share of human sympathies, but he no longer influences other people. Twenty years in all pass. A sudden rain catches him at his own doorstep. Seeing his wife's matronly shadow on the ceiling above her merry hearth fire, he enters his home again. We do not follow. Instead let us consider the moral: by stepping outside the harmonious system of inter-dependent lives, one may become the outcast of the universe.

Wakefield, Mrs. Wakefield.

"The Wedding Knell," 1836.

In the time of the narrator's grandmother, a church in New York was the scene of a curious marriage. Mrs. Dabney, twice married and twice a widow, returns to her once-youthful lover Mr. Ellenwood, whom unrequited love has rendered self-centered, scholarly, and disordered. The two now plan to wed. As the bride separately enters the church, a funeral bell begins to toll. The colorful bridal guests are perturbed. Then the groom enters, in his funeral shroud, and tells worldly Mrs. Dabney that they should marry and then go into their graves. Aghast at first, she then agrees. They wed. The bell tolls on, but the organ pours out a wedding anthem.

Mrs. Dabney, Ellenwood, Julia.

"The White Old Maid," 1835.

In a moonlit chamber containing the corpse of a young man come first a proud young woman, who kneels and kisses the corpse, and then a gentler young woman, named Edith. The two women argue. The proud one tries to order away Edith, who she says had the young man when he was alive. But Edith says that the dead is hers. The proud one fears betrayal, but Edith tells her to go away for a period of years and return at a time they agree on and then tell of her life. Her token will be a lock of the dead man's hair. They clasp hands over his corpse. The proud one leaves. Then Edith departs, lighted down the stairs by a Negro servant (later named Caesar) just as the young clergyman of the town is ascending. Years pass. Meanwhile, a lonely woman of the town passes from youth to age garbed in a kind of winding sheet and developing the habit of attending all funerals. She gradually becomes known as the "Old Maid of the Winding Sheet." She blesses the hillocks of her favorite dead. More years pass. Then late one afternoon a figure garbed in funeral white paces down the street and prepares to enter a lonely old mansion. The aged clergyman of the town tells her gently that not since Colonel Fenwicke's funeral, which she attended fifteen years ago, has the place been lived in. But she approaches the door, a step seems to be heard on the other side, and she enters. Some witnesses claim they saw at the door old Caesar, dead these thirty years. Now a grand, old-fashioned coach wheels up, bearing an aristocratic widow, who alights, a stately ruin, proud though wretched looking. She enters the mansion. Again Caesar is said to be at the door. Some say that it is all a delusion. Did a third visitant rap at the door? Some say yes. Everyone hears a shriek. The venerable clergyman, with a torchbearer, walks up the stairs bowing as though passing through a throng of people, and approaches the chamber where, years ago, he sat at the deathbed of a fine young man. The clergyman flings open the door so hastily that the torch is extinguished. There, in the moonlight, is the Old Maid, before whom the strange, aristocratic lady kneels, clutching a lock of hair. Both are dead.

Caesar, Edith "the Old Maid in the Winding Sheet," Colonel Fenwicke, Fenwicke.

The Whole History of Grandfather's Chair, 1841.

Grandfather sits in an old armchair. At various times and in different seasons, the kind, eloquent old man relates stories of colonial Massachusetts to twelve-year-old bookworm Laurence, his mild, ten-year-old cousin Clara, tough little nine-year-old Charley, and even littler, five-year-old, sleepy Alice. Each of the various historical persons mentioned has purportedly owned or at least sat in the curiously carved chair, the oak for which grew in the park of the English Earl of Lincoln. Events in the lives of the following persons figure in Grandfather's informative stories, told roughly in chronological order: the Lady Arbella and her husband Mr. Johnson, Roger Williams, Mrs. Anne Hutchinson, Henry Vane and other early Governors of Massachusetts (including Winthrop, Dudley, Bellingham, and Endicott), President Dunster of Harvard, William Hawthorne [Hathorne] of the House of Representatives, Captain John Hull the mint-master, Mary Dyer the martyred Quakeress, the Rev. Mr. John Eliot of Roxbury, old Simon Bradstreet, and Sir William Phipps the seeker after sunken Spanish treasure. Next, Grandfather summarizes the careers of the schoolmaster Ezekiel Cheever, the school-minister Cotton Mather, Governor William Shirley, and Governor William Pepperell of Louisberg fame; and tells about the Acadian exiles, various Old French War battles including the siege of Quebec, and the politician-historian Thomas Hutchinson. Grandfather also dramatically tells the attentive children about the Stamp Act, the Liberty Tree, the Hutchinson mob, the Boston Massacre, brilliant revolutionaries like Benjamin Franklin, several loyalists, the Boston Tea Party, the Continental Congress, Lexington and Bunker Hill, General George Washington (who sat in Grandfather's chair) and his officers and Tory opponents (including Sir William Howe) and their various battles, old loyalist Chief Justice Peter Oliver, Mr. Pierce the barber (who shaved Washington in the old chair), the Fourth of July and the Declaration of Independence, late battles (including Saratoga and Yorktown), and then Captain Shays' war, and finally the auction of the estate of old Samuel Adams and how Grandfather purchased the old chair at that time. Laurence expresses a wish that the venerable chair could speak. Grandfather, struck by the notion, concludes by telling the children that he has made up a fable. One night the chair did speak, from the lion's head carved on it, as the flickering fire made its oaken frame appear to be wriggling and alive. The chair explained that it occasionally spoke, but that its auditors later mistook its actions for dreams, then named a few of its occupants whom Grandfather had neglected to mention. The chair added that it could use a new cushion and a bit of varnish here and there, and then more seriously advised Grandfather that justice, truth, and love are the chief ingredients of every happy life. The chair then seemed to put its leg on the toe of Grandfather, who awakened to find that his walking-stick had fallen across his foot.

Alice, Charley, Clara, Grandfather, Laurence.

"The Wives of the Dead," 1834.

Calm, gentle Mary and lovely, irritable Margaret married brothers, one a sailor and the other a soldier. The two couples lived in a Bay Province seaport in one house with a common parlor and two separate bedrooms. It chanced that on two successive days Mary learned that her husband had been drowned during a storm on the Atlantic Ocean and Margaret learned that her husband had been killed in a Canadian skirmish. The two sisters-in-law weep together and then retire to their separate bedrooms. In the night, while Margaret is groaning bitterly, a knock at the street door takes her to the window. Outside in the misty darkness is the innkeeper Goodman Parker, who tells her that her husband was erroneously reported slain and that he is really well and sound. Margaret rushes to tell Mary but quickly decides against disturbing her with happy tidings which can only deepen her own personal misery. So Margaret lies down again and soon has dreams of bliss. Later the same night, Mary is aroused from sleep by eager knocking. It is Stephen, a former suitor and a sailor like her husband; he reports that her husband survived the wreck of his ship, was picked up by a brig from England, and will be home by daylight. Mary rushes to share her good news with Margaret, whom, however, she decides against awakening from a happy dream to a sense of her own misery. But a tear falls on her cheek, and the girl wakes up.

Margaret, Mary, Goodman Parker, Stephen.

A Wonder-Book for Girls and Boys, 1852. (See also "The Gorgon's Head," "The Golden Touch," "The Paradise of Children," "The Three Golden Apples," "The Miraculous Pitcher," and "The Chimaera.")

On the porch of Mr. and Mrs. Pringle's country-seat of Tanglewood, in the Berkshires, near Monument Mountain and not far from the Dome of Taconic, the college lad Eustace Bright one fine autumn morning tells the classical story of "The Gorgon's Head" to a dozen young children. Let us call the children Blue Eye, Buttercup, Clover, Cowslip, Dandelion, Huckleberry, Milkweed, Periwinkle, Plantain, Primrose, Squash-Blossom, and Sweet Fern, since it is sometimes dangerous for an author to use real names. By the time the delightful story is finished, the children notice that the morning has cleared. Between Tanglewood and the lake, the autumnal foliage is as high-colored as a shawl. With Eustace at their head, the children scamper to Shadow Brook, gather nuts, have a picnic, and induce the story-teller to speak again. This time he tells of King Midas and his "Golden Touch." The children discuss Midas and wonder how much Marygold weighed when she was all gold. Then they gather more nuts. October gives way to November and then December. At Christmas time Eustace returns from college and, kept from skating by a wild snow-storm which delights the frolicsome children – about a half dozen now – gathers them into the Tanglewood play-room and tells them about Pandora and Epimetheus, when the world was new and all summery. The story is called "The Paradise of Children." The listeners are pleased, but Sweet Fern thinks that there could not be enough trouble in the whole world for a big box three feet long. Two days later the storm stops, and the area is blanketed with snow. The children go out and slide, dig a cave in a drift, and throw snowballs. Eustace wanders away from them and delights in the lonely loveliness of winter. That evening the children interrupt his writing, drag him to the fireside of Mr. and Mrs. Pringle, and listen to his story of "The Three Golden Apples." Mr. Pringle laughingly criticizes the story as Gothicized, whereupon Eustace defends his redaction on the grounds that the Greeks held no monopoly on fables, which are the common property of the world. In May, on spring vacation from college and sporting a moustache now, the young man takes the children part way up a hill. The day is sweet, and wild flowers are everywhere. When the smallest of his charges get tired climbing, he stops and tells them about "The Miraculous Pitcher." When asked, Eustace explains that the pitcher was broken about 25,000 years ago, is mended now, but is not the same any more. Leaving the younger children with their dog, he then takes the older ones to the top of the hill — Bald-Summit — points out the distant sights, and then tells them about Pegasus, the winged horse, in the story called "The Chimaera," which especially moves Primrose, who cries a little. Eustace says that if he had Pegasus now, he would fly over to visit some fellow authors, including Herman Melville and Holmes. When Primrose asks about another literary man [Nathaniel Hawthorne], who lives in a red house near Tanglewood Avenue, Eustace wants her not to bother him, because he could burn some papers and destroy her and all the other children here. As the party climbs down the hill, Eustace says that he intends to write out the stories and gain fame when they are published by J. T. Fields of Ticknor & Co. Primrose says that Eustace Bright is in for a disappointment.

[Hammatt] Billings, Blue Eye, Eustace Bright, Luther Butler, Buttercup, Clover, Cowslip, Dandelion, Dr. [Orville] Dewey, J[ames]. T. Fields, [Nathaniel Hawthorne], [Dr. Oliver Wendell] Holmes, Huckleberry, [George Payne Rainsford] James, [Henry Wadsworth] Longfellow, Herman Melville, Milkweed, Periwinkle, Plantain, Primrose Pringle, Pringle, Mrs. Pringle, Captain Smith, Squash-Blossom, Sweet Fern, [William Davis] Ticknor.

"Young Goodman Brown," 1835.

At sunset one night only three months after his marriage, Goodman Brown bids his pretty, pink-ribboned wife Faith good-night and, in spite of her protests but with her blessing, walks into the dark forest beyond Salem. He meets with a soberly clad personage who seems about fify years of age and who tells him that he once helped Brown's Quaker-lashing grandfather and his Indian-fighting father. When young Brown expresses reluctance to consort with the curious person and then to be seen by the town minister, the elder traveler bursts into wild laughter. Brown says that his wife Faith might be deeply hurt by all this, at which the other expresses sympathy. Then Brown spies pious Goody Cloyse, who taught him his catechism, in the wild woods and marvels at the sight. He takes a short cut to avoid her eye, and the other man touches Goody Cloyse with his wriggling staff and converses with her familiarly. She has heard that a nice young man will be taken into their dark community this night. Brown rejoins the stranger, soon refuses to go farther, but then sees his minister and Deacon Gookin riding by, talking also of the imminent meeting. A goodly young woman is to be inducted. The sky overhead is windless, but a black cloud sails by and the air is suddenly full of lamentations. Brown shouts for Faith but is greeted by laughter, and then down from above flutters a pink ribbon. Brown concludes that his Faith is gone, there is no good on earth, and sin is only a name. He seizes the absent stranger's discarded staff and rushes with fiendish speed through the dark wilderness toward a red glare. He hears a rolling hymn and sees a sylvan altar or pulpit luridly lighted by four blazing, candle-like pine trees. A congregation is assembled, including high dames, wives, widows, persons who are evidently members of Brown's Salem church, and spotted, vicious sinners. The winds roar, and the pines blaze higher. The figure of a grave New England divine appears and orders the converts to be brought forth. Is Brown beckoned forward by the figure of his dead father? Is he warned back by his mother? The evil communicants are welcomed by the somber leader and are told that they will soon know the secret deeds of church elders, women eager to be widows, patricidal youths, and infant-killing damsels. "Evil is the nature of mankind. Evil must be your only happiness." As Brown steps forward with Faith to a bloody baptismal basin, he urges her to look to heaven and resist. Instantly, he is alone in calmness, darkness, and dewy cold. The next morning Brown returns to the village, shrinks from the approaching minister, fears for a child being catechized by Goody Cloyse, and refuses to kiss his happy, pink-ribboned wife Faith. Did he fall asleep in the forest and only dream a wild dream of a witch-meeting? Think so if you wish. But it was a dream of evil omen for him. He becomes a desperate man hearing evil and blasphemy in church anthems and sermons. He scowls when his wife and children kneel in prayer. And later they carve no verse on his tomb, because his last hour was gloom.

> Mrs. Faith Brown, Goodman Brown, Brown, Brown, Mrs. Brown, Martha Carrier, Goody Cloyse, Goody Cory, the Devil, Deacon Gookin.

"The Young Provincial," 1830 (may not be by Hawthorne).[10]

The old man's children ask their father to tell them about the war. He does. The young provincial, a Minute Man, is called from his house one April night by a signal which means that the British are marching from Boston to capture military stores in Concord. He joins his group, and they move toward Lexington, see the enemy, and begin to fire. He weeps beside a mortally wounded British soldier. He fights later, however, at Bunker Hill, and is wounded, beaten, captured, and taken first to a prison in Boston and then to another one up in Halifax. After four weeks of digging at the masonry, he and some fellow-prisoners escape. Only he and one other elude recapture, by hiding in a swamp. They travel only in the dark and after seven nights encounter a kind old Canadian farmer, who feeds them, lets them rest, and then puts them aboard a whaleboat to Falmouth, from which the

---

[10]See Blanck, *Bibliography of American Literature,* IV, 1.

young provincial returns home, like one emerging from the grave, to the ecstatic delight of his family.

(No named characters.)

CHARACTERS

Abbott, Eliakim. "Passages from a Relinquished Work." A timid leader of religious meetings who accompanies the story-telling narrator.

Achilles. "The Golden Fleece." Mentioned as a pupil of Chiron the centaur.

Adam. "The New Adam and Eve." A new Adam who wanders with Eve through Boston after the destruction of mankind.

Adams, Anna. "Old News." A woman who sells clothes in Boston (about 1760).

Adams, John. "A Book of Autographs." The author of several letters in the collection.

Adams, Samuel. "A Book of Autographs." The author of a fragment of a letter in the collection.

Aeetes, King. "Circe's Palace." Mentioned as wicked Circe's brother. "The Golden Fleece." The cruel king of Colchis, from whom, and with the help of whose daughter Medea, Jason takes the Golden Fleece.

Aegeus, King. "The Minotaur." The King of Attica and father of Theseus; he lives in Athens with wicked Queen Medea.

Aeolus. "Circe's Palace." Mentioned as the ruler of the winds which troubled Ulysses.

Aesculapius. "The Golden Fleece." Mentioned as a physician who was once a pupil of Chiron the centaur.

Aeson, King. "The Golden Fleece." Mentioned as the dethroned King of Iolchos and father of Jason.

Aethra. "The Minotaur." The kind mother of Theseus.

Agenor, King. "The Dragon's Teeth." The King of Phoenicia who orders his sons, Cadmus, Phoenix, and Cilix, to search for

lost Europa and not return home until they find her; his
wife Queen Telephassa accompanies them and dies during
the unsuccessful search.

Ainsworth, Mrs. *Dr. Grimshawe's Secret,* Preliminary Studies.
Mentioned in connection with the bloody footstep.

Alcott, [Bronson]. "The Custom House." Mentioned as a friend
of the author.

Alicampion, Miss. *Dr. Grimshawe's Secret,* First Draft. A name
by which Warden Brathwaite addresses Elsie (which see).

Alice. *The Whole History of Grandfather's Chair.* The little
five-year-old girl who sits in Grandfather's lap, delights in
his stories, but often falls asleep.

Allston, Washington. "A Book of Autographs." The author of a
brief letter in the collection.

Amherst, Sir Jeffrey. "Old News." A military leader who advertises in the Boston newspapers (about 1760) for
batteaux-men to be employed on the lakes.

Aminadab. "The Birthmark." The scientist Aylmer's earthy laboratory assistant who admires Georgiana but laughs when
she dies.

Andros, Sir Edmund. "Dr. Bullivant." The Governor-General of
New England and New York during the rule of King
James II but a prisoner before the monarch's abdication.
"The Gray Champion." The hated Governor of Massachu-
setts under King James II and a hated soldier whose loss of
power the Gray Champion predicts in April, 1689. "Howe's
Masquerade." The royal tyrant whose shade appears in the
mysterious pageant at Sir William Howe's fancy-dress ball.

Angelo, Father. *Dr. Grimshawe's Secret,* First Draft. The highly
cultivated personal priest of the Italianate Brathwaite of
Brathwaite Hall. (Also called Father Antonio.)

Annie. "Little Annie's Ramble." A sweet little five-year-old girl
with whom the narrator has a refreshing walk through the
streets and into the circus.

Antaeus. "The Three Golden Apples." The giant whom Hercules

defeats by holding him up from the earth, which is the source of his strength. "The Pygmies." The pygmies' big brother whom Hercules kills.

Antonio, Brother (Father). *The Marble Faun.* The spectral figure whose mysterious and unexplained past relationship to Miriam Schaefer causes him to do penance as a Capuchin monk but also to continue shadowing her as her model; at a signal from Miriam, Donatello flings him from the Tarpeian Rock to his death. (Also called the Spectre of the Catacomb, the Shadow, and the Demon.)

Antonio, Father. *Dr. Grimshawe's Secret,* First Draft. See Father Angelo.

Apollyon. "The Celestial Railroad." John Bunyan's character who is now the engineer of the Celestial Railroad.

Arabella, Lady. "Main Street." A pale lady who seeks her grave in virgin soil near Naumkeag.

Archdale. *Dr. Grimshawe's Secret,* First Draft. The treacherously treated lover of the Brathwaite girl; he left the country and is thought by Warden Brathwaite to be Dr. Etherege (which see).

Argus. "The Golden Fleece." The skillful ship-builder of Iolchos who builds the Argo for Jason.

Ariadne. "The Minotaur." The beautiful, tender-hearted daughter of King Minos of Crete; she helps Theseus get into the labyrinth to kill the Minotaur and then helps him escape.

Arnold, [General Benedict]. "A Book of Autographs." The author of a note in the collection. *Septimius Felton.* The American Revolutionary War leader whose campaign against Quebec Robert Hagburn joins.

Atalanta. "The Golden Fleece." A beautiful, fierce mountain-woman who becomes an Argonaut.

Atlas. "The Three Golden Apples." The giant who gives Hercules the sky to hold while he goes to the garden of the Hesperides for the three golden apples.

Aylmer. "The Birthmark." The perfectionist scientist who sacrifices his beautiful wife in an experiment to remove her birthmark and thus make her perfect in appearance.

Babcock, Jonathan. "The Bald Eagle." A member of the militia of the Connecticut Valley village which Lafayette does not visit.

Bacon, Friar. *Septimius Felton.* Reputed to be a friend of Septimius Felton's learned ancestor who wrote the recipe for the elixir of life.

Bacon. *The Scarlet Letter.* An English lawyer mentioned as a former associate of Governor Bellingham.

Baglioni, Professor Pietro. "Rappaccini's Daughter." Dr. Giacomo Rappaccini's academic rival and Giovanni Guasconti's family friend; he mixes the "antidote" which kills Beatrice Rappaccini.

Balch. "Main Street." An early neighbor of Jeffrey Massey of Naumkeag.

Barberini, Prince. *The Marble Faun.* The owner of Guido Reni's "Beatrice Cenci" who forbids all copying of it.

Barboni, Luca. *The Marble Faun.* The mysterious recipient of the packet of letters which Miriam Schaefer entrusts to Hilda for delivery; he lives in the Palazzo Cenci.

Barlow, Joel. "P.'s Correspondence." An American epic-writer thought by P. to be about a hundred years old.

Bartlett. "The Village Uncle." The owner of the store in which Uncle Parker spins his yarns.

Bartram. "Ethan Brand." The sluggish lime-burner who replaced Ethan Brand when the latter went in search of the unpardonable sin.

Bates, Judge. "The Haunted Quack." A judge in the region from which Hippocrates Jenkins, mistakenly thinking that he was wanted for murder, escaped temporarily.

Battleblast, Rev. Mr. "The Great Stone Face." The minister whose loud prayer precedes the sylvan banquet held in Old Blood-and-Thunder's honor.

Baucis. "The Miraculous Pitcher." The hospitable old wife of

Philemon; she turns into a linden tree after her death.

Bayard, [James]. "A Book of Autographs." The recipient with Leroy of a letter from Jefferson in the collection.

Beautiful Woman, A. "A Select Party." A beautiful woman without pride or coquetry who is a fanciful guest.

Beautineau, Deacon. "Old News." A man who lives near Alice Quick.

Beauty of the Golden Locks, The. *Dr. Grimshawe's Secret,* First Draft. The legendary maiden whose corpse turned into golden hair in her coffin. (See also Evelyn, Miss Brathwaite, and Dr. Etherege.)

Beelzebub, Prince. "The Celestial Railroad." The devil who has ceased shooting at pilgrims toiling toward heaven but whose subjects are now employed at the station-house of the Celestial Railroad.

Belcher, [Jonathan]. "Old News." The Massachusetts Governor who is reported as having made a proclamation against dissolute people in the Boston area. "The Minister's Black Veil." The Governor for whom the Rev. Mr. Hooper delivers an impressive, conservative election sermon. "Howe's Masquerade." The Rev. Mr. Mather Byles's patron whose shade appears in the mysterious pageant at Sir William Howe's fancy-dress ball.

Bellamont, The Earl of. "Howe's Masquerade." A gracious Governor of Massachusetts during the time of King William; his shade appears in the mysterious pageant at Sir William Howe's fancy-dress ball.

Bellerophon. "The Chimaera." The hero who with the help of Pegasus, the winged horse, destroys the malevolent Chimaera.

Bellingham, [Richard]. "Howe's Masquerade." An anti-royalist in the mysterious pageant at Sir William Howe's fancy-dress ball. *The Scarlet Letter.* A lawyer, soldier, and statesman, and then Governor of the Massachusetts colony at the beginning of the novel; when he tries to take Pearl away from Hester Prynne, the Rev. Mr. Arthur Dimmesdale pleads eloquently for the unhappy mother; the Governor's sister, Mistress Hibbins, is later executed as a witch.

Bernard, Sir Francis. "Old News." The Massachuestts Governor who is met between Dedham and Boston by a multitude of coaches and chariots (about 1760). "Howe's Masquerade." A former Massachusetts Governor whose shade appears in the mysterious pageant at Sir William Howe's fancy-dress ball.

Bertram. "The Custom House." A former Salem merchant.

Bewilderment, Rev. Mr. "The Celestial Railroad." An easy preacher in Vanity Fair.

Billings, [Hammatt]. *A Wonder-Book for Girls and Boys*. Mentioned by Eustace Bright as a possible illustrator for his book.

Black Man, The. *The Scarlet Letter*. The head of the company of merry sinners who, according to Mistress Hibbins, meet in the forest at night; Pearl at one point equates him with Roger Chillingworth. "The Dolliver Romance." Reputed to be the leading professor in the apothecaries' medical school. *Septimius Felton*. According to Aunt Keziah, the grand leader of the wizards in the forest; he once tempted her unsuccessfully, she boasts.

Blackstone, Rev. Mr. [William]. "The May-Pole of Merry Mount." Rumored to be the "Priest of Baal" at the Merry Mount wedding of Edgar and Edith. *The Scarlet Letter*. Mentioned as an almost mythologically early settler in the Boston area.

Blagden, Miss [Isa]. *Dr. Grimshawe's Secret*, First Draft. A name inexplicably mentioned in one of Hawthorne's notes to himself.

Blathwaite, Dr. *Dr. Grimshawe's Secret*, First Draft. See Warden Brathwaite.

Blood-and-Thunder, General. "The Great Stone Face." See Old Blood-and-Thunder.

Blue Eye. *A Wonder-Book for Girls and Boys.* One of Eustace
Bright's older auditors. *Tanglewood Tales, for Girls and
Boys.* Mentioned as having had scarlet fever.

Boaz. "The Bald Eagle." A Negro inhabitant of the Connecticut
Valley village which Lafayette does not visit; he is
supposed to signal the Marquis's approach along the
highroad.

Bonaparte, Napoleon. "P.'s Correspondence." A nervous old
ex-emperor now walked by two policemen in Pall Mall.

Bourne, Cyrus. "Roger Malvin's Burial." The fifteen-year-old son
of Reuben Bourne; Reuben accidentally kills the boy
beneath the rock at which Reuben left Roger Malvin to die.

Bourne, Mrs. Dorcas Malvin. "Roger Malvin's Burial." The daughter of fatally wounded Roger Malvin; believing that
Reuben Bourne is a hero, she marries him and gives him a
son, Cyrus.

Bourne, Reuben. "Roger Malvin's Burial." The wounded Indian
fighter who abandons fatally wounded Roger Malvin, father
of his fiancee Dorcas; by failing to tell the truth, Reuben
creates a situation in which he seems to himself to be more
sinful than he really was; later he accidentally kills his son
Cyrus as a kind of unconscious sacrificial act.

Brackett. *The Scarlet Letter.* Hester Prynne's jailer.

Bradstreet, Colonel [John]. "A Bell's Biography." An officer
during the Old French War; his scouts find the bell beside
the skeleton of Deacon Lawson.

Bradstreet, [Simon]. "The Gray Champion." The old former
Governor of Massachusetts who councils patience and is
later seen to embrace the Gray Champion. "Howe's
Masquerade." The last of the Puritans, whose shade
appears in the mysterious pageant at Sir William Howe's
fancy-dress ball. "Main Street." The ninety-four-year-old
former Governor whose funeral takes place on Main
Street. *The Scarlet Letter.* Mentioned as a Massachusetts
Governor. "The Dolliver Romance." The patriarchal
Governor who once blessed Dr. Dolliver long ago.

Bradstreet, Mrs. "Main Street." The Naumkeag widow of Captain Gardner who marries Governor Bradstreet.

Brand, Ethan. "Ethan Brand." The simple, loving lime-burner who left his home in search of the unpardonable sin, only to find it in his own heart.

Brathwaite, Sir Edward. *Dr. Grimshawe's Secret*, First Draft. The victim of Dr. Etherege, who mysteriously paralyzed him by poison and somehow had a hand in rendering him a lifelong prisoner in a secret chamber of Brathwaite Hall; he may have violated the doctor's wife somehow; Edward Etherege is imprisoned briefly with him.

Brathwaite, Sir Humphrey. *Dr. Grimshawe's Secret*, First Draft. Named as the ancient founder of Brathwaite Hospital for pensioners. (Also spelled Brathwayte.)

Brathwaite, Lord. *Dr. Grimshawe's Secret*, First Draft. The dark, Italianate, Catholic resident of Brathwaite Hall and claimant to the title Lord Hinchbrooke; he has a mysterious past, attends Warden Brathwaite's banquet for Edward Etherege, invites the American to his manor-house, and poisons and tries to imprison him there.

Brathwaite. *Dr. Grimshawe's Secret*, First Draft. One of the Italianate Brathwaite's forefathers; he emigrated to the Continent with King James (II).

Brathwaite. *Dr. Grimshawe's Secret*, First Draft. The son of Brathwaite of Brathwaite Hall; he is now at a Catholic college in America.

Brathwaite, Miss. *Dr. Grimshawe's Secret*, First Draft. The beloved of Archdale; their match was broken by the treacherous Brathwaite family; she is perhaps Evelyn (which see).

Brathwaite, Miss. *Dr. Grimshawe's Secret*, First Draft. The daughter of Brathwaite of Brathwaite Hall; she is now in a Catholic convent in America.

Brathwaite, Warden. *Dr. Grimshawe's Secret*, First Draft. The physician warden of Brathwaite Hospital, for pensioners;

he befriends and finally helps to save Edward Etherege. (Also called Dr. Blathwaite, the Master, Dr. Oglethorpe, and Dr. Gibb[le]ler [all of which see].)

Brathwayte, Sir Humphrey. *Dr. Grimshawe's Secret,* First Draft. See Sir Humphrey Brathwaite.

Bright, Eustace. *A Wonder-Book for Girls and Boys. Tanglewood Tales, for Girls and Boys.* An eighteen-year-old Williams College student who during his vacations tells the children at Tanglewood various stories; he aspires to literary fame.

Brome, Walter. "Alice Doane's Appeal." An unfortunate victim, who is inspired by a wizard to tempt his unknown sister Alice Doane and who is then murdered by his twin-brother Leonard Doane.

Brown, [Charles] Brockden. "P.'s Correspondence." An American writer praised by P.

Brown, Mrs. Faith. "Young Goodman Brown." The pretty, pink-ribboned wife of Goodman Brown; he sees or imagines that he sees her at the witch-meeting.

Brown, John. "Peter Goldthwaite's Treasure." The rich former partner of Peter Goldthwaite who kindly purchases the Goldthwaite mansion at last.

Brown, Zechariah. "The Old Manse." Mentioned as a native of Concord who helped bury two British soldiers killed at the Revolutionary War battle there.

Brown, Goodman. "Young Goodman Brown." The young Salem husband who leaves his wife Faith and attends a disillusioning witch-meeting in the forest.

Brown. "Young Goodman Brown." Goodman Brown's grandfather, who, according to the devil figure, was a Quaker-lasher.

Brown. "Young Goodman Brown." Goodman Brown's father, who, according to the devil figure, was an Indian-fighter in King Philip's War; Goodman Brown sees or imagines that he sees his father at the witch-meeting.

Brown, Mrs. "Young Goodman Brown." Goodman Brown's

mother, whom Goodman Brown sees or imagines that he sees the witch-meeting.

Browne. " 'Browne's Folly.' " A royalist who built a foolishly magnificent pleasure-house on a hill near Salem and then fled to England during the Revolutionary War.

Bryant, [William Cullen]. "The Antique Ring." An American anthologist who praises Edward Caryl. "P.'s Correspondence." An American poet thought dead by P.

Buchanan, President [James]. *Dr. Grimshawe's Secret,* First Draft. A name inexplicably mentioned in one of Hawthorne's notes to himself.

Buffum, Joshua. "Main Street." A Quaker prisoner in Salem.

Bulfinch, Captain. "Old News." A seller of Negro servants in Boston.

Bullfrog, Mrs. Laura. "Mrs. Bullfrog." Thomas Bullfrog's bald and toothless wife who has five thousand dollars from a breach of promise suit.

Bullfrog, Thomas. "Mrs. Bullfrog." The effeminate little drygoods man who overlooks his bald and toothless wife's defects for her money.

Bullivant, Dr. " 'Pothecary." "Dr. Bullivant." A humor-loving apothecary, temporarily in favor during Governor-General Sir Edmund Andros's tenure but then imprisoned briefly just before calm is restored by William and Mary. "The Gray Champion." Sir Edmund Andros's mocking, cavalier associate.

Burgoyne, [General John]. "A Book of Autographs." Mentioned in a letter by John Adams in the collection.

Burnet, [William]. "Howe's Masquerade." A learned, fever-stricken Governor of Massachusetts whose shade appears in the mysterious pageant at Sir William Howe's fancy-dress ball.

Burns, Robert. "P.'s Correspondence." The eighty-seven-year-old Ayrshire poet, now a white-haired and crickety patriarch, according to P.

Burr, Aaron. "The Christmas Banquet." A banquet guest at the time when his ruin and loneliness are complete. "A Book of Autographs." The author of a letter in the collection. *Dr. Grimshawe's Secret,* Preliminary Studies. A treasonous friend of the old doctor's swindling brother.

Burroughs, Rev. Mr. George. "Main Street." A holy, learned man of Salem, condemned to hang for supposedly being tempted by Satan; he counsels Martha Carrier, a condemned witch.

Burroughs, Martha. "Fancy's Show Box." The girl whom Smith in imagination ruined; she married David Tomkins.

Butler, Luther. *A Wonder-Book for Girls and Boys.* A neighbor of the Pringles living near Tanglewood.

Butler. *Fanshawe.* The dead father of the villainous Butler; his harshness is partly responsible for the son's later viciousness.

Butler, Mrs. "Sister Butler." *Fanshawe.* The demented mother of the villainous Butler; she dies just as her son returns to her cottage.

Butler. *Fanshawe.* The thirty-year-old villainous son of Mrs. Butler, who was befriended by John Langton, turned evil and associated at sea with Hugh Crombie, returned to the Harley College region, and abducted Ellen Langton to ruin her and take her fortune; while climbing a cliff to kill Fanshawe, he falls to his death.

Buttercup. *A Wonder-Book for Girls and Boys.* One of Eustace Bright's older auditors. *Tanglewood Tales, for Girls and Boys.* Mentioned as having had scarlet fever.

Byles, Rev. Mr. Mather. "Howe's Masquerade." A somewhat fun-loving Presbyterian friend and guest of Sir William Howe.

Byron, Lady. "P.'s Correspondence." Lord Byron's wife; the two are reconciled, according to P.

Byron, Lord. "P.'s Correspondence." P.'s friend, aged sixty years, fat, gouty, and conservative.

Cacaphodel, Dr. "The Great Carbuncle." The scientist who seeks the carbuncle for chemical analysis; he has to content himself with a piece of mountain granite.

Cadmus. "The Dragon's Teeth." The son of King Agenor and Queen Telephassa, and lost Europa's most faithful brother; he consults the oracle at Delphi, abandons the search for his sister, marries Harmonia, and founds a kingdom. "The Golden Fleece." Mentioned as an earlier sower of dragon's teeth.

Caesar. "The Bald Eagle." A Negro hostler employed by Jonathan Dewlap, proprietor of the Bald Eagle.

Caesar. "Old News." An escaped Negro slave in Boston.

Caesar. "The White Old Maid." The ghostly Negro servant in the house containing the corpse of the young man.

Caine, Mrs. Henrietta Maria. "Old News." A Boston milliner (about 1760).

Calcraft, [William]. *Dr. Grimshawe's Secret,* First Draft. The famous British executioner, under whom the Italianate Brathwaite may have served as an apprentice.

Calhoun, [John]. "A Book of Autographs." The author of a fragmentary letter in the collection.

Campbell, [Thomas]. "P.'s Correspondence." An old poet thought by P. to be planning a trip to Wyoming.

Caner, Dr. "Old News." The old Tory's High-Church authority.

Canning, [George]. "P.'s Correspondence." A peer whom P. says he heard speak in the House of Lords in 1845.

Cario, Michael. "Old News." A jeweler in Boston.

Carrier, Martha. "Young Goodman Brown." A sinner evidently promised the throne of hell. "Main Street." A Salem witch, thought to be the queen of hell; she cursed Mercy Parris.

Carrier, The. "Time's Portraiture." The newspaper carrier who addresses his patrons on the subject of time in the hope of a tip.

Carvill, Josias. "A Book of Autographs." Mentioned as a Maryland volunteer in a letter by John Adams in the collection.

Cary, Mother. "A Select Party." A fanciful guest who deserted her chickens to attend the Man of Fancy's party.

Caryl, Edward. "The Antique Ring." Clara Pemberton's fiance, a New England lawyer and writer, who reads her his legend of the diamond ring which he has given her.

Castor. "The Golden Fleece." A brave Argonaut, Pollux's twin brother.

Catharine. "The Gentle Boy." The Quaker mother who neglects her gentle son Ilbrahim to pursue her fanatical religion.

Celeus, King. "The Pomegranate Seeds." The King of Eleusis, whose son Demophoon is nursed back to health by Mother Ceres.

Ceres, Mother. "The Pomegranate Seeds." Proserpina's mother, who has charge of all crops.

Channing, [Dr. William] Ellery. "The Old Manse." Mentioned as a friend who goes boating with Hawthorne on the Concord and Assabeth rivers. "The Custom House." Mentioned as a speculative camping companion along the Assabeth River. "P.'s Correspondence." A poet admired by P.

Charity, Miss. "The Celestial Railroad." Now a dry old maid.

Charles I, King. *Dr. Grimshawe's Secret*, First Draft. The English king possibly beheaded by the blood-tracking Brathwaite. *Dr. Grimshawe's Secret*, Second Draft. The beheaded English king in whose blood Thomas Colcord is supposed to have stepped.

Charley. *The Whole History of Grandfather's Chair*. The tough little nine-year-old boy who delights in Grandfather's stories.

Chatsworth. *Dr. Grimshawe's Secret*, Preliminary Studies. Mentioned as the name of the American whose ancestor emigrated to America two hundred years earlier. (See Edward Etherege and Edward Redclyffe.)

Cheltenham, Miss. *Dr. Grimshawe's Secret,* First Draft. A name once used by Warden Brathwaite to address the daughter of the pensioner Pearson. (See Elsie.)

Chickering, Goody. *Septimius Felton.* Evidently a witch, known by Aunt Keziah.

Chief Marshal, The. "The Procession of Life." The leader of the procession; he is Death and deserts us short of our ultimate goal.

Child Unborn, The. "A Select Party." A frolicking, fanciful guest.

Chillingworth, Roger. *The Scarlet Letter.* The wronged husband of Hester Prynne, who through his sinful desire for revenge transforms himself into a crooked old fiend; the real name of this cold, scholarly physician is Prynne.

Chiron. "The Golden Fleece." The good and wise centaur tutor of Jason and many other heroes.

Cilix. "The Dragon's Teeth." Lost Europa's brother who abandons the search for her.

Circe. "Circe's Palace." The beautiful but wicked enchantress who turns twenty-two of Ulysses's gluttonous men into swine but whom Ulysses forces to undo her mischief. "The Golden Fleece." Mentioned as the sister of King Aeetes of Colchis and aunt and instructress of the enchantress Medea.

Clara. *The Whole History of Grandfather's Chair.* The mild ten-year-old child who delights in Grandfather's stories; she is Laurence's cousin.

Clark, Rev. Mr. "The Minister's Black Veil." A young minister from Westbury who attempts to administer to the veiled Rev. Mr. Hooper on his deathbed.

Clarke, Rev. Mr. Peter. "Old News." Reported as in a controversy in Boston on baptism.

Clarke, Dr. "Lady Eleanore's Mantle." The physician and champion of the popular party who first notices that Lady Eleanore is stricken with smallpox.

Clay, Henry. "A Book of Autographs." The author of a letter in the collection.

Clerk of the Weather, The. "A Select Party." One of the Man of Fancy's guests.

Clerk of the Weather, The. "A Visit to the Clerk of the Weather." The giant whose cave the narrator visits.

Clinton, [George]. "A Book of Autographs." Mentioned in a letter by John Adams in the collection.

Clog-the-spirit, Rev. Mr. "The Celestial Railroad." An easy preacher in Vanity Fair.

Clover. *A Wonder-Book for Girls and Boys.* One of Eustace Bright's older auditors. *Tanglewood Tales, for Girls and Boys.* Mentioned as having been troubled with her second teeth.

Cloyse, Goody. "Young Goodman Brown." Goodman Brown's catechism teacher in his youth; she evidently attends the witch-meeting, to his dismay.

Cobbett, [William]. "P.'s Correspondence." A clod-hopper whom P. says he heard speak in the House of Commons in 1845.

Coke. *The Scarlet Letter.* An English lawyer mentioned as a former associate of Governor Bellingham.

Colburn, Adam. "The Shaker Bridal." The calmly desperate middle-aged farmer lover of Martha Pierson; now he wants only to be her Shaker brother and with her to lead the Shakers at Goshen.

Colcord, Seymour. *Dr. Grimshawe's Secret,* Second Draft. A thin, mild schoolteacher who is descended from the Quaker Thomas Colcord; he is injured by a mob which is fighting Dr. Grimshawe; the doctor aids him, and he briefly tutors Edward Redclyffe and Elsie; later he turns up as a pensioner in the hospital in England and befriends Edward Redclyffe.

Colcord, Thomas. *Dr. Grimshawe's Secret,* Second Draft. The Quaker ancestor of Seymour Colcord; he was driven out of England, changed his name in New England to Thomas Colcord, and died in 1687; at his gravesite Edward Redclyffe finds a silver key.

Colcord. *Dr. Grimshawe's Secret,* First Draft. Named as the person in quest of whom Mountford has come to America.

Coleman, Ann. "Main Street." A Quaker prisoner in Salem punished by exposure, whipping, and forest exile.

Coleridge, [Samuel Taylor]. "P.'s Correspondence." An untalkative poet who, says P., has just finished "Christabel."

Colman, Rev. Dr. "Old News." Reported as trying to raise funds in Boston to support missionaries to the Indians; he is also a sermon writer.

Conant, Roger. "Main Street." The first settler in Naumkeag.

Conant, Mrs. "Main Street." The wife of Roger Conant, first settler in Naumkeag.

Conscience. "Fancy's Show Box." The power which stabs Smith when Fancy shows him sins he has only imagined.

Copley, [John Singleton]. "Drowne's Wooden Image." The famous Boston painter who admires the uniquely fine artistry of Drowne's wooden image.

Copley. "The Ancestral Footstep." The name of the family living in the neighborhood of Eldredge's estate.

Cory, Goody. "Young Goodman Brown." A witch accused by Goody Cloyse of stealing her broomstick.

Count of Monte Beni, The. *The Marble Faun.* See Donatello.

Coverdale, Miles. *The Blithedale Romance.* An inquisitive, intelligent, self-effacing observer of his fellow Blithedale Arcadians; he is in his late twenties at the outset, is a poet, despises Hollingsworth's evil single-mindedness, offers to help Zenobia, and is secretly and uselessly in love with Priscilla.

Cowslip. *A Wonder-Book for Girls and Boys.* A fun-loving, six-year-old child, one of Eustace Bright's younger auditors. *Tanglewood Tales, for Girls and Boys.* Mentioned as having had the measles or something like them.

Crambo. *Dr. Grimshawe's Secret,* First Draft. A name inexplicably mentioned in one of Hawthorne's notes to himself.

Cranfield, Ralph. "The Threefold Destiny." The tall, dark, courteous wanderer who finally finds his destined work, wealth, and joy near home.

Cranfield, Mrs. "The Threefold Destiny." The wanderer Ralph Cranfield's patient mother, in whose land her son finally finds wealth by tilling it.

Crawford, Ethan. "Sketches from Memory." The huge mountaineer landlord at the Notch in the White Mountains.

Crawford, [Thomas]. *The Marble Faun.* A sculptor ridiculed by Miriam Schaefer.

Crawford. "Sketches from Memory." The vigorous old father, aged seventy-five years, of Ethan Crawford, landlord at the Notch in the White Mountains.

Crombie, Hugh. *Fanshawe.* A semi-reformed sailor who at about forty years of age is the landlord of a disreputable tavern near Harley College; he reluctantly aids Butler in his scheme to abduct Ellen Langton.

Crombie, Mrs. Sarah. *Fanshawe.* The fifty-year-old widow of Hutchins; her having a tavern was an inducement for Hugh Crombie to marry her.

Crombie. *Fanshawe.* Hugh Crombie's father, whom the son supported loyally until his death.

Crusty Hannah. *Dr. Grimshawe's Secret,* Second Draft. See Hannah, Crusty.

Cunkey. *Dr. Grimshawe's Secret,* First Draft. A name inexplicably mentioned in one of Hawthorne's notes to himself.

Cunningham, Allan. "P.'s Correspondence." A friend of Robert Burns who urged the poet to sing his song to Mary in heaven.

Curwen [Corwin], Captain [George]. "Main Street." The sheriff of Essex who escorts condemned witches to Gallows Hill.

Cynic, The. "The Great Carbuncle." The cynical man who hopes not to find the carbuncle but is blinded by it.

Cyzicus, King. "The Golden Fleece." A monarch whose land is plagued by six-armed giants, some of whom the Argonauts kill.

Dabney, Colonel. "The Dolliver Romance." The choleric old man who visits Dr. Dolliver's shop, speaks of a bloody footstep plaguing his family, demands the rejuvenating cordial by pointing a pistol at Dr. Dolliver, drinks from it, and drops dead.

Dabney, Mrs. "The Wedding Knell." The worldly, twice-widowed bride of Ellenwood.

Dacy, Sibyl. *Septimius Felton.* The eighteen-year-old niece of Dr. Jabez Portsoaken; when Septimius Felton kills her fiance Cyril Norton, she leaves Boston, goes to Concord, plans to poison Septimius, but instead falls in love with him and drinks the poisonous elixir herself.

Daedalus. "The Minotaur." Mentioned as the deviser of the intricate labyrinth in which Theseus locates and kills the Minotaur.

Daffydowndilly, Little. "Little Daffydowndilly." The little boy who runs away from Mr. Toil's school, encounters Mr. Toil's brothers everywhere, returns to school, and learns to appreciate diligence.

Danae. "The Gorgon's Head." The mother of the hero Perseus.

Dandelion. *A Wonder-Book for Girls and Boys.* One of Eustace Bright's littlest auditors. *Tanglewood Tales, for Girls and Boys.* Mentioned as having had the whooping-cough.

Danforth, Annie Hovenden. "The Artist of the Beautiful." The somewhat insensitive daughter of sneering old Peter Hovenden; Owen Warland loves her vainly, since she marries the muscular blacksmith Robert Danforth.

Danforth, Robert. "The Artist of the Beautiful." The blacksmith whose practical muscularity Annie Hovenden prefers to Owen Warland's delicacy and idealism.

Danforth. "The Artist of the Beautiful." The stolid, lumpish infant son of Robert and Annie Danforth who destroys Owen Warland's mechanical butterfly.

Davenport, Miss. *The House of the Seven Gables.* See Mrs. Pyncheon.

David. "An Old Woman's Tale." The young man who shares an identical dream with Esther, digs where the old woman dug in the dream, and finds something.

Davidson, Margaret. "A Book of Autographs." The author of a letter in the collection.

Davies. "A Book of Autographs." Mentioned in Hamilton's letter in the collection.

Davis, Thomas. "The Old Manse." Mentioned as a native of Concord who helped bury two British soldiers killed at the Revolutionary War battle there.

Davy Jones. "A Select Party." A fanciful guest.

D[awson]., William. *Dr. Grinshawe's Secret,* Preliminary Studies. Mentioned in connection with grave clothes.

Death. "The Procession of Life." See the Chief Marshal.

Delphi, The Oracle of. "The Dragon's Teeth." The famous Oracle who windily advises Cadmus to abandon the search for his sister Europa and to make his home where the cow lies down.

Demon, The. *The Marble Faun.* See Brother Antonio.

Demophoon, Prince. "The Pomegranate Seeds." The sickly son of King Celeus and Queen Metanira of Eleusis, whom Mother Ceres cures by bathing him and then putting him into a bed of red-hot coals.

Denton, Martha. *Septimius Felton.* A dead witch whom Aunt Keziah says she would like to see.

Deputy Collector. "The Custom House." A customs officer.

Derby, King. "The Custom House." A former Salem merchant.

Derby, Richard. " 'Browne's Folly.' " An in-law of Browne who took care of Browne's foolish house during the Revolutionary War.

Devil, The. "Young Goodman Brown." Meets with Goodman
Brown in the forest and entices him to the witch-meeting
there.

Devonshire, The Duke of. *The House of the Seven Gables.* The
owner of Chatsworth, where a portrait of Alice Pyncheon
by a Venetian artist is preserved.

Dewey, Dr. [Orville]. *A Wonder-Book for Girls and Boys.*
Mentioned by Eustace Bright as one of his literary
neighbors, near Taconic.

Dewlap, Jonathan. "The Bald Eagle." The proprietor of the Bald
Eagle, a tavern in the Connecticut Valley which Lafayette
does not visit.

Dewlap, Mrs. Jonathan. "The Bald Eagle." The landlady and wife
of the proprietor of the Bald Eagle, a tavern in the
Connecticut Valley which Lafayette does not visit.

Dickens, [Charles]. "P.'s Correspondence." A promising author
who died young, according to P.

Dickon. "Feathertop." An invisible and apparently impish helper
of Mother Rigby the witch.

Dickson. "The Haunted Quack." A lawyer of the region from
which Hippocrates Jenkins, mistakenly thinking that he
was wanted for murder, escaped temporarily.

Digby, Sir Kenelm. *The Scarlet Letter.* Mentioned as a famous
scientist known by Roger Chillingworth.

Digby, Richard. "The Man of Adamant." The stony-hearted man
who spurns the rest of mankind, including Mary Goffe,
and turns to stone in his hidden sepulchral cave.

Dighton. "Howe's Masquerade." The drum-major who is not
responsible for the funeral music at Sir William Howe's
fancy-dress ball.

Dimmesdale, Rev. Mr. Arthur. *The Scarlet Letter.* The brilliantly
intellectual, sensitive minister of Boston, the former secret
lover of Hester Prynne, and the father of her daughter
Pearl; because of secret remorse and the subtle psychological torture of Roger Chillingworth, he confesses and
then dies.

Diocletian, Emperor. *The Marble Faun.* The early anti-Christian ruler of Rome under whose orders Memmius penetrated St. Calixtus's catacomb.

Dipper. "Old News." A Boston concert singer and performer on musical instruments (about 1760).

Dixey. *The House of the Seven Gables.* A laborer who periodically comments on the unlikelihood of Hepzibah Pyncheon's success in her cent-shop.

Doane, Alice. "Alice Doane's Appeal." The innocent sister of Leonard Doane, who erroneously believes that Walter Brome has violated her honor.

Doane, Leonard. "Alice Doane's Appeal." Unknowingly the twin-brother of Walter Brome, killed by Doane in the erroneous belief that Brome has violated Doane's sister Alice Doane's honor.

Dobbin. *Dr. Grinshawe's Secret,* First Draft. The name of a family living near Brathwaite Hall.

Doe, Joel. "A Select Party." A fanciful guest.

Dolliver, Bessie. "The Dolliver Romance." Dr. Dolliver's wife, deceased these fifty years and buried in a graveyard adjacent to the doctor's home.

Dolliver, Edward. "The Dolliver Romance." The dead grandson of Dr. Dolliver and father of Pansie; he was the brilliant scientist who deciphered the manuscript left to Dr. Dolliver by Dr. John Swinnerton.

Dolliver, Mrs. Edward. "The Dolliver Romance." The young wife of the brilliant scientist who mixes the cordial; she is Pansie's mother and dies shortly after her husband.

Dolliver, Pansie. "The Dolliver Romance." The charming three-year-old great-granddaughter of Dr. Dolliver, who wishes to stay alive only to support her.

Dolliver, Dr. "Grandsir." "The Dolliver Romance." The eighty-five-year-old apothecary and former pupil of diabolically learned Dr. John Swinnerton and inheritor from him of a mysterious manuscript concerning a rejuvenating elixir; he is tempted to use this elixir, perfected by his brilliant scientist grandson Edward Dolliver, to stay alive to support his great-granddaughter Pansie Dolliver.

Dolly. *Fanshawe.* One of the two chambermaids at Harley College; she is short, gray-haired, round-faced, and gossipy.

Donatello, The Count of Monte Beni. *The Marble Faun.* The twenty-year-old count whose family goes back to pre-Etrurian Tuscany; his fresh, primitive nature makes him resemble the marble faun of Praxiteles; his murder of the spectral monk, Brother Antonio, at a signal from Miriam Schaefer, is responsible for his transformation to suffering but also to mature moral choice; at the end, he is imprisoned.

Dora. "The Snow-Image." The maid of the Lindseys, ordered to clean up the melted snow at the end of the miracle.

Dove, The. *The Marble Faun.* See Hilda.

Downing, Emanuel. "Main Street." A grave and worthy inhabitant of Main Street.

Downing, George. "Main Street." Emanuel Downing's shrewd son, destined for a high position.

Dream, The. "A Select Party." An incredibly beautiful woman, one of the Man of Fancy's guests.

Drowne, Deacon. "Drowne's Wooden Image." The stolid wood-carver who attains his truest level of greatness by carving a uniquely beautiful wooden figurehead, modeled after Captain Hunnewell's Portuguese ward, with whom Drowne falls in love. (Deacon Drowne is mentioned in "Howe's Masquerade" but does not participate in the action.)

Dudley, Esther. "Old Esther Dudley." The venerable supernumerary to whom Sir William Howe gives the key to the Province House; she later drops it at the feet of Republican Governor [John] Hancock and then dies.

Dudley, [Thomas]. "The Gray Champion." The shamefaced,

Massachusetts-born associate of hated Governor Sir Edmund Andros. "Howe's Masquerade." A clever politician in Massachusetts whose shade appears in the mysterious pageant at Sir William Howe's fancy-dress ball. *The Scarlet Letter.* Mentioned as a Massachusetts Governor.

Duke, The. *The Marble Faun.* See the Grand Duke, Florence.

Duke, The. *The Marble Faun.* See the Grand Duke, Tuscany.

Duston, Mrs. Hannah. "The Duston Family." The Haverhill wife who in 1698 was captured by Indians but murdered them with a tomahawk, took their scalps, and claimed the bounty.

Duston, Goodman. "The Duston Family." The frontiersman of Haverhill who in 1698 abandoned his wife Hannah and their new-born baby in order to lead their seven other children to the safety of the garrison during an Indian raid.

Duston. "The Duston Family." One of the saved Duston children.

Duston. "The Duston Family." One of the saved Duston children.

Duston. "The Duston Family." One of the saved Duston children.

Duston. "The Duston Family." One of the saved Duston children.

Duston. "The Duston Family." One of the saved Duston children.

Duston. "The Duston Family." One of the saved Duston children.

Duston. "The Duston Family." One of the saved Duston children.

Duston. "The Duston Family." The new-born Duston baby killed by an Indian during a raid on Haverhill in 1698.

Dwight, Timothy. "A Book of Autographs." The author of a letter in the collection.

Earl. *Dr. Grimshawe's Secret,* Preliminary Studies. Mentioned as lying unburied.

Edgar. "The May-Pole of Merry Mount." The Lord of the May at Merry Mount, husband of Edith, and finally captive of John Endicott.

Edith. "The May-Pole of Merry Mount." The Lady of the May at Merry Mount, wife of Edgar, and finally captive of John Endicott.

Edith. "The White Old Maid." The gentle woman who mourns the death of her lover by remaining in the town and becoming the "Old Maid of the Winding Sheet."

Egerton, Faith. "The Threefold Destiny." The village girl who keeps the heart-shaped brooch which Ralph Cranfield gave her and welcomes him home again with her love.

Eldredge, Edward. "The Ancestral Footstep." The second son of Eldredge, Middleton's English ancestor; he fought his older brother for a woman engaged or married to that brother; he left the bloody footstep on the threshold of Smithell's Hall and went to America with her and changed his name to Middleton; the two married, and Middleton is one of their descendants.

Eldredge, Squire. "The Ancestral Footstep." The present ostensible owner of Smithell's Hall (also called Pemberton Hall) and Middleton's fierce enemy; he is a Catholic, has lived in Italy, and has a sister or daughter named Miss Eldredge.

Eldredge. "The Ancestral Footstep." An English ancestor of Middleton; he has three sons, two of whom fight over one woman.

Eldredge. "The Ancestral Footstep." The oldest son of Eldredge, Middleton's English ancestor; this son was engaged or married to a woman taken from him after a fight by Edward, his younger brother; the oldest son later dies childless.

Eldredge. "The Ancestral Footstep." The third son of Eldredge, Middleton's English ancestor; because his oldest brother dies childless and his second oldest brother, Edward, disappears, this third son's heirs, now specifically Squire Eldredge, whom Middleton meets, can claim Smithell's Hall.

Eldredge, Miss. "The Ancestral Footstep." The Italian-born sister or daughter of the present ostensible owner of Smithell's Hall; Middleton may leave the estate to her.

Eliot, Apostle [John]. *The Scarlet Letter.* A missionary among the Massachusetts Indians; the Rev. Mr. Arthur Dimmesdale meets Hester Prynne in the forest after he has visited Eliot.

Elizabeth. "The Minister's Black Veil." The fiancee of the Rev. Mr. Hooper; when he refuses to remove his veil, she refuses to marry him, but she nurses him on his deathbed.

Elizabeth, Queen. "The Antique Ring." The Queen of England for whose forgiveness the Earl of Essex tries unsuccessfully to appeal by means of the diamond ring which she gave him.

Ellenwood. "The Wedding Knell." The scholarly, sixty-five-year-old eccentric who waits forty years for his worldly bride, the twice-widowed Mrs. Dabney.

Elliston, Roderick. "Egotism." Rosina's jealous husband, whose diseased self-contemplation takes the form of a snake in his bosom. "The Christmas Banquet." The narrator, called only Roderick, of the story about cold Gervayse Hastings.

Elliston, Mrs. Rosina. "Egotism." The cousin of George Herkimer and Roderick Elliston's lovely wife, whose adjuration to Roderick to forget himself and think of her cures the snake-afflicted egotist. "The Christmas Banquet." The narrator's wife, called only Rosina, who criticizes the insubstantial story.

Elsie. *Dr. Grimshawe's Secret,* First Draft. "Ned" Etherege's childhood companion in the doctor's home; she is left part of the doctor's estate in his will, in which she is identified as Elsie Lyndhurst, the daughter of his brother James; it is hinted later, at which time she sketches, that she is the pensioner's daughter and is in love with Etherege. (She is also Miss Alicampion, Miss Cheltenham, and Miss Pearson [all of which see].)

Elsie. *Dr. Grimshawe's Secret,* Second Draft. The playmate of Edward "Ned" Redclyffe when they are young and are being cared for by Dr. Grimshawe, who provides for Ned's education but plans to use him to obtain revenge on the Redclyffe family in England.

Emerson, [Ralph Waldo]. "The Old Manse." Praised as a poet but not as a philosopher. "The Custom House." Mentioned as a subtle intellectual influence.

Endicott, John. "A Rill from the Town Pump." Mentioned as drinking from the spring. "The May-Pole of Merry Mount." The Puritan leader who invades Merry Mount, cuts down the maypole, and arrests the leaders. "Endicott and the Red Cross." The bold soldier who cuts the Red Cross of England from the flag to symbolize Salem's repudiation of Pope and Tyrant (about 1630). "Howe's Masquerade." An anti-royalist whose shade appears in the mysterious pageant at Sir William Howe's fancy-dress ball. "Main Street." The sturdy early Governor of the colony; he grows old and white-bearded. *The Scarlet Letter.* The unnamed Governor of the Massachusetts colony who succeeds Governor Winthrop and at whose inauguration the Rev. Mr. Arthur Dimmesdale preaches his eloquent Election Sermon.

Endicott, Mrs. Anna Gower. "Main Street." The rosy first wife of Governor Endicott; she dies childless.

Ephraim, Father. "The Shaker Bridal." The sick old leader of the Shakers at Goshen who passes the rule over to Adam Colburn.

Epimetheus. "The Paradise of Children." Pandora's playmate.

Ernest. "The Great Stone Face." The simple but profound native of the valley who ultimately is recognized as resembling the Great Stone Face and thus fulfilling the prophecy.

Espy, Professor. "The Hall of Fantasy." An inventor who has a storm in a rubber bag.

Essex, The Earl of. "The Antique Ring." The fallen British courtier who gives his diamond ring, originally a gift of Queen Elizabeth, to the deceitful Countess of Shrewsbury with the request that she use it to intercede on his behalf with the Queen; when the Countess fails to do so, he is beheaded.

Esther. *Fanshawe.* The maid of Melmoths.

Esther. "An Old Woman's Tale." The young lady who shares an identical dream with David, who digs where the old woman dug in the dream and finds something.

Esther. "The Ambitious Guest." The wife and mother of the family swept to ruin by the landslide.

Esther. "Ethan Brand." The daughter of old Humphrey; after Ethan Brand ruined her in a psychological experiment, she ran away from the village and joined a circus as an equestrienne.

Etheredge, Edward. *Dr. Grimshawe's Secret,* First Draft. See Edward Etherege.

Etherege, Edward "Ned." *Dr. Grimshawe's Secret,* First Draft. The doctor's foster son, a small boy at the beginning of the story and the ambassador-to-be to Hohen Linden, aged twenty-seven or twenty-eight years, at the end; he was an almshouse lad, taught by the doctor and led to believe that he was really the descendant of the aristocratic British family of Brathwaite; he is Elsie's companion and seems to be in love with her at the end; he is befriended by the pensioners, especially when he is imprisoned by Brathwaite in Brathwaite Hall.

Etherege, James. *Dr. Grimshawe's Secret,* First Draft. See James.

Etherege, Sylvia "Sylph." "Sylph Etherege." Mrs. Grosvenor's romantic young ward, seventeen years of age or a little more, who so falls in love with her image of her absent cousin fiance, Edgar Vaughan, that when he presents himself in reality as Edward Hamilton, she rejects him because she prefers her ideal.

Etherege, Dr. *Dr. Grimshawe's Secret,* First Draft. The first-used name of the forty-five-year-old doctor who lives near the Charter-Street graveyard, cares for Ned and Elsie, loves spiders and antiquarianism, and hatches the plot to gain revenge on the Brathwaite family of England because of an insulting crime perpetrated by an earlier Brathwaite against his English forebear or the lady whom that man or the doctor himself loved. (Also called Archdale, Dr. Gibber, Dr. Gibb[le]ler, Norman Hanscough, Dr. Ingle-field, and Uncle [all of which see].)

Etherege, Mrs. *Dr. Grimshawe's Secret,* First Draft. The wife of the doctor; she is mysteriously violated by Sir Edward Brathwaite and may have committed suicide. (See also Miss [Evelyn] Brathwaite and Evelyn.)

Etherege. *Dr. Grimshawe's Secret,* Second Draft. The name used once to refer to Edward Redclyffe (which see).

Etheridge. *Dr. Grimshawe's Secret,* Preliminary Studies. Mentioned as the name of the hero. (See Edward Etherege and Edward Redclyffe.)

Eurylochus. "Circe's Palace." Ulysses's sage officer who hangs back and therefore escapes being transformed into a swine by Circe.

Eurystheus, King. "The Pygmies." Mentioned as having ordered Hercules to obtain the three golden apples from the garden of the Hesperides.

Evangelist. "The Celestial Railroad." The ticket agent at the first station-house on the railroad line toward the Celestial City.

Eve. "The New Adam and Eve." A new Eve who wanders with Adam through Boston after the destruction of mankind.

Evelyn. *Dr. Grimshawe's Secret,* First Draft. Mentioned once as the name of the dead girl whose corpse turned into golden hair in her coffin; she is perhaps Miss Brathwaite (which see).

Fairfield, Daniel. "Main Street." A Naumkeag meeting-house prisoner condemned to wear a halter.

Fancy. "Fancy's Show Box." The mysterious being which opens its show box and reveals to Smith sins which he imagined.

Fane, General Edward. "Edward Fane's Rosebud." The fiance of Rose Grafton; when his mother breaks up their engagement, he goes on to become a general and later calls for his Rosebud when he is dying.

Fane, Mary. "Edward Fane's Rosebud." Edward Fane's three-year-old sister, who dies attended by Rose Grafton.

Fane, Mrs. "Edward Fane's Rosebud." Edward Fane's rich and haughty mother, who breaks up his engagement to Rose Grafton.

Fanshawe. *Fanshawe*. The proud, pale, self-possessed twenty-year-old scholar of Harley College; he hopelessly loves Ellen Langton and rescues her from Butler; he gratefully rejects her proposal and studies himself to death.

Far Niente, Signore. "Little Daffydowndilly." The idle brother of Mr. Toil.

Fauntleroy. *The Blithedale Romance*. The name assigned to Old Moodie (which see) when Miles Coverdale summarizes the story which that man has told him.

Fauntleroy. *The Blithedale Romance*. The name assigned to the rich brother of Old Moodie (which see) when Miles Coverdale summarizes the story which that man has told him; Old Moodie's brother dies and leaves his estate to Zenobia.

Fauntleroy, Mrs. *The Blithedale Romance*. The name assigned to the first wife of Old Moodie (which see) and the high-society mother of Zenobia, when Miles Coverdale summarizes the story which that man has told him; she dies.

Fauntleroy, Mrs. *The Blithedale Romance*. The name assigned to the second wife of Old Moodie (which see) and the seamstress mother of Priscilla, when Miles Coverdale summarizes the story which that man has told him; she dies.

Fauntleroy, Priscilla. *The Blithedale Romance.* See Priscilla.

Fauntleroy, Zenobia. *The Blithedale Romance.* See Zenobia.

Faun, The. *The Marble Faun.* See Donatello.

Fay, Lilias "Lilly." "The Lily's Quest." The fragile object of Adam Forrester's love; just as they build their Temple of Happiness, she dies.

Feathertop. "Feathertop." The illusory creature of sticks and rags which the witch Mother Rigby creates and with which she fools Polly Gookin; he commits suicide by breaking his life-giving pipe.

Felton, Gaspar. *Septimius Felton.* Septimius Felton's old ancestor, reputedly the discoverer of and author of the recipe for the elixir of life.

Felton, Septimius "Seppy." *Septimius Felton.* The young man of Concord whose search for the elixir of life turns him into an aloof monomaniac; he is part Indian and part English, his ancestors having arrived in New England ahead of the Puritans; he loves and wishes to share his elixir with Sibyl Dacy, who, however, drinks it alone instead and then dies.

Fenwicke, Colonel. "The White Old Maid." The man whose death fifteen years before the climax of the story closes the gloomy family mansion.

Fenwicke. "The White Old Maid." Probably the family name of the young man over whose corpse Edith and her proud rival join hands; the death of Colonel Fenwicke is followed by the closing of the family mansion.

Fields, J[ames]. T. *A Wonder-Book for Girls and Boys.* Mentioned by Eustace Bright as his possible publisher.

Finch. *The Scarlet Letter.* An English lawyer mentioned as a former associate of Governor Bellingham.

Flimsy-faith. "The Celestial Railroad." The imperfect repairer of the Castle of Despair.

Foot-it-to-heaven. "The Celestial Railroad." An old-fashioned, Bunyanesque pilgrim who makes it to the Celestial City.

Forester, Ellen. "The New England Village." The first child of the Foresters.

Forester, Mrs. Mary. "The New England Village." The charming, hard-working wife of Forester; she accompanies him as he moves from place to place, cares for him in his final sickness, and then marries the minister of the village of N—.

Forester, William. "The New England Village." The second child of the Foresters.

Forester. "The New England Village." The pseudonym of the ex-convict who cannot find happiness with his charming wife and their two children because he is followed by a blackmailing fellow ex-convict.

Forman, Doctor. *The Scarlet Letter.* A reputed acquaintance of Roger Chillingworth implicated in the celebrated murder case of Sir Thomas Overbury in London.

Forrester, Adam. "The Lily's Quest." The lover of fragile Lilias Fay; when she dies, he understands that eternal bliss is built on human affliction.

Forrester, Simon. "The Custon House." A former Salem merchant.

Forrester, Sir. *Septimius Felton.* In Sibyl Dacy's legend, the seeker for eternal life who must sacrifice an innocent young life to gain his ends and whose bloody foot causes the bloody footstep on the threshold of — Hall.

Foster, Silas. *The Blithedale Romance.* The grim, garrulous old farmer who acts as overseer at Blithedale.

Foster, Mrs. Silas. *The Blithedale Romance.* The fat old wife of the overseer at Blithedale.

Foster, Goody. "Main Street." A woman suspected in Salem of being a witch.

Fowler, Mrs. "Widow." *Fanshawe.* The mother of the girl supposedly seen at Hugh Crombie's tavern; the girl there is really Ellen Langton.

Fowler, Miss. *Fanshawe.* The girl named as the one seen at

Hugh Crombie's tavern; the girl there is really Ellen Langton.

Fox, George. *Dr. Grimshawe's Secret,* First Draft. Named as perhaps the peaceful friend and teacher of the original proscribed Brathwaite who migrated to America. *Dr. Grimshawe's Secret,* Second Draft. A teacher of Seymour Colcord's proscribed ancestor who is named Thomas Colcord.

Franklin, [Benjamin]. "A Book of Autographs." The author of two letters in the collection.

Franklin, Madam [Benjamin]. "A Book of Autographs." The recipient of a letter from Franklin in the collection.

Frost, John "Jack." "A Visit to the Clerk of the Weather." The icy dwarf who has Boston and the rest of the world in his icy grip.

Frost, Mrs. John. "A Visit to the Clerk of the Weather." The wife of John Frost; her desire for a polar bear as a pet causes her husband to delay releasing the world from his icy grip.

Furness, Jonathan. "Old News." The owner of a prized black gelding in Boston.

Gage, [General Thomas]. "Howe's Masquerade." A British general whose shade appears in the mysterious pageant at Sir William Howe's fancy-dress ball. "A Book of Autographs." Mentioned in a letter by John Adams in the collection.

Gardner, Captain. "Main Street." A brave Naumkeag fighter against King Philip; he is destined to die attacking the fortress of the Narragansetts; his widow marries Governor Bradstreet.

Gardner, Mrs. "Main Street." See Mrs. Bradstreet.

Garfield, Rose. *Septimius Felton.* At one point, the pretty fiancee at Concord of Septimius Felton, whose search for the elixir of life leads him to neglect her; at another point, Septimius Felton's half-sister who marries Robert Hagburn, an American Revolutionary War soldier; she is a schoolteacher.

Gascoigne, Walter. "The Lily's Quest." The shadowy relative of Lilias Fay who warns her against building a Temple of Happiness with her lover Adam Forrester.

Gascoigne. "Dr. Heidegger's Experiment." An old politician who drinks Dr. Heidegger's water of youth and spouts patriotic rhetoric.

Gathergold. "The Great Stone Face." The miser whose grand return to the valley misleads some people into thinking for a time that he resembles the Great Stone Face.

Georgiana. "The Birthmark." Aylmer's beautiful wife; through love of her husband and admiration for his scientific aspirations, she lets him try to remove her birthmark and thus dies.

Geryon. "The Three Golden Apples." Mentioned as the six-legged man whom Hercules met.

Giant Transcendentalist. "The Celestial Railroad." See Transcendentalist.

Gibber, Dr. *Dr. Grimshawe's Secret,* First Draft. Mentioned by Warden Brathwaite as the author of a book on antiquarianism; perhaps Dr. Gibber is Dr. Etherege (which see).

Gibbins, Dr. *Dr. Grimshawe's Secret,* First Draft. Another name for Dr. Etherege (which see).

Gibb[le]ler, Dr. *Dr. Grimshawe's Secret,* First Draft. A name once used by Miss Cheltenham (which see) to address Warden Brathwaite.

Gibbliter, Dr. *Dr. Grimshawe's Secret,* First Draft. Thought of by Edward Etherege as an authority on spiders. (See Dr. Etherege.)

Gibson, [John]. *The Marble Faun.* The sculptor whose habit of coloring his statues Miriam Schaefer deplores.

Gibson, Captain. *Dr. Grimshawe's Secret,* Preliminary Studies. Mentioned.

Gifford, [William]. "P.'s Correspondence." An old man of decayed intellect, according to P.

Giles. "Ethan Brand." A crippled but courageous village lawyer turned drunkard soap-boiler.

Gill, Counsellor. "A Select Party." A fanciful guest who reports the after-dinner speeches at the Man of Fancy's party.

Girard, Stephen. "The Christmas Banquet." The rich man whose burden of wealth make him miserable and hence entitled to admittance to the banquet.

Girolamo. *The Marble Faun.* The cook at Donatello's home in Tuscany.

Glover. *Fanshawe.* A Harley College student who frequents Hugh Crombie's tavern with Edward Walcott on the rainy night during which Ellen Langton is there.

Gobbledown, Squire. "The Haunted Quack." The friend of Dr. Ephraim Ramshorne at whose home the doctor dines just before his death.

Goffe, Mary. "The Man of Adamant." The radiant follower of Richard Digby whose spirit unsuccessfully begs him to return to mankind.

Goldthwaite, Peter. "Peter Goldthwaite's Treasure." The imaginative, ever-optimistic, but impoverished former partner of John Browne who fails to find any precious metals in the walls of his run-down ancestral mansion and hence must finally sell the place to Brown.

Gookin, Deacon. "Young Goodman Brown." A pious man who evidently rides with the Salem minister to the witch-meeting, much to Goodman Brown's dismay.

Gookin, Polly. "Feathertop." The simple, pretty daughter of Justice Gookin who falls in love with Feathertop until she sees him in a mirror for what he is.

Gookin, Justice. "Feathertop." The rich merchant who evidently consorted with evil once and therefore has to let Feathertop court his pretty daughter Polly.

Gordon, Bill. "The Haunted Quack." The blacksmith husband of

Granny Gordon whose threat to kill Hippocrates Jenkins caused the authorities to be suspicious of him when Jenkins disappeared.

Gordon, Mrs. Bill "Granny." "The Haunted Quack." The patient of "Doctor" Hippocrates Jenkins whose apparent death from an overdose of one of his worthless nostrums caused him to flee, feel haunted, and then return home to the authorities.

Grafton, Rose "Rosebud." "Edward Fane's Rosebud." See Mrs. Toothaker.

Graham. "The Haunted Quack." The sheriff of the region from which Hippocrates Jenkins, mistakenly thinking that he was wanted for murder, escaped temporarily.

Le Grand, M. "Count." *Dr. Grimshawe's Secret,* Second Draft. The French tutor of young Edward Redclyffe in New England.

Grandfather. *The Whole History of Grandfather's Chair.* The kindly, well-informed old man who tells stories of historical events and personages to Alice, Charley, Clara, and Laurence.

Grand Duke of Florence, The. *The Marble Faun.* The owner of one of Raphael's Madonnas.

Grand Duke of Tuscany, The. *The Marble Faun.* The generous patron of strolling entertainers in the region of Donatello's home.

Grantly. *Dr. Grimshawe's Secret,* First Draft. Named as the family involved in the legend of the bloody footstep.

Gray, Billy. "The Custom House." A former Salem merchant.

Gray Champion, The. "The Gray Champion." The venerable old Puritan patriarch who mysteriously appears before Sir Edmund Andros, Governor of Massachusetts, and forces him back by announcing the imminent end of the rule of James II.

Gray, Goodman. "The Minister's Black Veil." A member of the Rev. Mr. Hooper's congregation.

Greatheart. "The Celestial Railroad." John Bunyan's character who has retired to the Celestial City.

Green. "Old News." A book seller, partner of Kneeland in Boston.

Greenough, [Horatio]. *The Marble Faun.* A sculptor ridiculed by Miriam Schaefer.

Gridley, Colonel. "A Book of Autographs." An engineer mentioned in a letter by General Warren in the collection.

Griffin, Dr. *Dr. Grimshawe's Secret*, First Draft. Thought of by Edward Etherege as an authority on English history. (See Dr. Etherege.)

Grim, Dr. *Dr. Grimshawe's Secret*, Second Draft. One of the nicknames of Dr. Grimshawe (which see).

Grimshawe, Dr. *Dr. Grimshawe's Secret*, Second Draft. The rough, grim titular hero of the novel, wronged in England and therefore an emigrant to New England; he is partly a quack, is scholarly, and is devoted to antiquarianism and spiders; he rears Ned (see Edward Redclyffe) and Elsie, befriends Seymour (see Seymour Colcord), and plots revenge on the Redclyffe family of England.

Grimsouth, Dr. *Dr. Grimshawe's Secret*, Second Draft. A name once used for Dr. Grimshawe (which see).

Griswold, [Rufus]. "The Antique Ring." An American editor who praises Edward Caryl. *The Blithedale Romance.* Mentioned as a literary critic who approves of Miles Coverdale's poetry.

Grosvenor, Mrs. "Sylph Etherege." Sylvia Etherege's guardian, who consents to Edgar Vaughan's fatal experiment.

Guasconti, Giovanni. "Dr. Rappaccini's Daughter." The shallow young Neapolitan who studies in Padua and falls in love with Beatrice Rappaccini.

Gubbins. *The House of the Seven Gables.* The husband of one of Hepzibah Pyncheon's irate customers.

Gubbins, Mrs. *The House of the Seven Gables.* One of Hepzibah Pycheon's irate customers.

Hagburn, Robert. *Septimius Felton.* The brawny friend of Septimius Felton who becomes an American Revolutionary army captain; at one point he is mildly jealous of Septimius Felton's success with Rose Garfield; at another point, when Rose Garfield becomes Septimius Felton's half-sister, Robert Hagburn returns to Concord and marries her.

Hagburn, Mrs. Rose Garfield. *Septimius Felton.* See Rose Garfield.

Hagburn, Mrs. *Septimius Felton.* Robert Hagburn's mother, nearly ninety years of age, who at one point gives room and board to wandering Sibyl Dacy; she is a close friend of Septimus Felton's Aunt Keziah.

Haldiman. "A Book of Autographs." Mentioned in a letter by John Adams in the collection.

Hall, Acquilla. "A Book of Autographs." Mentioned as a Maryland volunteer in a letter by John Adams in the collection.

Halleck, [Fitz-Greene]. "P.'s Correspondence." An American poet thought strange by P.

Hallowell, Captain. "Old News." An officer who advertises in the Boston newspapers (about 1760) for able-bodied seamen to serve in His Majesty's navy.

Hamilton, [Alexander]. "A Book of Autographs." The author of a letter in the collection.

Hamilton, Edward. "Sylph Etherege." The name assumed by Edgar Vaughan (which see), when he first visits Sylvia Etherege.

Hammond, Alice. "The Ancestral Footstep." The bright, free-thinking, easy-going American-born daughter (or granddaughter) of the hospitaler Hammond (who is also called Rothermel and Wentworth); she urges Middleton in England to prefer an exciting American future to a conservative retirement in an English ancestral home.

Hammond. "The Ancestral Footstep." A former swindler in America who once cheated Middleton's father; he is Alice

Hammond's father (or grandfather); he is now a hospitaler and an antiquarian who takes Middleton to Smithell's Hall. (He is also called Rothermel and Wentworth.)

Hammond, Warden. *Dr. Grimshawe's Secret,* Second Draft. The brusque, intelligent director of the hospital to which Edward Redclyffe is brought when he is shot.

Hammond. *Dr. Grimshawe's Secret,* First Draft. The name once used in New England in place of that of Mountford (which see); in England Hammond calls on Edward Etherege at the hospital and is later the mechanical, horror-stricken servant of Brathwaite of Brathwaite Hall during Etherege's visit and subsequent imprisonment there.

Hannah. "The Great Carbuncle." The young bride who with her husband Matthew finds the carbuncle but decides to leave it on the mountain.

Hannah, Crusty. *Dr. Grimshawe's Secret,* Second Draft. Dr. Grimshawe's witch-like servant, who is part East Indian and part Negro.

Hannah. *Dr. Grimshawe's Secret,* First Draft. The doctor's servant. (Also called Hannah Lord and Sukey.)

Hancock, [John]. "Old Esther Dudley." The Republican Governor of Massachussetts whose arrival at the Province House is the indirect cause of Esther Dudley's death. "A Book of Autographs." The author of an envelope in the collection.

Hanscough, Norman. *Dr. Grimshawe's Secret,* First Draft. A name mentioned by Edward Etherege to Sir Edward Brathwaite in their prison chamber; it is evidently another of the names of Dr. Etherege (which see).

Harmonia, Queen. "The Dragon's Teeth." King Cadmus's beautiful queen.

Harper, [Fletcher, James, John, and Joseph]. "The Antique Ring." American publishers who are interested in the writings of Edward Caryl.

Harris, Rev. Dr. "The Ghost of Doctor Harris." An eighty-year-old minister from Dorchester, whose ghost the narrator regularly sees sitting in the old Boston Athenaeum reading-room.

Hastings, Gervayse. "The Christmas Banquet." The cold and distant banquet guest whose misery it is to be warm and intimate with no one and to believe that everything about him is a shadow.

Hawkwood, Squire. "The Threefold Destiny." The venerable village sage who offers Ralph Cranfield the infinitely influential position of village schoolmaster.

[Hawthorne, Nathaniel.] *A Wonder-Book for Girls and Boys.* Mentioned by Eustace Bright as an author living nearby who could by burning some papers destroy all the children to whom Eustace has been telling his wonderful stories.

Hawthorne [Hathorne], Major [William]. "Main Street." A Salem persecutor of Quakers.

Haynes, [John]. "Howe's Masquerade." An anti-royalist whose shade appears in the mysterious pageant at Sir William Howe's fancy-dress ball.

Heber, Dr. Reginald. "P.'s Correspondence." A former Bishop of Calcutta, now in England and now Shelley's friend, according to P.

Hecate. "The Pomegranate Seeds." A dog-headed old hag who offers Mother Ceres the comfort of more melancholy.

Heidegger, Dr. "Dr. Heidegger's Experiment." The physician-wizard who gives his four guests the water of youth and then watches them grow temporarily young and make fools of themselves.

Helle. "The Golden Fleece." Mentioned as a boy rescued with Phrixus by the Boeotian ram with the Golden Fleece; he later drowns.

Helwyse, Jervase. "Lady Eleanore's Mantle." The unrequited lover of Lady Eleanore who makes a footstool of himself for her but who also warns her to become a part of mankind instead of wrapping herself in pride; he finally burns her mantle.

Henry. "David Swan." The dead son of the merchant and his wife who are momentarily tempted to adopt David Swan.

Hercules. "The Three Golden Apples." The hero who obtains the three golden apples by tricking Atlas. "The Pygmies." The killer of Antaeus, who makes the mistake of opposing the hero on his way to the garden of the Hesperides. "The Golden Fleece." A pupil of Chiron and an Argonaut with Jason.

Herkimer, George. "Egotism." The sculptor friend of Roderick Elliston and his wife Rosina, who is Herkimer's cousin; he brings Rosina back to effect a cure of the morbid egotist Elliston. "The Christmas Banquet." The unnamed sculptor who quietly listens with Rosina as her husband Roderick tells the story.

Hewen, Ebenezer. *Dr. Grimshawe's Secret,* Second Draft. The gravedigger of the Charter-Street graveyard near which Dr. Grimshawe lives; he tries to help Mountford.

Hewes, Robert. "Old News." A Boston soap-maker whose revolutionary tendencies the old Tory deplores.

Hibbins. *The Scarlet Letter.* Mentioned as a Boston magistrate, now dead; his widow, Governor Bellingham's sister, is later executed for witchcraft.

Hibbins, Mistress. *The Scarlet Letter.* The sister of Governor Bellingham and a magistrate's widow who occasionally taunts Hester Prynne; she is later executed for witchcraft.

Hide-sin-in-the-heart. "The Celestial Railroad." A materialistic friend of Smooth-it-away.

Higginbotham, Miss. "Mr. Higginbotham's Catastrophe." The pretty schoolteacher niece of Squire Higginbotham who marries Dominicus Pike.

Higginbotham, Squire. "Mr. Higginbotham's Catastrophe." The wealthy squire of Kimballton who is not murdered by three ruffians, or even by one, but is saved by Dominicus Pike.

Higgins, Ned. *The House of the Seven Gables.* The little boy who eats cookies obtained in Hepzibah Pyncheon's cent-shop.

Higginson, Rev. Mr. [Francis]. "A Rill from the Town Pump." Mentioned as using the spring water to baptize the first town-born child. *The House of the Seven Gables.* An ecclesiastical friend of Colonel Pyncheon and one of the guests at the opening of the Pyncheon house.

Hilda "The Dove." *The Marble Faun.* The young New England-born, Puritanical girl who spends about three years as a copyist in Rome; she lives in a tower far above the heat and dust of the streets, surrounded by white doves and near a shrine to the Virgin; when she accidentally witnesses the murder of Brother Antonio, she repudiates Miriam Schaefer and Donatello but is transformed into a person aware of the pervasiveness of evil; at the end, she returns to America as Kenyon's bride.

Hillard, [George Stillman]. "The Antique Ring." A Boston editor who praises Edward Caryl. "The Old Manse." Mentioned as having supposedly heard with Hawthorne the rustle of a ghost in the Old Manse. "The Custom House." Mentioned as a cultured, refined companion.

Hiller, Abigail. "Old News." A teacher of ornamental work in Boston (about 1760).

Hinchbrooke, Lord. *Dr. Grimshawe's Secret,* First Draft. The title to which Brathwaite, the incumbant at Brathwaite Hall, is claimant.

Hippodamia, Princess. "The Gorgon's Head." Mentioned as the possible fiancee of wicked King Polydectes.

Hippolyta. "The Three Golden Apples." Mentioned as the queen of the Amazons whom Hercules conquers.

Hobart, Peggy. "Drowne's Wooden Image." A Boston merchant's daughter whom some of Drowne's wooden statues resemble.

Holgrave. *The House of the Seven Gables.* The twenty-one-year-old daguerrotypist who rooms in the seven-gabled

Pyncheon house; he resists using his hypnotic powers on Phoebe Pyncheon, whom he ultimately marries; he begins with radical notions but humorously becomes conservative; he is really a Maule, descended from Matthew Maule, who ruinously hypnotized Alice Pyncheon.

Hollingsworth. *The Blithedale Romance.* A former blacksmith, later an egotistically and sinfully single-minded would-be reformer of criminals who wants to use Zenobia's wealth and Blithedale farm for his purpose; he attracts Priscilla to him and is thus morally responsible for Zenobia's suicide by drowning.

Holmes, [Dr. Oliver Wendell]. *A Wonder-Book for Girls and Boys.* Mentioned by Eustace Bright as one of his literary neighbors and a poet worthy of riding Pegasus.

Hooper, Rev. Mr. "The Minister's Black Veil." The sinful or sorrowful minister who suddenly puts on a black veil and thus disturbs his congregation; he loses his fiancee Elizabeth but develops into a persuasive minister.

Hope. "The Paradise for Children." The rainbow-winged creature released last from the mysterious box which Pandora opens.

Hopnort. "The Ancestral Footstep." The name of a family living in the neighborhood of Eldredge's estate.

Hosmer, Harriet. *The Marble Faun.* The sculptress whose rendition of the clasped hands of Robert Browning and his wife Elizabeth Barrett Browning is admired by Miriam Schaefer.

Hovenden, Annie. "The Artist of the Beautiful." See Annie Hovenden Danforth.

Hovenden, Peter. "The Artist of the Beautiful." A retired watchmaker whose cold sneer discomfits Owen Warland and whose daughter Annie marries Robert Danforth.

Howe, Sir William. "Howe's Masquerade." The last royal Governor of Massachusetts, who is frightened by the ghostly funeral procession at his fancy-dress ball. "Old Esther

Dudley." The last royal Governor, who gives the key to the Province House to Esther Dudley and leaves for Halifax. "A Book of Autographs." Described as an unprincipled miscreant in a letter by John Adams in the collection.

Howorth. "Edward Randolph's Portrait." Mentioned as a picture-cleaner in the New England Museum who might be able to clean the blackness of time from Edward Randolph's portrait.

Hubbard, Mother. *Dr. Grimshawe's Secret,* First Draft. Mentioned by the sexton as buried later in the old Colcord grave.

Huckleberry. *A Wonder-Book for Girls and Boys.* An elfish little girl, one of Eustace Bright's older auditors. *Tanglewood Tales, for Girls and Boys.* Mentioned as having had the whooping-cough.

Huggins, Susan. "Howe's Masquerade." A chambermaid at the Province House.

Humphrey. "Ethan Brand." An old man who has become demented because his daughter Esther ran away and joined a circus after Ethan Brand ruined her in a psychological experiment.

Hunnewell, Captain. "Drowne's Wooden Image." The sea captain who commissions Drowne to carve a figurehead for his ship with his mysterious Portuguese ward as the model.

Hunt. "The Custom House." A former Salem merchant.

Hutchins, Sarah. *Fanshawe.* See Mrs. Sarah Crombie.

Hutchins. *Fanshawe.* The dead husband of tavern-owner Sarah Hutchins, who later marries Hugh Crombie.

Hutchinson, Ann (Anne). "Main Street." A female preacher surrounded by an attentive audience in Naumkeag. *The Scarlet Letter.* Mentioned as once a saintly prisoner in the Boston jail where Hester Prynne and her illegitimate daughter Pearl are imprisoned.

Hutchinson, [Thomas]. "Howe's Masquerade." A former Governor of Massachusetts whose shade appears in the mysterious pageant at Sir William Howe's fancy-dress ball. "Edward Randolph's Portrait." The Lieutenant-Governor of Massachusetts who signs the order to bring British regiments into Boston and thus starts the Boston Massacre.

Ilbrahim. "The Gentle Boy." The gentle little boy, about six years old at the beginning of the story, who dies because of persecution by anti-Quaker children and because of neglect by his fanatical Quaker mother Catharine.

Ingersoll, Miss [Susan?]. *Dr. Grimshawe's Secret,* First Draft. A name inexplicably mentioned in one of Hawthorne's notes to himself.

Inglefield, John. "John Inglefield's Thanksgiving." The rugged old widowered blacksmith whose wayward daughter Prudence returns to him, but only temporarily.

Inglefield, Mary. "John Inglefield's Thanksgiving." The twin sister of Prudence Inglefield, the wayward daughter of John Inglefield who returns momentarily to him.

Inglefield, Prudence. "John Inglefield's Thanksgiving." The sinful, shamed sixteen-year-old daughter of John Inglefield who returns to him for Thanksgiving dinner but then answers the dark summons of sin again; she is Mary Inglefield's twin sister.

Inglefield, Dr. *Dr. Grimshawe's Secret,* First Draft. Mentioned as the man with whom Edward Etherege lives near the graveyard and who tells him the story of the bloody footstep. (See Dr. Etherege.)

Inglefield. "John Inglefield's Thanksgiving." The theology-student son of John Inglefield who is soon to go to the islands of the Pacific Ocean as a missionary.

Inspector. "The Custom House." A customs officer of more than eighty years of age, later killed in a fall from a horse.

Inspector. "The Custom House." Mentioned as a customs officer who knows many stories about sea captains and tells them well to Hawthorne.

Intelligencer, The. "The Intelligence Office." The grave man with mysterious spectacles who records all that is wanted in his Book of Wishes.

Iobates, King. "The Chimaera." The King of Lycia who asks Bellerophon to rid his land of the destructive Chimaera.

Irving, Washington. "A Book of Autographs." The signer of an indorsement on a draft in the collection.

Jackson, Andrew. "A Book of Autographs." An author of a letter in the collection.

Jackson, Mary. "Old News." A woman who sells butter in Boston (about 1760).

Jacobs, George. "Main Street." A forlorn old man condemned in Salem to hang for supposedly selling his soul to Satan.

James (I), King. *The Scarlet Letter.* Mentioned as the King of England during Governor Bellingham's vain youth at court. *Dr. Grimshawe's Secret,* First Draft. The English king once entertained by the hereditary patron of the hospital.

James (II), King. *Dr. Grimshawe's Secret,* First Draft. The English king who once dined in the banquet hall of the hospital; when he emigrated to the Continent, the Italianate Brathwaite's father accompanied him.

James, [George Payne Rainsford]. *A Wonder-Book for Girls and Boys.* Mentioned by Eustace Bright as one of his literary neighbors, in Stockbridge.

James. *Dr. Grimshawe's Secret,* First Draft. Mentioned in the doctor's will as his distinguished but scheming brother and the father of Elsie Lyndhurst.

Jason. "The Golden Fleece." The son of dethroned King Aeson of Iolchos who takes the Golden Fleece from King Aeetes of Colchis, with the help of his fellow Argonauts and Medea.

Jay, Judge [John]. "A Book of Autographs." The author of a letter or two and the recipient of a letter in the collection.

Jefferson, [Thomas]. "A Book of Autographs." The author of a letter in the collection.

Jehu. "Mrs. Bullfrog." The coach driver of the Bullfrogs.

Jenkins, Hippocrates "Hippy" "Doctor." "The Haunted Quack." The apprentice quack under Dr. Ephraim Ramshorne, whose death enabled Jenkins to take over his practice until he thought that he had killed Granny Gordon with poisonous nostrums; then he was haunted until he learned that she had not died.

Jenkins, Robert. "Old News." A notions merchant in Boston.

Jew of Nuremberg, The. "Ethan Brand." The German Jewish showman who entertains Joe but then annoys Ethan Brand by suggesting that he is carrying the Unpardonable Sin in his diorama.

Job, Father. "The Canterbury Pilgrims." Mentioned by Josiah as a rigorous old Shaker leader.

Joe. "Ethan Brand." The sensitive little son of the sluggish lime-burner Bartram; Joe cries when he thinks of Ethan Brand's loneliness.

Johnson, Isaac. *The Scarlet Letter.* The early settler of Boston on whose lot the first cemetery was established.

Joliffe, Colonel. "Howe's Masquerade." The tough old Whig who watches with unfeigned pleasure the ghostly funeral march at Sir William Howe's fancy-dress ball.

Joliffe, Miss. "Howe's Masquerade." Colonel Joliffe's brave, outspoken granddaughter.

Jones, Daniel. "Old News." A Boston haberdasher who advertises in the newspapers (about 1760) to sell uniforms to British officers.

Jones, Davy. "A Select Party." See Davy Jones.

Josiah. "The Canterbury Pilgrims." The stalwart young Shaker lover who decides not to return home but instead to go with Miriam away from their village and marry her.

Juba. "Old News." The Governor's Negro slave, who escapes in Boston.

Julia. "The Wedding Knell." An attractive young member of Mrs. Dabney's wedding party.

Kean, [Edmund] the elder. "P.'s Correspondence." An actor whom P. says he saw play the part of Hamlet's ghost at the Drury Lane Theatre in 1845.

Keats, [John]. "P.'s Correspondence." An old poet rumored to be writing a Miltonic epic, according to P.

Kemble, John. "P.'s Correspondence." Mrs. Siddons' decrepit old brother, seen by P., he says, at the Drury Lane Theatre in 1845.

Kenyon. *The Marble Faun.* The American sculptor who resides and works in Rome, admires Miriam Schaefer, tries to help Donatello, and falls in love with Hilda; his initial coldness and professionalism are transformed in the course of the novel, and he becomes sympathetic and devout.

Keziah, Aunt "Kezzy." *Septimius Felton.* Septimius Felton's old, yellow-skinned aunt who brews vile concoctions with nearby herbs, using a recipe handed down to her from her Indian ancestors.

Killigrew, Colonel. "Dr. Heidegger's Experiment." The gouty old sinner who gets flirtatious after he sips Dr. Heidegger's water of youth.

Kimball. "The Custom House." A former Salem merchant.

Kneeland. "Old News." A book seller, partner of Green in Boston.

Knox, Henry. "A Book of Autographs." The author of a letter in the collection.

Lafayette, General Marquis. "The Bald Eagle." The French hero of the American Revolutionary War who does not visit the Bald Eagle, a tavern in a village in the Connecticut Valley. "A Bell's Biography." The revered French officer whose return to America after half a century the bell noted. "A Book of Autographs." The author of a letter in the collection.

Langford, Captain. "Lady Eleanore's Mantle." The British officer who escorts Lady Eleanore and therefore is one of the first to be stricken by smallpox.

Langton, Ellen. *Fanshawe*. The eighteen-year-old daughter of the merchant John Langton, during whose absence she becomes the ward of President Melmoth of Harley College, falls in love with Edward Walcott, attracts the notice of Fanshawe, and is abducted by Butler; she is rescued by Fanshawe and later marries Walcott.

Langton, John. *Fanshawe*. A rich merchant; absent at the beginning of the novel, he asks President Melmoth of Harley College to act as guardian of his daughter Ellen.

Langton, Mrs. John. *Fanshawe*. The wife of the merchant John Langton; her death contributes to his reluctance to return to America.

Laurence. *The Whole History of Grandfather's Chair*. The twelve-year-old bookworm who delights in Grandfather's stories; he is Clara's cousin.

Laurens, Henry. "A Book of Autographs." The author of a letter in the collection.

Lawson, Deacon. "A Bell's Biography." A soldier who wants to take the bell back to his church but is killed by Indians on his way home.

Lee, General [Henry]. "A Book of Autographs." Mentioned in a letter by John Adams in the collection.

Leroy. "A Book of Autographs." The recipient with Bayard of a letter from Jefferson in the collection.

Leutze, [Emanuel]. "Chiefly about War Matters." The painter

observed by Hawthorne in Washington painting a vast scene of the Rocky Mountains.

Leverett, [Sir John]. "Howe's Masquerade." An anti-royalist whose shade appears in the mysterious pageant at Sir William Howe's fancy-dress ball.

Lincoln, President Abraham "Uncle Abe." "Chiefly about War Matters." The President of the United States, met by Hawthorne at the White House.

Lincoln, General [Benjamin]. "A Book of Autographs." The author of a hasty letter in the collection.

Lincoln, Captain Francis. "Edward Randolph's Portrait." Lieutenant-Governor Hutchinson's kinsman who, as provincial captain of Castle William, unsuccessfully implores the Lieutenant-Governor not to sign the order bringing British troops into Boston.

Lindsey, Peony. "The Snow-Image." The fat younger child, a son, of the Lindseys; he and his older sister Violet make a sister of snow.

Lindsey, Violet. "The Snow-Image." The older child, a daughter, of the Lindseys; she and her younger brother Peony make a sister of snow.

Lindsey. "The Snow-Image." The well-meaning but too common-sensible father of Violet and Peony Lindsey, whose snow-sister he disastrously warms before the fire in their house.

Lindsey, Mrs. "The Snow-Image." The delicate, imaginative, loving mother of Violet and Peony Lindsey, whom she sees — or seems to see — dancing with the snow-sister they made.

Lisabetta, Dame. "Rappaccini's Daughter." Giovanni Gusaconti's landlady, who shows the young man a secret entrance to Dr. Rappaccini's poisonous garden.

Little Daffydowndilly. "Little Daffydowndilly." See Daffydowndilly, Little.

Little Pickle. "Passages from a Relinquished Work." A mischievous friend of the story-telling narrator.

Live-for-the-world. "The Celestial Railroad." A materialistic friend of Smooth-it-away.

Longfellow, [Henry Wadsworth]. "P.'s Correspondence." A delicate American poet thought by P. to be dead of overwork. "The Custom House." Mentioned as a poetic friend of Hawthorne's. *A Wonder-Book for Girls and Boys.* Mentioned by Eustace Bright as one of his literary neighbors, at the Ox-Bow.

Lord, Hannah. *Dr. Grimshawe's Secret,* First Draft. See Hannah.

Lord of the Celestial City, The. "The Celestial Railroad." The Ruler who has refused to incorporate the Celestial Railroad.

Lord of Vanity Fair, The. "The Celestial Railroad." The chief patron of Vanity Fair.

Lowell, James Russell. "P.'s Correspondence." A friend of P.'s correspondent and an admirer of Keats. "The Old Manse." Mentioned as having told Hawthorne a story about a lad from Concord who irrationally killed with an axe a British soldier wounded at the Revolutionary War battle there.

Lucas, John. "Old News." A Boston coachmaker who rents his black coach for funerals.

Ludlow, Elinor. "The Prophetic Pictures." The bride of Walter Ludlow warned by the eminent artist that Walter is fated to desire to kill her.

Ludlow, Walter. "The Prophetic Pictures." The Bostonian who hires the eminent painter to paint his portrait, only to have the painter prophecize in a sketch Walter's coming desire to kill Elinor, his beloved.

Lynceus. "The Golden Fleece." The sharp-eyed Argonaut who can see through stones.

Lyndhurst, Elsie. *Dr. Grimshawe's Secret,* First Draft. See Elsie.

Lyndhurst, James. *Dr. Grimshawe's Secret,* First Draft. See James.

McClellan, General [George B.]. "Chiefly about War Matters." The Union general whom Hawthorne closely observes as he reviews his troops at the Fairfield Seminary in Virginia, outside Washington.

Mackintosh, James. *Dr. Grimshawe's Secret*, First Draft. A name inexplicably mentioned in one of Hawthorne's notes to himself.

Mackintosh, Miss. *Dr. Grimshawe's Secret*, First Draft. A name inexplicably mentioned in one of Hawthorne's notes to himself.

Malbone, [Edward Greene]. *The House of the Seven Gables*. The reputed painter of a miniature of Clifford Pyncheon.

Malvin, Dorcas. "Roger Malvin's Burial." See Mrs. Dorcas Malvin Bourne.

Malvin, Roger. "Roger Malvin's Burial." The fatally wounded father of Dorcas who urges his fellow Indian-fighter Reuben Bourne to abandon him to die but to return to bury him.

Man in the Moon, The. "A Select Party." The being which lights departing guests of the Man of Fancy as they return home.

Man of Fancy, The. "A Select Party." The builder of a castle in the air and host at the select party there.

Man of Intelligence, The. "The Intelligence Office." See the Intelligencer.

Man of Straw, A. "A Select Party." A fanciful guest who has no existence except as a voter in close elections.

Margaret. "The Wives of the Dead." A lively, irritable girl whose soldier husband, the brother of Mary's husband, is mistakenly reported killed in a Canadian skirmish; she lives with Mary.

Married Pair, A. "A Select Party." A married couple whose life together has never been disturbed; they are fanciful guests.

Martha. "The Dolliver Romance." The servant of Dr. Dolliver

and his great-granddaughter Pansie Dolliver.

Mary. "The Wives of the Dead." A calm, gentle girl whose sailor husband, the brother of Margaret's husband, is mistakenly reported drowned during a storm on the Atlantic Ocean; she lives with Margaret.

Marygold. "The Golden Touch." King Midas's happy daughter who is temporarily turned to gold by her father's kiss.

Massey, Jeffrey. "Main Street." An early settler in Naumkeag and the father of John Massey, the first child born there.

Massey, Goodwife. "Main Street." The wife of Jeffrey Massey and the mother of John Massey, the first child born in Naumkeag.

Massey, John. "Main Street." The first-born child of Naumkeag; he ages as Main Street develops and dies at about eighty years of age.

Master, The. "The Ancestral Footstep." The manager of the hospital for retired, intelligent, impoverished wanderers, including Hammond; he is Middleton's host and informant at one point.

Master, The. *Dr. Grimshawe's Secret,* See Warden Brathwaite.

Master Genius, The. "A Select Party." The genius for whom our country prays; he is a fanciful guest.

Mather, Cotton. "Alice Doane's Appeal." Depicted as the triumphant and diabolical witch-persecutor of Gallows Hill, Salem. "The Duston Family." The Puritan writer who, according to Hawthorne, delighted in accounts of Indian deaths because most Indians in his time had been converted to Catholicism by French missionaries. "Main Street." A scholar who tells the people of Salem that the witches have been properly condemned, for the good of New England. *The House of the Seven Gables.* The minister at whose hands Matthew Maule, the accused wizard, suffers.

Mather, Increase. "Dr. Bullivant." A New England author who writes scornfully of Dr. " 'Pothecary" Bullivant. *The*

Scarlet Letter. Mentioned as an example of a politically successful priest.

Mather, Nathanael. *Fanshawe.* The dead scholar whose epitaph Fanshawe's friends copy for his gravestone.

Mathew, Father [Theobald]. "Earth's Holocaust." The leader of the liquor-burners at the holocaust.

Matthew. "The Great Carbuncle." The young husband who with his bride Hannah finds the carbuncle but decides to leave it on the mountain.

Matthews, Charles. "P.'s Correspondence." A victim of paralysis seen by P. at the Drury Lane Theatre in 1845.

Maule, Matthew. *The House of the Seven Gables.* The accused wizard whose house-site Colonel Pyncheon covets; as he is about to be hanged for witchcraft, he curses the Pyncheon family; his son Thomas Maule later builds the house of the seven gables.

Maule, Matthew. *The House of the Seven Gables.* The only grandson, a carpenter, of Matthew Maule the hanged wizard; thirty-seven years after the Pyncheon house is built he is summoned by Gervayse Pyncheon and ruinously hypnotizes that proud man's daughter Alice Pyncheon.

Maule, Mrs. Matthew. *The House of the Seven Gables.* The wife of wizard Matthew Maule's only grandson; Alice Pyncheon waits humbly upon her at her wedding and shortly thereafter dies.

Maule, Thomas. *The House of the Seven Gables.* The son of the executed wizard Matthew Maule; he is the architect and builder of the Pyncheon house, and hid the Pyncheon deed to the Indian lands behind Colonel Pyncheon's portrait; he is the father of Matthew Maule, who ruins Alice Pyncheon.

Maule. *The House of the Seven Gables.* A child of the wizard Matthew Maule in addition to his carpenter son Thomas Maule.

Maule. *The House of the Seven Gables.* See Holgrave.

Mayor, The. "The Ancestral Footstep." The neighborhood official who gives a dinner celebrating the ambassadorial appointment of Middleton, who meets Ethredge there.

Mayor, The. *Dr. Grimshawe's Secret,* Preliminary Studies. Mentioned as giving a public dinner at which the American hero is called upon to speak.

Mayor, The. *Dr. Grimshawe's Secret,* First Draft. The mayor of a town near the hospital; he attends the banquet in Edward Etherege's honor.

Medbourne. "Dr. Heidegger's Experiment." The ruined merchant who when he partakes of Dr. Heidegger's water of youth begins immediately to make plans for a new commercial venture.

Medea. "The Minotaur." The wicked queen who lives in Athens with old King Aegeus until she is exposed by Theseus; then she escapes in a flaming chariot. "The Golden Fleece." The daughter of King Aeetes of Colchis, niece of Circe, odd enchantress, and wily helper of Jason when he takes the Golden Fleece. "Circe's Palace." Mentioned as wicked Circe's daughter.

Medus. "The Minotaur." The son of Medea.

Medusa. "The Gorgon's Head." The Gorgon with the snaky head beheaded by Perseus.

Melmoth, Mrs. Sarah. *Fanshawe.* The shrewish wife of President Melmoth of Harley College.

Melmoth, Dr. *Fanshawe.* The President of Harley College; almost sixty years of age, he is the philosophical, religious, and impractical guardian of Ellen Langton, the daughter of his old friend John Langton.

Melville, Herman. *A Wonder-Book for Girls and Boys.* Mentioned by Eustace Bright as one of his literary neighbors, who lives near Pittsfield and is writing *The White Whale.*

Memmius. *The Marble Faun.* The spy who under Emperor Diocletian's orders penetrated St. Calixtus's catacomb;

after he rejected the opportunity to kneel before the cross there, he became a proscribed spectre of the catacomb somehow related to Brother Antonio later.

Memory. "Fancy's Show Box." The power which reminds Smith that he has indeed imagined the sins which Fancy shows him.

Metanira, Queen. "The Pomegranate Seeds." King Celeus's queen, whose son Demophoon is nursed back to health by Mother Ceres.

Midas, King. "The Golden Touch." The king of ancient times who suffers the curse of possessing the golden touch.

Middleton. "The Ancestral Footstep." See Edward Eldredge.

Middleton. "The Ancestral Footstep." The American claimant Middleton's father, whom Hammond swindled.

Middleton. "The Ancestral Footstep." An American Congressman who learns from his father about the swindler Hammond and the bloody footstep, and is thus tempted to claim Smithell's Hall from Squire Eldredge, who tries to kill him; Alice Hammond urges Middleton to prefer an exciting American future to a conservative retirement in an English ancestral home; after Eldredge's death, Middleton may assign the Hall to Miss Eldredge, the Squire's sister or daughter.

Middleton, Mrs. "The Ancestral Footstep." The shamed wife of Edward Eldredge (which see); she was engaged or married to Edward Eldredge's older brother, accompanied Edward to America, and thus became Middleton's oldest female American forebear.

Milkweed. *A Wonder-Book for Girls and Boys.* One of Eustace Bright's older auditors. *Tanglewood Tales, for Girls and Boys.* Mentioned as having had the whooping-cough.

Miller, General [James]. "The Custom House." A rough but kindly old customs officer, almost seventy years of age.

Miller, Father [William]. "The Hall of Fantasy." A gloomy man who predicts the imminent destruction of the world.

"The Christmas Banquet." A banquet guest entitled to admittance because of his despair at the delay in the ending of the world.

Minos, King. "The Minotaur." The ruler of Crete who has demanded annual human tribute of defeated Athens; Theseus kills his voracious Minotaur.

Minotaur. "The Minotaur." The roaring creature with the horned head of a bull and the body of a man; Theseus kills it.

Miriam. "The Canterbury Pilgrims." The beautiful young Shaker girl who decides not to return home but instead to accompany Josiah away from their village and marry him.

Miriam. "Old News." The comely daughter of a newspaper-reading merchant in Boston.

Miriam. *The Marble Faun.* See Miriam Schaefer.

Miroir, Monsieur du. "Monsieur du Miroir." The musing narrator's reflective alter ego.

Mirth. "The Seven Vagabonds." The beautiful, mirthful damsel who accompanies the tall, dark, foreign fiddler.

Molineux, Robin. "My Kinsman, Major Molineux." The "shrewd" eighteen-year-old country lad who seeks the help of his kinsman the Tory Major Molineux, only to find him tarred and feathered and being dragged out of town in an open cart.

Molineux, Major. "My Kinsman, Major Molineux." Robin Molineux's Tory kinsman, who cannot give aid promised to the lad because the rebellious colonists have tarred and feathered him and are carting him out of town.

Monte Beni, The Count of. *The Marble Faun.* See Donatello.

Moodie, Old. *The Blithedale Romance.* The penitant, self-effacing father of the half-sisters Zenobia and Priscilla; over a bottle of wine he tells Miles Coverdale the story of his life; when Coverdale summarizes the story, he gives Old Moodie the name of Fauntleroy (which see).

Moore, Robert. "John Inglefield's Thanksgiving." The once affectionate friend of Prudence Inglefield, John Inglefield's wayward daughter; he is now a journeyman blacksmith.

Moore, [Thomas]. "P.'s Correspondence." A brilliant but reprehensible man whom Byron ejected from his house, according to P.

Morehead, Sarah. "Old News." A teacher of drawing and painting in Boston (about 1760).

Morris, Robert. "A Book of Autographs." The author of a brief letter in the collection.

Morton, [Thomas]. "Main Street." The wild gallant of Merry Mount, soon to be Governor Endicott's prisoner.

Moseby. *Dr. Grimshawe's Secret,* First Draft. The name of a family living near Brathwaite Hall.

Mountford. *Dr. Grimshawe's Secret,* First Draft. An Englishman who interviews the doctor in an effort to find information at the grave in New England of a man named Colcord. (Also called Hammond [which see].)

Mountford. *Dr. Grimshawe's Secret,* Second Draft: A young British lawyer who comes to New England to find information about Thomas Colcord, the Quaker ancestor of Seymour Colcord.

Mudge, Hezekiah. "My Kinsman, Major Molineux." Mentioned in a wanted poster as an escaped colonial bound-servant.

Mumpson, Mary. *Dr. Grimshawe's Secret,* First Draft. A name inexplicably mentioned in one of Hawthorne's notes to himself.

Murray, John. "P.'s Correspondence." Coleridge's old publisher, according to P.

Naval Officer, The. "The Custom House." Mentioned as a fellow employee and a conversationalist.

Neal, John. "P.'s Correspondence." A wild American writer, admired by P. and thought by him to be dead.

Ned. *Dr. Grimshawe's Secret,* First Draft. See Edward Redclyffe.

Neff, Mrs. Mary. "The Duston Family." The widow who is

captured by Indians while nursing Mrs. Hannah Duston during her confinement; they later murder their captors and escape.

New Year, The. "The Sister Years." The sister of the Old Year; she has a basket of hopes.

Nightingale. "Passages from a Relinquished Work." The owner of a drygoods store in the story-telling narrator's native village. "Fragments from the Journal of a Solitary Man." Mentioned as a drygoods storekeeper in Oberon's native village.

Nightmare, Sister. "The Gorgon's Head." See the Three Gray Women.

Nobody. "A Select Party." The impossibly able guest of the Man of Fancy.

Norman. "Main Street." An early neighbor of Jeffrey Massey of Naumkeag.

Norris, Rev. Mr. "Main Street." A venerable minister of Naumkeag.

Norton, Cyril. *Septimius Felton.* The handsome young British officer who impertinently kisses Rose Garfield on the road in front of Septimius Felton, is later shot by Septimius in a kind of military duel, and bequeaths his killer a miniature of Sibyl Dacy, a key to Aunt Keziah's old iron chest, and a manuscript which contains rules of egotistic life and a recipe for the elixir of life; Dr. Jabez Portsoaken seeks to obtain revenge for Norton against Septimius.

Norton. "Chippings with a Chisel." A rich customer for the tombstone carver of Martha's Vineyard.

Noye. *The Scarlet Letter.* An English lawyer mentioned as a former associate of Governor Bellingham.

Noyes, Rev. Mr. "Main Street. A nasal Salem minister.

Nymphs, The. "The Gorgon's Head." Beautiful creatures who help Perseus.

Oberon. "The Devil in Manuscript." The frustrated author who burns his unwanted manuscripts and sets the town on fire. "Fragments from the Journal of a Solitary Man." The young writer and journal-keeper who wanders from his native village apart from mankind but returns to die.

Oglethorpe, Richard. *Dr. Grimshawe's Secret*, First Draft. The name on a tombstone with the date 1613, which Miss Cheltenham, Warden Brathwaite, and Edward Etherege examine in the town near the hospital.

Oglethorpe. *Dr. Grimshawe's Secret*, First Draft. A name once used by Miss Cheltenham to address Warden Brathwaite.

Old Blood-and-Thunder. "The Great Stone Face." The illustrious retired general who for a time some inhabitants of the valley wrongly think resembles the Great Stone Face.

Oldest Inhabitant, The. "A Select Party." The Man of Fancy's guest who recalls forgotten men and things.

Old Harry. "A Select Party." A fanciful guest, more respectfully known at the party as Venerable Henry.

Old Maid, The. "The White Old Maid." See Edith.

Old Maid in the Winding Sheet, The. "The White Old Maid." See Edith.

Old Man of the Sea, The. "The Three Golden Apples." The myriad-shaped sea-creature whom Hercules wrestles with to obtain information. (Also called "The Old One.")

Old Moodie. *The Blithedale Romance*. See Moodie, Old.

Old One, The. "The Three Golden Apples." See the Old Man of the Sea.

Old Spider-winder. *Dr. Grimshawe's Secret*, Second Draft. One of the nicknames of Dr. Grimshawe (which see).

Old Stony Phiz. "The Great Stone Face." The eminent but gloomy statesman mistakenly thought for a time to resemble the Great Stone Face.

Old Year, The. "The Sister Years." The worn-out sister of the New Year.

On-Dit, Monsieur. "A Select Party." The gossiping guest of the Man of Fancy.

Oracle of Delphi, The. "The Dragon's Teeth." See Delphi, the Oracle of.

Ormskirk, Dr. *Dr. Grimshawe's Secret,* Second Draft. One of the other names of Dr. Grimshawe (which see).

Orpheus. "The Golden Fleece." The sweetly singing Argonaut.

Overbury, Sir Thomas. *The Scarlet Letter.* The victim of a celebrated murder in London; Roger Chillingworth is reputed to have been friendly with Dr. Forman, who was implicated; Ann Turner was hanged for the murder.

P. P. "The Custom House." Mentioned as an autobiographically inclined parish clerk whose example Hawthorne follows.

P. "P.'s Correspondence." The narrator's mentally disordered friend, who mixes fact and fancy, past and present.

Pain, Harriet. "Old News." A Boston milliner (about 1760).

Palfrey, Peter. "The May-Pole of Merry Mount." John Endicott's "ancient" or lieutenant, who helps his Puritan leader break up festivities at Merry Mount. "Main Street." An early neighbor of Jeffrey Massey of Naumkeag.

Palmer, General. "A Book of Autographs." The recipient of many letters in the collection.

Palmer, The. *Dr. Grimshawe's Secret,* First Draft. See Pearson.

Pan. "The Pomegranate Seeds." A horned, hairy-eared, goat-footed flutist who cannot give Mother Ceres any information about Proserpina.

Pandora. "The Paradise of Children." The inquisitive girl friend of Epimetheus who disobeys orders and opens the mysterious box full of miseries.

Panini. *The Marble Faun.* An artist who paints a popular picture showing Hilda in a blood-stained white robe.

Parker, Goodman. "The Wives of the Dead." The innkeeper who tells Margaret that her husband has not been killed.

Parker, Uncle. "The Village Uncle." A tall, gnarled old yarn-spinner in Bartlett's village store.

Parris, Mercy. "Main Street." A minister's daughter in Salem, supposedly smitten by the witch Martha Carrier's curse.

Patriot, A. "A Select Party." An incorruptibly patriotic fanciful guest.

Pearl. *The Scarlet Letter.* See Pearl Prynne.

Pearson, Mrs. Dorothy. "The Gentle Boy." The Puritan wife of Tobias Pearson who tries to be a mother to Ilbrahim, the gentle boy.

Pearson, Tobias. "The Gentle Boy." The former Puritan soldier who adopts Ilbrahim, the gentle boy, and turns Quaker because of his quiet influence.

Pearson. *Dr. Grimshawe's Secret,* First Draft. The mysterious and gentle pensioner at Brathwaite Hospital; he rescues the hero after he is shot, is evidently the father of Elsie, is an antiquarian, and finally is seen to be the descendant of the bloody-footed emigrant and the true heir to the Brathwaite estate. (See also Hammond and the Palmer.)

Pearson, Miss. *Dr. Grimshawe's Secret,* First Draft. Presumably the name of the daughter of the pensioner Pearson. (See Elsie.)

Pelias, King. "The Golden Fleece." The dethroner of King Aeson and present monarch of Iolchos whom Aeson's son Jason determines to dethrone; he sends Jason to Colchis for the Golden Fleece.

Pemberton, Clara. "The Antique Ring." The fiancee of Edward Caryl, who reads her his legend of the diamond ring which he has given her.

Percy, Lord. "Howe's Masquerade." The frightened officer who remains near Sir William Howe at the latter's fancy-dress ball.

Periwinkle. *A Wonder-Books for Girls and Boys.* A ten-year-old girl, one of Eustace Bright's older auditors. *Tanglewood Tales, for Girls and Boys.* Mentioned as maturing.

Perseus. "The Gorgon's Head." The son of Danae who beheads the Gorgon Medusa and with it turns wicked King Polydectes and his wicked people into stone.

Peters, Hugh. "Main Street." A fiery, restless, energetic man of Naumkeag who later becomes Cromwell's chaplain.

Philemon. "The Miraculous Pitcher." The hospitable old husband of Baucis; he turns into an oak tree after his death.

Phillips, Sir William. "Howe's Masquerade." A versatile Massachusetts Governor whose shade appears in the mysterious pageant at Sir William Howe's fancy-dress ball. *The House of the Seven Gables.* The Governor of Massachusetts who participated in the persecution of witches and wizards, including Matthew Maule.

Phillips. "The Custom House." A former Salem merchant.

Philoctetes. "The Golden Fleece." Mentioned as a pupil of Chiron the centaur.

Phineus. "The Golden Fleece." A blind Thracian whom the Argonauts rescue from the Harpies.

Phoebus. "The Pomegranate Seeds." The sunny-faced singer-poet who tells Mother Ceres that Pluto has kidnapped her daughter Proserpina.

Phoenix. "The Dragon's Teeth." Lost Europa's brother who abandons the search for the girl.

Phrixus. "The Golden Fleece." Mentioned as a boy rescued with Helle by the Boeotian ram with the Golden Fleece.

Pickering, [Timothy] "Old Tim." "A Book of Autographs." The author of a letter in the collection; known by the author years ago.

Pickering. *Dr. Grimshawe's Secret,* Second Draft. Dr. Grimshawe's lawyer.

Picus, King. "Circe's Palace." A preening king whom Circe turned into a bird but who earns the friendship of Ulysses by trying to warn him; therefore Ulysses forces Circe to transform him back again.

Pierson, Martha. "The Shaker Bridal." The woman who loves

Adam Colburn, grows into middle age enduring a variety of vicissitudes, and as she promises to be his sister and help him lead the Shakers at Goshen falls dead at his feet.

Pietro. *The Marble Faun.* A young boy who lives on a street near the Palazzo Cenci.

Piety, Miss. "The Celestial Railroad." Now a dry old maid.

Pigsnort, Ichabod. "The Great Carbuncle." The rich merchant who wants the carbuncle for profit but who is kidnapped by Indians during his search for it.

Pike, Dominicus. "Passages from a Relinquished Work." A manufacturer of tobacco products in the native village of the story-telling narrator. "Mr. Higginbotham's Catastrophe." The gossipy peddler who recounts false stories of Higginbotham's murder but who because of his curiosity saves the squire from murder; he marries Higginbotham's pretty niece. "Fragments from the Journal of a Solitary Man." Mentioned as a grocer in Oberon's native village.

Pingree. "The Custom House." A former Salem merchant.

Pitcher, Moll. *The House of the Seven Gables.* Reported to have imprisoned Judge Jaffrey Pyncheon's grandfather in a supposedly enchanted chair.

Pittheus, King. "The Minotaur." The King of Troezene and grandfather of Theseus.

Plaisir, Monsieur le. "Little Daffydowndilly." The fiddling brother of Mr. Toil.

Plantain. *A Wonder-Book for Girls and Boys.* One of Eustace Bright's older auditors. *Tanglewood Tales, for Girls and Boys.* Mentioned as having had scarlet fever.

Platt, Judge. *Dr. Grimshawe's Secret,* Preliminary Studies. Mentioned.

Pluto, King. "The Pomegranate Seeds." The King of the Underground who kidnaps Proserpina and can keep her six months a year because she ate six pomegranate seeds while in his domain.

Poet, A. "A Select Party." A never-jealous poet, a fanciful guest.

Poet, The. "The Great Carbuncle." The poet who seeks the carbuncle in order to write an immortal poem about it; later he must content himself with a piece of ice.

Pollux. "The Golden Fleece." A brave Argonaut, Castor's twin brother.

Polly. "A Book of Autographs." Mentioned in Franklin's letter to his wife in the collection.

Polydectes, King. "The Gorgon's Head." The wicked King of the Island of Seriphus who is turned to stone by Perseus.

Polyphemus. "Circe's Palace." Mentioned as the one-eyed Cyclops who troubled Ulysses.

Pompey. "Old News." An escaped Negro slave in Boston.

Poore, Major Ben Perley. "Chiefly about War Matters." A note-taker with whom Hawthorne meets President Abraham Lincoln at the White House.

Popgun, Peleg. "The Bald Eagle." A member of the militia of the Connecticut Valley village which Lafayette does not visit.

Porter, Tabitha "Tabby." "Peter Goldthwaite's Treasure." The sixty-year-old companion and domestic servant of Peter Goldthwaite; she shrewdly advises him to tear down his kitchen last in his useless search for an ancestral treasure in the walls of his old mansion.

Portingale, Dr. *Dr. Grimshawe's Secret*, Second Draft. The physician who tends Edward Redclyffe when he is shot; the doctor is a friend of Warden Hammond of the hospital.

Portsoaken, Dr. Jabez. *Septimius Felton*. A retired British army surgeon who later practices medicine and magic in Boston; he seems to befriend Septimius Felton but in reality helps Sibyl Dacy, his niece, in an abortive plot to poison Septimius; the doctor wants to aid the cause of a British claimant to Smithell's Hall.

Posterity. "A Select Party." A very popular guest at the party given by the Man of Fancy.

Powers, [Hiram]. *The Marble Faun*. A sculptor in Florence whom Miriam Schaefer knows.

Pownall, Governor [Thomas]. "Old News." A leader who places military orders in the advertising columns of Boston newspapers (about 1760). "Howe's Masquerade." A former Governor of Massachusetts whose shade appears in the mysterious pageant at Sir William Howe's fancy-dress ball.

President of the United States, The. *Dr. Grimshawe's Secret,* First Draft. The chief executive who writes Edward Etherege about his ambassadorial appointment.

Price. "The Ancestral Footstep." The name of a family living in the neighborhood of Eldredge's estate.

Priest, A. "A Select Party." A priest without worldly ambition, a fanciful guest.

Primrose. *A Wonder-Book for Girls and Boys. Tanglewood Tales, for Girls and Boys.* See Primrose Pringle.

Pringle, Primrose. *A Wonder-Book for Girls and Boys.* A pert, bright, saucy little twelve- or thirteen-year-old daughter of Mr. and Mrs. Pringle of Tanglewood; one of Eustace Bright's older auditors. *Tanglewood Tales, for Girls and Boys.* Mentioned as maturing.

Pringle. *A Wonder-Book for Girls and Boys.* A fifty-year-old classical scholar, the owner of Tanglewood, and the father of Primrose Pringle.

Pringle, Mrs. *A Wonder-Book for Girls and Boys.* The wife of the owner of Tanglewood and mother of Primrose Pringle.

Priscilla. *The Blithedale Romance.* The pallid, teen-age younger daughter of Old Moodie, who attaches herself to Zenobia, knowing that they are half-sisters; her love for Hollingsworth is stronger than her love for Zenobia; Priscilla is the Veiled Lady whom Westervelt victimizes for a time; she is the object of Miles Coverdale's hopeless love.

Procrustes. "The Minotaur." A robber who cuts or stretches people to make them fit into his bed; Theseus rids the country of him.

Proctor, Mrs. Elizabeth. "Main Street." A Christian condemned with her husband John Proctor to hang in Salem for witchcraft.

Proctor, Goodman John. "Main Street." A Christian condemned with his wife Elizabeth Proctor to hang in Salem for witchcraft.

Proserpina. "The Pomegranate Seeds." Mother Ceres's daughter, who is kidnapped by King Pluto and must spend six months annually with him in the Underground because she ate six pomegranate seeds while in his domain.

Prudence, Miss. "The Celestial Railroad." Now a dry old maid.

Prynne, Hester. "The Custom House." The central figure in the account by Surveyor Jonathan Pue concerning the scarlet letter. *The Scarlet Letter.* The secretly renounced wife of Roger Chillingworth and natural mother of Pearl by the Rev. Mr. Arthur Dimmesdale; because of social ostracism, this strong, passionate, beautiful woman becomes a free-thinker but also self-sacrificial and deeply sympathetic to others in trouble.

Prynne, Pearl. *The Scarlet Letter.* The beautiful, intuitively intelligent, wild-tempered natural daughter of Hester Prynne and the Rev. Mr. Arthur Dimmesdale; she is humanized by grief at her father's confession and death.

Prynne. *The Scarlet Letter.* The real name of Roger Chillingworth (which see).

Pue, Surveyor Jonathan. "The Custom House." One of Hawthorne's predecessors, dead more than eighty years, at the Salem Custom House, whose package containing the faded scarlet letter with an accompanying manuscript account inspires Hawthorne to write about Hester Prynne. *The Scarlet Letter.* Mentioned as the investigator of Hester Prynne's case a century afterwards.

Pyncheon, Alice. *The House of the Seven Gables.* The Europeanized daughter of Gervayse Pyncheon who plants the seeds of posies brought from Europe, plays the harpsichord, and is ruinously mesmerized by Matthew Maule, the carpenter grandson of the wizard Matthew Maule, immediately after whose wedding she catches a fatal cold; she is Phoebe Pyncheon's great-great-grand-aunt.

Pyncheon, Arthur. *The House of the Seven Gables.* Phoebe Pyncheon's dead father, whose wife was a woman of no family or property; Phoebe resembles him less than she does her mother.

Pyncheon, Mrs. Arthur. *The House of the Seven Gables.* Phoebe Pyncheon's mother, whose remarriage following the death of her husband Arthur Pyncheon causes Phoebe to leave home and stay with Hepzibah Pyncheon; Phoebe resembles her mother more than she does her father.

Pyncheon, Clifford. *The House of the Seven Gables.* The nephew of the bachelor Jaffrey Pyncheon, whose death of natural causes he is unjustly blamed for through the machinations of his cousin Jaffrey Pyncheon; following a thirty-year imprisonment he is released and begins to live with his spinster sister Hepzibah Pyncheon; his faculties are ruined, but he retains his love of beauty and is tenderly cared for by Phoebe Pyncheon.

Pyncheon, Gervayse. *The House of the Seven Gables.* The handsome, foreign-bred grandson of Colonel Pyncheon, whose daughter Alice Pyncheon is ruinously mesmerized by Matthew Maule, the grandson of the hanged wizard.

Pyncheon, Mrs. Gervayse. *The House of the Seven Gables.* The rich, British wife of Gervayse Pyncheon and mother of Alice Pyncheon; she dies before her husband.

Pyncheon, Hepzibah "Old Maid." *The House of the Seven Gables.* The sixty-year-old spinster cousin of Judge Jaffrey Pyncheon and of Phoebe Pyncheon; she has been granted the right to reside in the house of the seven gables during the remainder of her lifetime; she has Holgrave as a roomer, opens the cent-shop but scowls most of her customers away, and cares tenderly for her partly demented brother Clifford Pyncheon.

Pyncheon, Jaffrey. *The House of the Seven Gables.* The bachelor uncle of Judge Jaffrey Pyncheon and Clifford Pyncheon who died of a seizure while observing the younger Jaffrey ransacking his desk for papers and money; his death was attributed to Clifford, who was therefore unjustly imprisoned for thirty years.

Pyncheon, Judge Jaffrey. *The House of the Seven Gables.* The hypocritical, sultrily smiling villain who causes his cousin Clifford Pyncheon's unjust imprisonment, tortures him in an effort to locate missing evidence of Pyncheon family rights to Indian lands, and dies alone in the parlor of the house of the seven gables.

Pyncheon, Mrs. Jaffrey. *The House of the Seven Gables.* Judge Jaffrey Pyncheon's wife, who died after three or four years of marriage; the Judge delays repairing her split tombstone.

Pyncheon, Jaffrey. *The House of the Seven Gables.* The dissipated son of Judge Jaffrey Pyncheon who dies abroad a week before his father dies.

Pyncheon, Phoebe. *The House of the Seven Gables.* The seventeen-year-old country cousin of Hepzibah Pyncheon, Clifford Pyncheon, and Judge Jaffrey Pyncheon; she is lovely, sunny, intellectually shallow, but spiritually sound; she and Holgrave marry at the end of the novel.

Pyncheon, Colonel. *The House of the Seven Gables.* The original Pyncheon, who covets Matthew Maule's house-site and contributes to the condemnation of the wizard to hang for witchcraft in order to seize the land and build the seven-gabled Pyncheon house on it; his corpse greets the first guests to enter the new house; he is the great-great-grandfather of Judge Jaffrey Pyncheon; his gloomy portrait dominates the parlor of the house.

Pyncheon, Mrs. *The House of the Seven Gables.* One of the three wives of Colonel Pyncheon; her maiden name was Davenport, and she had teacups which were rare in colonial days; she is Phoebe Pyncheon's great-great-great-great-grandmother.

Pyncheon, Mrs. *The House of the Seven Gables.* Another of Colonel Pyncheon's three wives.

Pyncheon, Mrs. *The House of the Seven Gables.* Another of Colonel Pyncheon's three wives.

Pyncheon, Rev. Mr. *The House of the Seven Gables.* A clergyman member of the Pyncheon family.

Pyncheon. *The House of the Seven Gables.* The son of Colonel Pyncheon who inherits the estate; his son is Gervayse Pyncheon, whose daughter Alice Pyncheon is ruined by the wizard Matthew Maule's grandson Matthew Maule.

Pyncheon. *The House of the Seven Gables.* The great-great-grand-father of Hepzibah and Clifford Pyncheon who started the cent-shop.

Pyncheon. *The House of the Seven Gables.* A member of the Pyncheon family who was a British army officer during the Old French War.

Pyncheon. *The House of the Seven Gables.* A member of the Pyncheon family whose death about a hundred years before the events of the novel was similar to that of Colonel Pyncheon.

Pyncheon. *The House of the Seven Gables.* Hepzibah Pyncheon's proud colonial grandfather, whom Uncle Venner remembers.

Pyncheon. *The House of the Seven Gables.* A member of the Pyncheon family who during the American Revolutionary War became a royalist, escaped, but repented in time to prevent the seven-gabled house from being confiscated.

Pyncheon. *The House of the Seven Gables.* The dead father of Hepzibah and Clifford Pyncheon.

Pyncheon, Mrs. *The House of the Seven Gables.* The dead mother of Hepzibah and Clifford Pyncheon, whom the latter is said to resemble.

Pyncheon. *The House of the Seven Gables.* The present head of the English branch of the Pyncheon family, a member of Parliament, and the owner of Pyncheon Hall.

Pyncheon, Miss. *The House of the Seven Gables.* The dead sister of Hepzibah and Clifford Pyncheon.

Quick, Alice. "Old News." A Boston crockery and hosiery dealer (about 1760).

Quicksilver. "The Gorgon's Head." The speedy stranger who aids Perseus; he has a wise, invisible sister who also helps. "The Paradise of Children." The messenger who leaves the mysterious box with Epimetheus with orders that it remain closed. "The Miraculous Pitcher." The nimble-footed guest of hospitable Philemon and Baucis who makes their milk pitcher perpetually full. "Circe's Palace." The nimble young man with the snaky staff who helps Ulysses discomfit Circe. "The Pomegranate Seeds." The nimble messenger with the snaky staff who persuades Pluto to release Proserpina from his underground domain.

Rachel. "The Vision of the Fountain." The "nymph" of water, wood, and fire, who the day after the narrator arrives must leave the area which he has come to live in; she returns.

Raikes, Robert. "A Good Man's Miracle." The Londoner who founds Sunday schools after he sees the plight of muddy slum children.

Ralle [Rale], Father [Sebastien]. "Bells." A martyred French priest whose chapel bell is hidden in the forest, and is then found and taken to the Bowdoin College Museum.

Ramshorne, Dr. Ephraim. "The Haunted Quack." The physician and apothecary, who was little better than a quack, under whom Hippocrates Jenkins studied.

Ramshorne, Mrs. Ephraim. "The Haunted Quack." The wife of Dr. Ephraim Ramshorne, an irresponsible physician and apothecary.

Ramshorne, Miss. "The Haunted Quack." The bookish daughter

of Dr. and Mrs. Ephraim Ramshorne.

Randolph, Edward. "Dr. Bullivant." A political associate of Sir Edmund Andros. "The Gray Champion." The hated cavalier enemy of Massachusetts, an associate of Sir Edmund Andros the Governor.

Rappaccini, Beatrice. "Dr. Rappaccini's Daughter." The daughter of Dr. Giacomo Rappaccini; she is pure in spirit but poisonous in body because of her father's diabolical experiment.

Rappaccini, Dr. Giacomo. "Dr. Rappaccini's Daughter." The diabolical botanist who feeds his daughter Beatrice Rappaccini a diet of poison to make her feared.

Redclyffe, Sir Edward. *Dr. Grimshawe's Secret,* Second Draft. Mentioned as a fighter in the War of the Roses.

Redclyffe, Edward. *Dr. Grimshawe's Secret,* Second Draft. The hero of the novel; as a youth he is the playmate of Elsie in Dr. Grimshawe's home; later he is sent to school by the doctor; after a varied career, he visits England, believing that he is the true heir of the Redclyffe title and lands, is shot, and is befriended by Seymour Colcord, now a palmer, living in the hospital and then by Warden Brathwaite of that hospital. (He is also called Etherege.)

Reformer, A. "A Select Party." A reformer untrammeled by his theory, a fanciful guest.

Rigby, Goodman. "Feathertop." The husband of Mother Rigby until she worried the life out of him.

Rigby, Mother. "Feathertop." The retired witch who cannot refrain from sending her scarecrow Feathertop, which she created, out into the world as an illusion of glittering greatness.

Roberts, [David?]. *Dr. Grimshawe's Secret,* First Draft. A name inexplicably mentioned in one of Hawthorne's notes to himself.

Robin. "My Kinsman, Major Molineux." See Robin Molineux.

Robinson, Emily. *Biographical Stories.* Edward Temple's seven-year-old friend and informal step-sister.

Rochcliffe, Lady Eleanore. "Lady Eleanore's Mantle." The haughty British ward of Colonel Shute; her mantle is the source of the smallpox plague which strikes Boston.

Roderick. "The Christmas Banquet." See Roderick Elliston.

Roe, Richard. "A Select Party." A fanciful guest.

Rogers, Rev. Mr. "A Bell's Biography." A minister for whose church Deacon Lawson wants the bell.

Rollins. *Dr. Grimshawe's Secret,* First Draft. The former sexton of the Charter-Street graveyard and father of the present sexton, whom the doctor knows.

Rollins. *Dr. Grimshawe's Secret,* First Draft. The present sexton of the Charter-Street graveyard and son of the former sexton; the doctor knows him; he is nearby when the silver key is found near the site of the Colcord grave.

Rosina. "The Christmas Banquet." See Rosina Elliston.

Rothermel, Alice. "The Ancestral Footstep." See Alice Hammond.

Rothermel. "The Ancestral Footstep." See Hammond.

Rugg, Peter. "A Virtuoso's Collection." The missing man, now the doorkeeper of the Wandering Jew's museum.

Rynders, Marshall [Captain Isaiah]. *Dr. Grimshawe's Secret,* First Draft. A name inexplicably mentioned in one of Hawthorne's notes to himself.

Sachem, The Squaw. "Main Street." See the Squaw Sachem.

Sally. "A Book of Autographs." Mentioned in Franklin's letter to his wife in the collection.

Salmon, Mary. "Old News." A person who shoes horses in Boston (about 1760).

Saltonstall, Sir Richard. "Main Street." The Lord Mayor of London who visits Main Street.

Saunders, Squire. "The Minister's Black Veil." An influential member of the congregation of the Rev. Mr. Hooper who refuses to invite his minister to customary Sunday dinner once he puts on his veil.

Scaly-conscience. "The Celestial Railroad." A materialistic friend of Smooth-it-away.

Scarecrow, Sister. "The Gorgon's Head." See the Three Gray Women.

Scarisbrooke. *Dr. Grimshawe's Secret,* Preliminary Studies. Mentioned.

Schaefer, Miriam. *The Marble Faun.* The mysterious artist of English, Jewish, and southern Italian blood whose beauty attracts Donatello; at a signal from her, Donatello murders the spectral monk, Brother Antonio, thus precipitating the transformation of Donatello.

Schlemihl, Peter. "The Intelligence Office." The man who inquires in the Intelligence Office for information about his lost shadow.

Scholar, A. "A Select Party." A scholar without pedantry, a fanciful guest.

Schuyler, General [Philip]. "A Book of Autographs." The author of a letter in the collection.

Scinis. "The Minotaur." A robber whom Theseus throws off a cliff.

Scipio. "Old News." An escaped Negro slave in Boston.

Scipio. "Egotism." Roderick Elliston's faithful Negro family servant.

Scipio. *The House of the Seven Gables.* Gervayse Pyncheon's Negro servant.

Scott, Sir Walter. "P.'s Correspondence." A paralytic old writer, no longer famous, according to P.

Scut, Captain. "Old News." A cloth merchant on Creek Lane in Boston.

Sealsfield, [Charles] [Karl Anton Postl]. "A Select Party." A fanciful guest, once thought to be a man of straw but later proved to be a resident of Germany.

Seeker, The. "The Great Carbuncle." The man who has made a lifelong task of seeking the carbuncle; upon seeing it, he dies beside its lake.

Selectman, The. "Edward Randolph's Portrait." A Boston selectman who speaks for the selectmen and unsuccessfully urges Lieutenant-Governor Hutchinson not to sign the order bringing British troops into Boston on the eve of the Boston Massacre.

Seward, Secretary [William Henry]. "Chiefly about War Matters." President Lincoln's Secretary of State, seen by Hawthorne in Washington.

Sewell [Sewall], Chief-Justice [Samuel]. "Main Street." The death-dealing Salem judge of John and Elizabeth Proctor.

Seymour. *Dr. Grimshawe's Secret.* See Seymour Colcord.

Shadow, The. *The Marble Faun.* See Brother Antonio.

Shakejoint, Sister. "The Gorgon's Head." See the Three Gray Women.

Shallow-deep, Rev. Mr. "The Celestial Railroad." An easy preacher in Vanity Fair.

Sheaffe, Timothy. "Old News." A tombstone carver in Cold Lane in Boston.

Sheepshanks, Tribulation. "The Bald Eagle." A member of the militia of the Connecticut Valley village which Lafayette does not visit.

Shelley, [Percy Bysshe]. "P.'s Correspondence." A conservative Church of England poet once rumored to have drowned in the Bay of Spezzia, according to P.

Shepard. "The Custom House." A former Salem merchant.

Shirley, [William]. "Howe's Masquerade." A former Governor of Massachusetts whose shade appears in the mysterious pageant at Sir William Howe's fancy-dress ball. "The Custom House." The Massachusetts Governor who appointed Jonathan Pue to be surveyor in the Salem Custom House.

Shrewsbury, The Countess of. "The Antique Ring." The scorned, deceitful courtesan who breaks her promise to use the diamond ring given her by the Earl of Essex to intercede on his behalf with Queen Elizabeth.

Shute, Colonel [Samuel]. "Howe's Masquerade." A Massachusetts Governor, once frightened out of the province by the people; his shade appears in the mysterious pageant at Sir William Howe's fancy-dress ball. "Lady Eleanore's Mantle." The Governor of Massachusetts and guardian of haughty Lady Eleanore Rochcliffe.

Siddons, Mrs. [Sarah]. "P.'s Correspondence." John Kemble's histrionic sister, seen by P. at the Drury Lane Theatre in 1845.

Smith, J. T. "A Book of Autographs." A presumably non-existent colonel under Andrew Jackson at the battle of New Orleans; mentioned in Jackson's letter in the collection.

Smith, Rev. Mr. Sydney. "Earth's Holocaust." A European who burns certain repudiated stocks in the holocaust.

Smith. "Fancy's Show Box." The silver-haired old man who over a glass of Madeira is shown his imagined sins by Fancy, reminded of their truth by Memory, and then tortured by Conscience.

Smith. "The Christmas Banquet." A red-faced banquet guest whose misery it is to want to laugh but who knows that any merriment will kill him; he dies.

Smith, Captain. *A Wonder-Book for Girls and Boys.* Presumably a neighbor of the Pringles.

Smith. *The House of the Seven Gables.* Mentioned as the town livery-stable keeper.

Smooth-it-away. "The Celestial Railroad." The narrator's companion on the railroad trip toward the Celestial City.

Southey, [Robert]. "P.'s Correspondence." Lord Byron's intimate friend and a diligent poet, according to P.

Southwick, Cassandra. "Main Street." A Quaker prisoner in

Salem.

Spectre of the Catacomb, The. *The Marble Faun.* See Brother Antonio.

Spencer, Edward. "Fancy's Show Box." A friend whom Smith tried to kill and therefore in imagination did kill.

Spinney, Keziah. "The New England Village." The spinster neighbor of the minister in the village of N— who gives up her ambition to marry him.

Spring. "A Visit to the Clerk of the Weather." The lovely damsel who lodges a complaint with the Clerk of the Weather against John Frost.

Squash-Blossom. *A Wonder-Book for Girls and Boys.* One of Eustace Bright's youngest auditors. *Tanglewood Tales, for Girls and Boys.* Mentioned as having had scarlet fever.

Squaw Sachem, The. "Main Street." A feminine Indian ruler from Mystic to Agawam, married to Wappacowett.

Squire, The. "An Old Woman's Tale." An elderly man with a sky-blue coat in the identical dream of David and Esther; he greets the old woman and questions her about her digging.

Stella. *The Marble Faun.* The maid at Donatello's home in Tuscany.

Stephen. "The Wives of the Dead." A sailor who tells Mary, whom he formerly courted, that her husband has not been drowned.

Steuben, Baron [von]. "A Book of Autographs." The author of a letter in the collection.

Stevenson, Mrs. "A Book of Autographs." Mentioned in Franklin's letter to his wife in the collection.

Stick-to-the-right. "The Celestial Railroad." An old-fashioned Bunyanesque foot-pilgrim who makes it to the Celestial City.

Story Teller, The. "Passages from a Relinquished Work." The narrator who leaves his guardian Parson Thumpcushion to become a wandering story-teller.

Straggler, The. "The Seven Vagabonds." The diabolical beggar, conjurer, and fortune-teller who temporarily joins the other vagabonds and then continues alone toward Stamford, Canada.

Stuart. *Dr. Grimshawe's Secret*, First Draft. The royal English family mentioned as having migrated to the Continent accompanied by one of the Brathwaite heirs.

Stumble-at-the-truth, Rev. Mr. "The Celestial Railroad." An easy preacher in Vanity Fair.

Sukey. *Dr. Grimshawe's Secret*, First Draft. See Hannah.

Susan. "The Village Uncle." The real or imaginary wife of the hearty old narrator.

Swan, David. "David Swan." The young man who on his way to Boston falls asleep and is approached by wealth. love, and death without knowing it.

Sweet Fern. *A Wonder-Book for Girls and Boys*. A good little boy, trouble-free and literal-minded, one of Eustace Bright's younger auditors. *Tanglewood Tales, for Girls and Boys*. Mentioned as having learned to read and write.

Swinnerton, Dr. John. *The House of the Seven Gables*. One of the physicians who examined the corpse of Colonel Pyncheon and rendered the verdict of "sudden death." "The Dolliver Romance." A diabolically skilled physician and the master of Dr. Dolliver; he was unprofessionally cynical and at his death bequeathed to Dr. Dolliver his property, herb garden, manuscripts, and brazen serpent. *Dr. Grimshawe's Secret*, Second Draft. A physician of a century before Dr. Grimshawe's time, near whose grave Dr. Grimshawe is buried.

Take-it-easy. "The Celestial Railroad." A resident of the Valley of the Shadow of Death who has decided to stay rather than go on to the Celestial City.

Talby, Dorothy. "Main Street." A meeting-house prisoner forced in Naumkeag to stand in the hot sun for raising her hand against her husband.

Talus, the Man of Brass. "The Minotaur." The human-looking creature who patrols the island of Crete until he falls into the sea while trying to strike Theseus's vessel.

Taylor, President [Zachary]. "The Custom House." The President of the United States whose election (in 1848) causes Hawthorne to lose his position as surveyor of the Salem Custom House.

Telephassa, Queen. "The Dragon's Teeth." Cruel King Agenor's queen, who accompanies their three sons — Cadmus, Cilix, and Phoenix — when he orders them to search for their lost sister Europa until they find her; Queen Telephassa dies during the long, unsuccessful search.

Temple, Edward "Ned." *Biographical Stories.* The temporarily blind, eight- or-nine-year-old boy who is told instructive anecdotes of real-life people by his father.

Temple, George. *Biographical Stories.* The brother, three or four years older, of Edward Temple.

Temple. *Biographical Stories.* The kindly, somewhat sententious man who tells his temporarily blinded son Edward Temple instructive anecdotes of real-life people.

Temple, Mrs. *Biographical Stories.* The devoted wife of Temple and the mother of temporarily blinded Edward Temple.

Thasus. "The Dragon's Teeth." A noble young friend of lost Europa who joins the unsuccessful search for her but later abandons it.

That-to-morrow, Rev. Mr. "The Celestial Railroad." An easy preacher in Vanity Fair.

Theodore. *The Blithedale Romance.* The gentleman in Zenobia's story "The Silvery Veil" who lifts the veil from the Veiled Lady's face and is thus doomed to pine forever for another sight.

Theseus. "The Minotaur." The son of King Aegeus of Attica and Queen Aethra, and killer of wicked King Minos's Minotaur on the island of Crete. "The Golden Fleece." The Minotaur-killing Argonaut.

This-to-day, Rev. Mr. "The Celestial Railroad." An easy preacher in Vanity Fair.

Thompson, [Cephas Giovanni]. *The Marble Faun.* The artist said by Hilda to have copied Guido Reni's "Beatrice Cenci" piecemeal.

Thoreau, [Henry David]. "The Old Manse." Mentioned as an expert on Indian relics and flowers in the region of Concord. "The Custom House." Mentioned as an expert on Indian relics and trees.

Three Gray Women, The. "The Gorgon's Head." Sister Scarecrow, Sister Nightmare, and Sister Shakejoint, whose one bright eye Perseus seizes to force them to help him.

Thumpcushion, Parson. "Passages from a Relinquished Work." The Puritan but well-meaning guardian of the story-telling narrator.

Tibula. "Main Street." An Indian hag, one of the Afflicted Ones, condemned as a witch to hang in Salem.

Ticknor, [William Davis]. "The Antique Ring." A distinguished American who praises Edward Caryl. *A Wonder-Book for Girls and Boys.* Mentioned as the publisher employing J. T. Fields; he might publish Eustace Bright's wonderful stories.

Tidy Man, The. "Main Street." The busy truant officer of Naumkeag.

Tiffany, Bela. "Howe's Masquerade." The elderly, unnamed story-teller at the Province House. "Edward Randolph's Portrait." The elderly story-teller at the Province House. "Lady Eleanore's Mantle." The narrator. "Old Esther Dudley." A story-teller who listens to the old loyalist's tale of Esther Dudley.

Tilton, Deacon. "The Antique Ring." A kind New England churchman in whose collection box the antique ring appears.

Time. "Time's Portraiture." A dapper fellow who associates with everything, not merely with hoary events of the past, and who must die.

Tiphys. "The Golden Fleece." A star-gazing Argonaut, helmsman of the Argo.

Toil, Mr. "Little Daffydowndilly." The toilsome master from whose school Little Daffydowndilly runs away for a while.

Tomaso. *The Marble Faun.* The white-haired butler at Donatello's home in Tuscany.

Tomkins, David. "Fancy's Show Box." The real-life husband of Martha Burroughs, whom Smith in imagination ruined.

Toothaker, Rose "Rosebud" Grafton. "Edward Fane's Rosebud." The disappointed fiancee of Edward Fane who later marries sick Toothaker and becomes a sick-room nurse.

Toothaker. "Edward Fane's Rosebud." Rose Grafton Toothaker's mortally palsied husband.

Transcendentalist. "The Celestial Railroad." A misty, shapeless, smoke-fed monster in the cavern formerly inhabited by John Bunyan's Pope and Pagan.

Trott, Deacon. "The Antique Ring." The nettlesome friend of Deacon Tilton, in whose collection box the antique ring appears.

Trumbull, Colonel [John]. "A Book of Autographs." The author of a letter in the collection.

Turner, Ann. *The Scarlet Letter.* Mentioned as having been hanged for the murder of Sir Thomas Overbury in London.

Ulysses. "Circe's Palace." The King of Ithaca, who with Quicksilver's help defies the enchantress Circe.

Uncle. *Dr. Grimshawe's Secret,* First Draft. The name by which Ned and Elsie know Dr. Etherege (which see).

Upton. "The Custom House." A former Salem merchant.

Vane, Alice. "Edward Randolph's Portrait." Lieutenant-Governor Hutchinson's niece, who urges the Lieutenant-Governor to be warned by the portrait of the unhappy Edward Randolph and who may have restored the time-blackened features of Randolph's mysterious portrait.

Vane, Sir Henry. "Howe's Masquerade." An anti-royalist whose shade appears in the mysterious pageant at Sir William Howe's fancy-dress ball. "Main Street." A man who appears on Main Street near Lady Arabella and Ann Hutchinson.

Van Pelt. "The Haunted Quack." A rheumatic patient of Dr. Ephraim Ramshorne.

Vaughan, Edgar. "Sylph Etherege." The absent cousin of Sylvia Etherege, who conjures up an impossibly romantic image of himself; in an unsuccessful attempt to cure her, he presents himself (as Edward Hamilton) as a rival, whose dark smile she rejects.

Veiled Lady, The. *The Blithedale Romance.* See Priscilla.

Venerable Henry. "A Select Party." See Old Harry.

Venner, Uncle. *The House of the Seven Gables.* The old, rheumatic laborer who is full of pithy philosophy and who instead of retiring to the workhouse joins Hepzibah Pyncheon, Clifford Pyncheon, Phoebe Pyncheon, and Holgrave when they move to the late Judge Jaffrey Pyncheon's country estate.

Vere, Lord de. "The Great Carbuncle." The haughty aristocrat who wants to decorate his ancestral halls with the carbuncle but who has to settle for a chandelier.

Vulcan. "The Minotaur." Mentioned as the metal worker who built Talus, the Man of Brass. "The Golden Fleece." Mentioned as the blacksmith who made the brass bulls for King Aeetes of Colchis.

Waite, Thomas. "Howe's Masquerade." The proprietor of the Province House in Boston. "Lady Eleanore's Mantle." The host of the Province House.

Wakefield. "Wakefield." A crafty Londoner who deserts his wife for twenty years, on an inexplicable whim, and then as inexplicably returns.

Wakefield, Mrs. "Wakefield." The "widow" of the crafty Londoner who whimsically deserts her for twenty years, then inexplicably returns to her.

Walcott, Edward. *Fanshawe.* The tall, handsome, slightly wild relative of President Melmoth of Harley College, which Walcott attends; he loves and later marries Ellen Langton.

Waldo, Samuel. "Old News." The agent who offers Irish lasses "for sale" as servants in Boston.

Walpole, Sir Robert. "The Antique Ring." A British statesman who gives the diamond ring to the wife of a legislator whom he wishes to dishonor.

Wandering Jew, The. "A Virtuoso's Collection." The icy-hearted curator of the museum of fabulous objects. "A Select Party." One of the Man of Fancy's guests, so common now and so out of place that he soon leaves.

Wanton Gospeller. "Endicott and the Red Cross." An independent interpreter of the Bible, punished for his deviation from orthodoxy.

Wappacowett. "Main Street." The second Indian husband of the Squaw Sachem.

Ward, Nathaniel. "Main Street." The cobbler wit of Agawam.

Ward, Sylvia. "Dr. Heidegger's Experiment." Dr. Heidegger's fiancee, who died by accident on her bridal evening fifty-five years before the time of the story.

Warden, The. *Dr. Grimshawe's Secret,* First Draft. See Warden Brathwaite.

Warland, Owen. "The Artist of the Beautiful." The delicate-fingered, idealistic artist who creates a mechanical butterfly which partially echoes his conception of the divinely beautiful.

Warren, General [Joseph]. "A Book of Autographs." The author of a letter in the collection.

Washington, General [George]. "A Bell's Biography." The Father of His Country who was welcomed by the bell. "A Book of Autographs." The author of one letter and the revered leader mentioned in other letters in the collection. *Septimius Felton.* Gives Sibyl Dacy permission to leave Boston and live in Concord for her health.

Weatherwise. "Old News." An almanac writer whose pro-Washington tendencies the old Tory deplores.

Webster, Noah. "A Book of Autographs." The author of a letter in the collection which tells an anecdote of General Washington at Mount Vernon.

Wentworth, Alice. "The Ancestral Footstep." See Alice Hammond.

Wentworth. "The Ancestral Footstep." See Hammond.

Westervelt, Professor. *The Blithedale Romance.* The handsome, diabolical mesmerist, apparently under thirty years of age but wizard-like in his dominance of Priscilla.

Whicher, David. "David Whicher." A peaceful old basket-weaver in seventeenth-century Maine, whose children Judith and Joshua are killed and scalped by four Indians; he traps the Indians and leaves them to perish.

Whicher, Joshua. "David Whicher." David Whicher's eighteen-month-old son, who is killed by four Indians in seventeenth-century Maine.

Whicher, Judith. "David Whicher." David Whicher's daughter, who is killed by four Indians in seventeenth-century Maine.

Whittier, [John Greenleaf]. "P.'s Correspondence." A fiery Quaker poet thought by P. to have been lynched in 1835.

Wiggins, Squire. "The Bald Eagle." A member of the militia of the Connecticut Valley village which Lafayette does not visit.

Wigglesworth, President [Edward]. "Old News." The (acting) President (of Harvard College) who is reported as trying to raise funds in Boston to support missionaries to the Indians.

Wigglesworth. "Chippings with a Chisel." The old sculptor who carves tombstones on Martha's Vineyard.

Wilkins, Betsey. "The Haunted Quack." The woman who swore that she heard Bill Gordon threaten to kill Hippocrates Jenkins if his wife Granny Gordon died as the result of taking Jenkins's prescribed nostrums.

Willard, John. "Main Street." A shrewd businessman in Salem condemned to hang for supposedly becoming a wizard.

William, King. *The House of the Seven Gables.* The British monarch represented at the opening of the Pyncheon house by the Lieutenant-Governor of Massachusetts.

Williams, Roger. "Endicott and the Red Cross." The elderly minister who brings John Endicott a letter from Governor Winthrop. "Main Street." A tolerant but strong-willed inhabitant of Main Street.

Willis, [Nathaniel Parker]. "P.'s Correspondence." An American writer thought by P. to have drowned in 1833.

Wilson, Rev. Mr. John. *The Scarlet Letter.* The oldest colleague of the Rev. Mr. Arthur Dimmesdale, scholarly and rather genial.

Wind-of-doctrine, Rev. Mr. "The Celestial Railroad." An easy preacher in Vanity Fair.

Winthrop, Governor [John]. "A Rill from the Town Pump." Mentioned as drinking from the spring. "Endicott and the Red Cross." The Governor of Massachusetts who sends word from Boston to Endicott that Charles I and Archbishop Laud are planning to appoint a Catholic Governor-General to New England. "Howe's Masquerade." An anti-royalist whose shade appears in the mysterious pageant at Sir William Howe's fancy-dress ball. "Main Street." A mild, venerable ruler who comes from Boston to Main Street. *The Scarlet Letter.* The Governor of Massachusetts colony who dies during the evening of the Rev. Mr. Arthur Dimmesdale's midnight vigil on the scaffold.

Woodbury. "Main Street." An early neighbor of Jeffrey Massey of Naumkeag.

Wordsworth, [William]. "P.'s Correspondence." A poet who died in 1845, according to P.

Wycherly, Mrs. Clara. "Dr. Heidegger's Experiment." The vain old widow who when she sips Dr. Heidegger's water of youth grows temporarily young and foolishly coquettish again.

Zenobia. *The Blithedale Romance.* The statuesque, darkly gorgeous older daughter of Old Moodie, to whom her initially unknown half-sister Priscilla attaches herself; she is characterized by wearing in her hair a fresh flower daily; because of her wealth, Hollingsworth selfishly professes to admire Zenobia, and his later preference for Priscilla causes Zenobia to drown herself; she was evidently victimized at one time by Professor Westervelt.

DATE DUE

3/2/83	reserve	
5/3/8		